JOHN A. KOUWENHOVEN, Professor of English at Barnard College, Columbia University, received his A.B. degree from Wesleyan University and his M.A. and Ph.D. degrees from Columbia. He is the author of *Adventures of America, 1857–1900, The Columbia Historical Portrait of New York, The Beer Can by the Highway;* has contributed articles to *Harper's, The Atlantic, The Yale Review, American Literature, The New England Quarterly, The Colophon, The Musical Quarterly* and *The Reader's Digest,* and is on the editorial board of *American Quarterly* and of *Technology and Culture. The Arts in Modern American Civilization* was first published in 1948 and has been reprinted in a Branford edition and in a slightly revised Anchor Books edition, from which the present text is taken.

The
Arts in Modern
American Civilization

JOHN A. KOUWENHOVEN

Introduction by MARK VAN DOREN

W · W · NORTON & COMPANY
New York · London

For my son,
Gerrit Wolphertsen Kouwenhoven,
and in memory of my daughter,
Ann Sherman Kouwenhoven

W. W. Norton & Company, Inc., 500 Fifth Avenue, New York, N.Y. 10110
W. W. Norton & Company Ltd., 37 Great Russell Street, London WC1B 3NU

First published in the Norton Library 1967
by arrangement with Doubleday & Company, Inc.

Originally published under the title *Made In America*

Published simultaneously in Canada by
Penguin Books Canada Ltd,
2801 John Street, Markham, Ontario L3R 1B4.

Books That Live

The Norton imprint on a book means that in the publisher's
estimation it is a book not for a single season but for the years.

W. W. NORTON & COMPANY, INC.

ISBN 0-393-00404-X

Printed in the United States of America

0

Contents

Illustrations

ILLUSTRATIONS

Introduction

Made in America forces attention as few books have done upon the main question which American art has long been putting to itself. What is its relation to American life? Or what ought to be its relation? The second question is not quite the same as the first, but under the illusion that it is, it has been asked with even greater anxiety, not to say vehemence. Not to say, also, conviction that the answer is easily known.

John Kouwenhoven makes it brilliantly clear to one reader that the answer is within reach. Mr. Kouwenhoven has his own answer, and everybody who is interested in American art should note it—indeed, will note it, for I cannot imagine that *Made in America* will fail to be widely discussed. But I should like to pay the book a still more serious tribute. It deserves to be deeply discussed. For its answer is of less weight at last than the care, the intelligent and responsible care, with which it frames the question. It is more important that we should think well about American life and art than that we should agree with Mr. Kouwenhoven. I often disagree with him. But never until I read his book had I seen the whole matter in the perspective it now occupies for me. This is what I call "making a contribution."

American art for Mr. Kouwenhoven is of course but a local phase of something much vaster in extent. His broadest view takes in all of Western civilization since the day when democracy and machinery got married and set up their modern house. It even foresees the universal triumph of this force, and I suppose there is no reason to doubt that even now such a triumph is taking place. The "vernacular" is on the march. Yet Mr. Kouwenhoven finds most of his instances in America, and sometimes his horizon is entirely bounded by our two oceans. That is why his book will touch us first of all. But there is no living mind to which it has not much to say, and there is no artist —painter, musician, architect, writer, sculptor, bridge builder, toolmaker, movie director, or house furnisher—to whom its author does not speak.

Europe has always been repudiating its past, but it was our distinction—if distinction—to cut ourselves off so completely from that past as not to know at last what we had repudiated. We did not criticize the immemorial ideas. We forgot them. And Mr. Kouwenhoven is happier about this than I am. His story is of how the arts in America have seldom known how to make themselves at home in an empty house. And certainly it is not often that they have had the air of being at home anywhere.

Toward the end of his book Mr. Kouwenhoven remarks that foreign movies have often been better than our own in spite of the fact that we invented the cinematic art. This might be for the simple reason that the rest of the world has not forgotten, as we have, how to feel and think tragedy and comedy. No idea, even an old one, ought to be alien to any man. Art in America seems to be stuck at some point between the past and now. Neither extreme is sacred in itself. The free artist is the one who can run the whole course, backward and forward, without stopping or stumbling.

The emphasis of Mr. Kouwenhoven is on the latter end of time. He is justified by the fact that so much American art has been old-fashioned. Not timeless, but out of date. It is true that we have not mastered our vernacular. That task remains to be done, and Mr. Kouwenhoven's book, more than any book I know, will assist the process. But what will the vernacular say when it has learned to talk? Something not too different, I suspect, from what great art has always said. Something more humane, certainly, than what America is saying for itself today.

I am not at all suggesting that Mr. Kouwenhoven has overlooked the point I made. Nor am I claiming that I have an answer which could be substituted for his. I have not even said in so many words what his answer is. The reader will find that out, and take delight in doing so. Better yet, he will thoroughly understand the problem before he is finished, either in his own terms or in those the author uses. For again it is Mr. Kouwenhoven's distinction that he has opened the question to its very heart.

Mark Van Doren

1 Art in America

To many Americans the arts have always seemed to have little connection with everyday life. Architecture, painting, literature, and the other arts have been regarded as rather remote things, vaguely foreign, no direct concern of ours. As a people we have been proud of American civilization and of its political and social institutions, but we have been less confident about our performance in the arts. There have been many respected American architects, painters, and poets, to be sure, but their total achievement, regarded from the conventional critical and historical points of view, has appeared to be only a somewhat crude dispersal of the western European tradition. There are, for example, still a good many institutions in our educational system where American art and literature are regarded as mere appendages to other—and, on the whole, weightier—matters.

Most historical and critical studies of the development of the arts in America have been based on some variant of John Fiske's theory of "the transit of civilization." Culture, the theory goes, is brought here from Europe by "carriers"—artists, writers, and musicians who migrate to this country from the Old World or natives who return after studying abroad. Thus American culture is regarded as an extension of western European culture, subject only to certain influences often thought of as more or less regrettable —inherent in the American environment.

The principal cramping or limiting influences to which culture has been subjected in America, according to this theory, have been the lack of leisure among a people engaged in conquering the wilderness, the gross materialism fostered by the frontier and by industrial capitalism, and the reputed anti-aesthetic bias of our Puritan intellectual inheritance. What is more, all three of these influences have been pictured as interacting with one another in a diabolic circle: Puritanism encouraging (if it did not actually breed) materialism, the frontier strengthening both, and everything conspiring to make leisure impossible.

Yet if we accept the view that American art is an integral part of a western European tradition which, in spite of national variants, is essentially a unity, we inevitably encounter a problem. On the one hand we find that although all the trends and movements and fashions of European art may be traced in work done by Americans, there is nevertheless a quality in the total sum of our painting, our architecture, our music, or our literature which is distinct from the comparative unity of tradition among the arts in the various countries of Europe. As Henry James noted, without enthusiasm, in the book which sums up the impressions he received during a visit to the United States after living abroad for almost a quarter of a century, the way things were done in America was "more different from all other native ways, taking country with country, than any of these latter are different from each other."

On the other hand, however, it is frequently said that in spite of this distinctively American element the arts have been inadequately representative of our national character. In one way or another almost everyone, native or foreign, who has commented on our artistic history has borne witness to the disparity between our achievements in the arts and in the realms of politics, economics, and social organization. That is what Jay B. Hubbell meant when he said that our literature "has always been less American than our history"—an observation that might be applied with equal force to any of our fine arts. For, as Stuart Sherman once summed the matter up, the national genius has never expressed itself "as adequately, as nobly, in music, painting, and literature, as it has, on the whole, in the great political crises." And thus the theory of a transplanted culture leads us at last to the paradoxical conclusion that though art in America is American it is singularly less so than the acts and institutions which embody our history. Fruitful as the study of the interrelationship between American and European art can be, therefore, it clearly must abandon the theory that one is merely a maimed offshoot of the other. There is obviously something left out of our concept of the arts if they are unrepresentative of the civilization which produced them; for it is in the arts that a civilization most compactly and fully expresses itself.

This book attempts to show that what has been left out is a tradition which was developed by people "who didn't know anything about art" but who had to deal with the materials of a new and unprecedented environment—a tradition which not only modified and obstructed the traditions carried over from western Europe but which contributed directly, as we shall see, to the evolution of new forms of artistic expression.

Men everywhere and at all times instinctively seek to arrange the elements of their environment in patterns of sounds, shapes, colors, and ideas which are aesthetically satisfying, and it is this instinct which underlies the creation of techniques and forms in which the creative imagination of the artist finds expression. In a given culture, such as that of western Europe, certain of these techniques and forms are more relevant than others to the life of the people, and from time to time these become institutionalized as schools of painting and sculpture, orders or styles of architecture, and types of music and literature. As long, therefore, as we are discussing a single, comparatively unified culture like that of western Europe from the Middle Ages to the Industrial Revolution, it is the tradition composed of these dominant techniques and forms which we have in mind when we talk about the arts. But in another culture, in a different kind of civilization, quite different forms and techniques might be in the ascendancy, and some of the arts which were most highly developed in western Europe might be relatively unimportant. The criteria of historical and critical judgments appropriate to the products of the western European tradition would not be adequate to the understanding or appreciation of an art produced in a different tradition. The capacity to enjoy and understand the music of Beethoven or Mozart, for example, is rooted in attitudes and sensibilities which provide little or no basis for an understanding or appreciation of the music of southern Asia.

So much is pretty obvious. Yet for a hundred and fifty years the historians and critics of American culture have, in effect, been applying the established western European criteria of value to the products of a civilization which has had less and less in common with that which produced the forms and techniques from which those criteria were deduced. To the cultural achievements, and specifically to the arts, of a civilization whose dynamics originate in technology and science, they have sought to apply the standards which were appropriate to those of civilizations founded upon agriculture or handicraft commerce.

The civilization which took form in the United States during the first century after the Declaration of Independence was, more than that of any European nation, the unalloyed product of those forces which throughout the world were creating what Charles Beard calls "technological civilization": that is, a civilization founded on power-driven machinery which indefinitely multiplies the capacity for producing goods, and upheld and served by science in all its branches. At most this civilization is two hundred years old, and there has never before been any order comparable to it.

Many people, including a good many historians, like to think of the United States as having been a nation of farmers and handicrafters, relatively untouched by the so-called Industrial Revolution, during a great part of its formative period. And it is, of course, true that until about the time of the Civil War the nation's economy was predominantly based upon agriculture. But it is easy to overestimate the agrarian aspects of our early history, and it

is well to be reminded that in significant respects our civilization has from the beginning been dependent upon
technology.

The least mechanized of all aspects of our society—the
lives of men and women on the advancing frontier—depended upon the machine-made rifles and revolvers which
enabled the pioneers to kill game and outfight the Indians,
upon the steamboats and railroads which opened up new
country for settlement, and upon the telegraph which
made rapid intercommunication possible. It was technological civilization which made it possible for our people
to conquer the wilderness and which ultimately built all
our continental diversities into what the Civil War made
clear was an indisseverable union. And as this civilization
spread westward across the New World it was free, in a
way that it could not have been free in any European
country, to develop with relatively little interference from
the habits of mind and social conventions which had been
developed in earlier civilizations, and which, like the artistic monuments they had created, persisted in Europe.

It is this fact which gives special significance to the
study of American arts. As this book tries to make clear,
it is not primarily because they are American that they
are worth our notice. Their importance lies in the fact that
because they are American, and because America is—for a
number of fortuitous reasons—the only major world power
to have taken form as a cultural unit in the period when
technological civilization was spreading throughout the
world—because of both these facts the arts in America
reveal, more clearly on the whole than the arts of any
other people, the nature and the meaning of modern civilization.

In other words, as the title of this book is intended
to suggest, we shall be concerned in the following pages
with what has happened and is happening to the arts in
modern civilization. We shall note the effects of democracy
and technology upon the older arts inherited from the
past, and we shall observe the development of new art

forms growing directly out of the new civilization's interests and techniques.

Both democracy and technology have, of course, been at work in Europe and Asia and the other Americas, as well as here—though not always collaborating with one another. What we call modern civilization is on the way to being global in a sense that no earlier civilization ever was. But it is, I think, fair to say that in America, and specifically in the United States, democracy and technology—the chief shaping forces of modern civilization—have for good or ill had the longest relatively uninhibited domination. As a matter of fact, with the Declaration of Independence there had been an abrupt and rapid orientation of the American environment away from the cultural heritage of Europe. As democratic political ideals evolved in practice and as technological civilization developed, the social environment became increasingly unlike that which had produced the western European patterns. The need for appropriate new patterns became increasingly acute.

Many Americans were aware of the need for new forms —for what they called a national literature, or art, or architecture. At first they tended to think in such nationalistic terms for the obvious reason that nationalism stood foremost in the consciousness of a people who had just fought a war for political independence. The answer to our needs seemed to many to be simply that we produce American versions of Shakespeare and paint pictures the way the European masters did—but of American subjects. Many of our early writers, on the other hand, began with a youthful determination to "forget Europe wholly," as James Russell Lowell urged in *A Fable for Critics,* and to write of native matters only, shaping their literature to the scale of the vast new continent, just as many painters like Bierstadt tried to develop an appropriate American art by simply increasing the size of their canvases. But they soon discovered that they could not forget Europe, and most of them found that they really didn't want to. The comfortable thing to do, then, was to relax into something approximating Longfellow's ultimate assumption that since Americans were really only "English under another sky" our literature needn't be expected to differ much from theirs. Of course, he added, the English stock in America was being mixed with other nationalities, and our English thoughts and feelings would therefore be tempered by German "tenderness," Spanish "passion," and French "vivacity." But he obviously assumed that we would remain essentially English, and that all that the writer and artist need do was carry on the old traditions. After all, he concluded, "all literature, as well as all art, is the result of culture and intellectual refinement."

Lowell stuck with the problem more tenaciously than that. "It is all idle to say that we are Englishmen," he wrote in 1854, because "we only possess their history through our minds, and not by life-long association with a spot and an idea we call England. History without the soil it grew in is more instructive than inspiring." But in everything that concerned art it seemed to Lowell that the Europeans had us at an immense disadvantage, for they were able to absorb cultural influences through their pores, as it were, from the whole atmosphere that surrounded them, while it required "weary years" for Americans to acquire these things from books and art galleries. The only good which might come of all this, he added rather lamely, was that, having been "thrown back wholly on nature," our literature might ultimately have a fresh flavor.

The nearest Lowell ever came to an answer which would prove fruitful to other writers and to himself was in his *Bigelow Papers*. Defending his use of dialect in these humorous poems and sketches of Yankee character, he declared in the preface to the second series (1867) that the first postulate of an original literature is that a people should use their language "as if it were a living part of their growth and personality, not as the mere torpid boon of education or inheritance." And in these dialect pieces Lowell did manage to capture some of the life and vigor and originality of native speech. But his formal poetry and essays were not much affected by this excursion into the vernacular; as far as style and manner are concerned, they could as well have been written in Cambridge, England, as in Cambridge, Massachusetts, and one feels that this, after all, was really the goal which Lowell wanted to achieve after the original nationalistic fervor wore off.

The quest for a national tradition in this spurious sense ended inevitably in failure. But all during the early years of the Republic we, and our European critics as well, debated the question of American art as if the problem were one of cultural independence. We argued stoutly that we could achieve it; most of the Europeans who came over here to inspect the strange new Republic argued that we could not. Yet both seemed to feel that beneath the surface manifestations of our society there were the elements of an indigenous culture—something singularly and essentially non-European expressed in our everyday life.

Many of the hundreds of books about America which issued so profusely from the pens of European visitors during the nineteenth century analyzed the non-European quality of our life with surprising keenness. But their authors frequently disliked it. It was alien to them and came as a point-blank challenge to the culture which had shaped their own lives. There were, of course, numbers of visitors who—like Harriet Martineau and Alexander Mackay—liked much of what they found here (and would have liked it wherever they found it); and a good deal of debate was carried on throughout the nineteenth century between our champions and our detractors. But those who had a vested interest in the survival of the ideals and customs of the older culture were frankly apprehensive about the growing influence of American ways. Here too, however, it was in terms of politics that the conflict was expressed. Captain Marryat, the popular English novelist whose *Diary in America* created a storm of protest among the Americans when it appeared in 1839, frankly announced that it had been his object "to do injury to democracy." And Mrs. Trollope, who emigrated from England to Cincinnati, where she kept a shop in frontier days, professed that her chief purpose in writing the *Domestic Manners of the Americans* (1832) had been to encourage the English people (who had seen enough of technology and tasted enough of democracy to need encouragement in those days of the Reform Bill) "to hold fast by a constitution that insures all the blessings which flow from established habits and solid principles," and to save them from the tumult and degradation incident to "the wild scheme of placing all the power in the hands of the populace."

Both these writers were keen observers of men and affairs, and their books are a vivid record of what they saw and how they felt about it. They saw men living under democratic institutions without the restraints imposed by an established social order, and they detested it. What little they found to praise was mostly confined to the longer-settled regions along the Eastern seaboard, where older English manners and customs had retained the greatest influence and where the "American" phenomena were most effectively diluted.

American people, still acutely aware of the newness of their nation, were eager to read what anyone wrote about them; hundreds of thousands of copies of books similar to Captain Marryat's and Mrs. Trollope's were sold and read in this country. Like other people, Americans don't enjoy being disliked; so the reaction to such attacks was immediate. Those whose cultural environment was least like that of Europe and who had therefore little emotional attachment to the manners and customs which the visitors were defending, turned bitterly against them, scorning their lack of understanding and their injustice, and were confirmed in distrust of the culture which such critics represented. It was this attitude, for example, which in 1835 led James Hall, the Cincinnati editor, to praise James K. Paulding on the grounds that his novels were "free from the blight of foreign influence."

Those, on the other hand, who still cherished in their homes furniture brought from the old country, whose education was patterned as closely as possible on that of their English cousins, or whose business or profession kept them in close contact with European society, tended often to react more with shame, or at worst with the anger which springs from shame. To them the long series of European attacks was a stimulus to mend their manners, to ape the ways of the older culture, and to adopt its externals so studiously that in the future they would appear less gross. Here was one of the sources of that development of conflicting traditions within American culture which this book traces.

Both types of response to the travelers' criticisms were unfortunate. Both hastened the already widening split between two divergent streams of national life. As we look at various aspects of our civilization we shall discover, over and over again, tragic evidence of how much it cost those who turned their backs on Europe to lose fruitful contact with the essential humanity embodied in the living masterpieces of Western culture; and just as vividly we shall become conscious of the enervation and sterility which resulted from rootless imitation here, as elsewhere, of long-established but no longer meaningful modes and surfaces. But it may also become clear that what seemed superficially to be a conflict between Europe and America was in reality quite another thing; that it was in essence only a more clear-cut and high-lighted version of a conflict which also existed within European culture itself.

It was easy, indeed almost inevitable, in nineteenth-century America to assume that art had little relation to the affairs of everyday life. Anyone familiar with American history will recall how remote Edgar Allan Poe and Henry James found themselves from the predominant concerns of their fellow Americans. But one need not assume —as some people do—that the things which interested Poe and James were of more aesthetic importance or of greater human value than those which preoccupied their countrymen. The world from which they were remote was, after all, the world of Abraham Lincoln.

Actually the chasm between art and everyday life may well prove to have been merely one manifestation of the catastrophic split which cut right through the whole of nineteenth-century society, both here and abroad. The conflict between the new science and the traditional religion produced an apparently unbridgeable gap between what man knew and what he believed. The development of industrial capitalism tended to divorce the production and distribution of goods from the political system, thus forcing men as unregulated economic beings to commit barbarous injustices which as political beings they had to cope with in terms of an inadequate traditional system. And finally, the tradition of western European art, like that of the Church, seemed to be seriously at odds with the social forces emerging chaotically from the Industrial Revolution.

So irreconcilable have art and technology seemed that many who believe in the creative discipline of form still cut themselves off deliberately from important areas of contemporary experience. One of the most influential modern critics holds that such willful isolation is imperative for the artist. Scientific knowledge, according to Mr. I. A. Richards, has made it impossible for us to believe countless poetic statements about God, the universe, and human nature. Furthermore, scientific knowledge, he maintains, is not of a kind upon which we can base an organization of the mind as "fine" (to use his own exceedingly vague term) as that which is based on prescientific thought. The solution which he offers—and which some of our most talented artists and writers have tried to accept—is that we must cut poetic and literary statements "free from belief, and yet retain them in this released state as the main instruments by which we order our attitudes to one another and to the world."[1]

[1] One of the bluntest expressions of this point of view, in this instance with Marxist overtones, was contained in Kenneth Burke's demand, in *Counter-Statement* (1931), "that the aesthetic ally itself with a Program which might be defined

For all its pseudo-scientific trappings, this is Victorian sentimentality in modern dress. So long as men persist in ordering their attitudes toward life in harmony with concepts which they merely wish were true, they will face life with emotional insecurity and dread. Only when men reckon with one another and the world in terms which take courageous account of what they *know* can they face life or death without fear.

Such wistful and perilous withdrawal from reality is evidence of a split between art and everyday life which, to many people, has seemed more complete in our generation than in any other in history. Actually that split, as has already been suggested, and as succeeding chapters try to make clear, is illusory. What we really have to reckon with, at home and abroad, is a conflict between two civilizations—one maturing, the other powerless to die. If in the United States for a century and a half the arts have seemed more strikingly unrepresentative of national life than in the countries of Europe, that is because here the art forms inherited from the older culture have had to cope with the new civilization in its most uninhibited aspects. What we have overlooked is the concomitant fact that in the United States—for that same reason—the new civilization has been freest to evolve its own artistic expression.

It is time we considered the frequently crude but vigorous forms in which the untutored creative instinct sought to pattern the new environment. It is in this unpretentious material that we may find the clearest expression of the vital impulses upon which the future of modern civilization depends.

---

roughly as a modernized version of the earlier bourgeois-Bohemian conflict." That program, designed to combat the "practical" values which the economic system imposes upon our society, should foster the following qualities: "inefficiency, indolence, dissipation, vacillation, mockery, distrust, 'hypochondria', nonconformity, bad sportsmanship." Mr. Burke did not defend these qualities as either admirable or "good" in themselves, but he urged adoption of the total attitude they reflect "because it could never triumph."

2   What Is Vernacular?

The forms we have so long neglected are in reality the products of a unique kind of folk art, created under conditions which had never before existed. They represent the unself-conscious efforts of common people, in America and elsewhere, to create satisfying patterns out of the elements of a new and culturally unassimilated environment; but this patternmaking is something altogether different from the folk arts which in recent years have been collected and studied with such enthusiasm. It has nothing in common with the balladry of the Kentucky mountaineers or the decorative crafts of the Pennsylvania Dutch. Unlike these, it is the art of sovereign, even if uncultivated, people rather than of groups cut off from the main currents of contemporary life. The patterns it evolved were not those which are inspired by ancient traditions of race or class; on the contrary, they were imposed by the driving energies of an unprecedented social structure. *In their least diluted form these patterns comprise the folk arts of the first people in history who, disinherited of a great cultural tradition, found themselves living under democratic institutions in an expanding machine economy.*

It is this unique factor of a democratic-technological vernacular which has been overlooked in our estimates of art in the United States. The development of folk-art forms is always hard to trace. No one bothers to note the patterns of colors, shapes, sounds, and ideas which plain people produce—at least no detailed record is kept until long after the patterns have crystallized and have become habitual. It is especially difficult to trace the emergence of this vernacular, for the patterns through which it evolved were not designed to be kept in frames on the wall, or cherished behind glass doors. These patterns formed tools, machines, buildings, and other objects for use in the routine of daily life. It was into the design of useful things that these people inevitably turned the universal creative instinct. Repressed artistic impulses found release in uncounted rudimentary and personal expressions.

The purest form of this vernacular, the form in which its characteristics are most clearly revealed and can be most readily defined, is represented by technological design. Here craft tradition had least influence and the characteristic impulses of the new civilization were freest to display their energy in patterns available to all the people, cultivated and uncultivated alike.

The men and women who built a civilization in the American wilderness had to relearn a truth which many of their European contemporaries had been able to get along without: the truth of function. They had to become familiar with the nature of materials and the use of tools. The frontier country was strange indeed to those who had been accustomed to the ways of the older culture. James Hall, writing in the *Illinois Monthly Magazine* for June 1831, warned the Western emigrant that he must abandon his predilections, prejudices, and local attachments. "Instead of bringing *society* with him," Hall wrote, "he should cultivate the intimacy of the inhabitants, and by imbibing their feelings and sentiments learn to relish *their* society." And like his predilections and prejudices, his customary tools also had ultimately to be abandoned.

The United States won its independence from Britain with the aid of a tool which had been developed, though not invented, on the frontier. When Washington took command of the Continental Army at Boston he brought with him fourteen hundred frontier riflemen from western Pennsylvania. The Massachusetts troops who watched these leather-jacketed irregulars assemble on Cambridge Common jeered at the incredibly long-barreled guns which the strangers carried; there was something absurd about the length of such weapons in comparison with the stubby, smooth-bore firelock muskets which both the English and

Massachusetts men were using. But Washington had been in western Pennsylvania some years before and had seen what those ungainly men could do with their ungainly weapons; and that afternoon on Cambridge Common the Massachusetts men saw too. The lanky Westerners drove seven-inch target posts into the ground and then strode off to take firing position: fifty yards, a hundred yards (at that distance a man with a smooth-bore musket could have hit such a small target only by sheer luck), a hundred and fifty yards, two hundred yards, *two hundred and fifty yards*. There they stopped, lined up in ragged order, and fired; and they hit the posts.

Here was a weapon which revolutionized fighting techniques. Men armed with these rifles didn't have to stand in line, like the British at Bunker Hill, firing volleys at short range and hoping some of the bullets hit someone. This was the Pennsylvania version of the German rifle-barreled gun, developed during the 1730s and 1740s by patient experiment among the gunsmiths around Lancaster, a hunting tool which could pick off a 'coon or a rabbit at long range in the lonely forests. And these rifles played a significant part in America's victory; for so greatly did the enemy dread their effectiveness that, as Roger Burlingame tells the story, Washington later asked other troops to wear the costume of the men who used them, even though there were nowhere near enough of the rifles to go around.

The tools whose design first showed the influence of the American environment were, as one would expect, those which were most widely used in getting food, clearing the land, and making it fertile. The men who came over from Europe brought with them axes, spades, hayforks, manure forks, and plows, and used them as long as they lasted. But when these tools wore out it was difficult to import others, and local blacksmiths hammered out new ones for their neighbors.

Changes in design under such circumstances are made only very gradually; it was quite a while before there was a noticeable difference between the tools used in America and those still used in Europe. But changes nevertheless occur, as old habits give way to new requirements. Fenimore Cooper observed in 1828 that American plows were more "graceful and convenient" and American axes more admirable "for form, for neatness, and precision of weight" than their English equivalents, and by the middle of the nineteenth century, when the Great Exhibition at the Crystal Palace in London provided the first general opportunity for comparative study of the products of all nations, differences were strikingly apparent.

Twenty-five years later the reports of European observers at the United States Centennial Exhibition, held in 1876 at Philadelphia, were filled with detailed descriptions of characteristic American designs. Among the reports of the British Commission, for example, there is a comparison of British and American tools. Commissioner David McHardy noted that the English axe was bulky, while the American was thinned considerably below the eye—a shape which "enables it to be more easily drawn out after the blow is given, and the body of the axe, being much firmer, is not liable to twist in working." Again, in his report on agricultural and laborers' tools, he expressed surprise that the great improvements which had been made in the United States had not been introduced into Europe many years before. The old-style hayfork, for example, with its iron ferrule and strong ash handle, was "a very cumbrous tool"; the manure fork, with its three prongs—usually flat and about an inch broad, but occasionally made in the more efficient V shape—was doubly so. "No accurate judgment," he wrote, "can be formed of the many advantages which have been conferred on the laborer by the introduction of the American steel spade, shovel, manure- and hayforks." An iron spade quickly became caked with dirt, an iron fork blunted its points easily; but the surfaces of the American steel tools remained clean, and the edges and points remained sharp. Furthermore, the new tools were much lighter; the difference of weight between the old-style and the new steel spades was from three to four pounds in favor of steel.

If, then, we are to judge from McHardy's report, European tools in 1876 had not yet adopted improvements which had been made in America at least sixty or seventy years earlier. For we have record that "long before" 1814 a member of the American Institute "left off the use of common iron spades and hoes," and employed a good workman to make his spade and hoe of trowel stuff, as he called it, "so hard that no stone could injure its edge, and so thin that the spade was driven by hand instead of foot, up to the hub, polished as a razor." With such spades, he testified, he could dig more in a day than two men with iron spades, "and dance in the evening."

Not all foreign observers admired the functional simplicity of American products at the Centennial. A member of the German delegation objected, for instance, that "certain objects of daily use which ought to be richly decorated, like grandfather clocks, show the sad state of American taste by the complete absence of ornamentation." At London's Crystal Palace a similar criticism had been implied in the official commentary on the American exhibits. "The expenditure of months or years of labour upon a single article, not to increase its intrinsic value, but solely to augment its cost or its estimation as an object of *virtu,* is not common in the United States," the exhibition catalogue had announced. On the contrary, both manual and mechanical labor were applied with direct reference to increasing the quantity of those articles which were suited to the wants of a whole people—with the result that the products of American industry seemed to the exhibition's officials to have "a character distinct from that of other countries."

It has frequently been said that Europe surpassed the United States in the mechanical sciences during the first half of the nineteenth century, and it is undoubtedly true that both England and Germany were far ahead of us in metallurgy and in the perfection and elaborateness of their heavy machinery. But to some extent, at least, the notion of European mechanical superiority in this period derives from the fact that technological history has been written chiefly by Europeans who were unfamiliar with American developments. There is ample evidence, however, that even in the first half of the century mechanical progress in America was in a number of important respects less inhibited than that in the Old World. In the development of machine tools, for instance, and of the precision gauges and accurate jigs and fixtures which made possible the mechanical duplication of metal parts for rifles, clocks, and a hundred other objects, the gunsmiths and mechanics of New England were far in advance of the Europeans. When Samuel Colt set up a factory in England in the early 1850s to supply the foreign market with mass-produced rifles and muskets and the famous Colt revolvers which he had been making in Hartford since 1848, he reluctantly discovered that he had to import from America both the machines and the men to operate them. English machines, as he told an investigating committee of the House of Commons, were not sufficiently precise, and skilled English workmen seemed to be unable to operate the machines made in America. Recognition of the superiority of American machine tools for precision work was given by the British government itself when it established the Royal Small Arms factory at Enfield Lock in 1853. It awarded the contract for practically all of the standard and special machine tools, and for the jigs, fixtures, and gauges required to mass-produce the Enfield rifle, to the firm of Robbins & Lawrence in Windsor, Vermont.

What was lacking among the European mechanics whom Colt had been unable to employ was the intense and daring mechanical imagination which foreign commentators repeatedly remarked as a characteristic of the American workman, and which remained such a distinctive feature of our industrial system that, no matter how decisively England maintained her world leadership in the scientific development of machines, America—as the London *Times* itself observed in 1878—nevertheless developed "more that is new and practical in mechanism than all Europe combined."

The whole subject of American mechanical history—or, to be more inclusive, technological history—has been too much neglected, especially those aspects of it which reflect its relationship to cultural history as a whole. The very materials from which such a history could be written are scattered, and in many cases have been lost. The scientist or the technical expert has little interest in regional or national variants in mechanism, as such; he is concerned chiefly with the discovery of mechanical principles (which have no nationality) and their efficient application. [In 1958, ten years after this was written, the first organization devoted to the serious study of the development and consequences of technology was established. Called the Society for the History of Technology, it publishes an international quarterly entitled *Technology and Culture*, with editorial offices at Case Institute of Technology, Cleveland, Ohio.]

Yet it is evident that machinery developed very differently in different countries. In the abstract, technology may be technology wherever it exists, but in actual practice its internationalism is a myth, or at best an ideal which has never been attained. During the nineteenth century wide divergence in national and regional practice existed, and much may be learned from a consideration of those differences of which evidence still remains. As early as 1840 the English author of a *True Guide* to the United States, published in London for the benefit of British mechanics and laborers who were planning to emigrate, summed up his experience of four years' work and five thousand miles of travel in the new nation by warning that a mechanic from the "Old Country" should be prepared to meet with "new and peculiar, if not improved, modes and ideas, and make up his mind also to their immediate adoption." But unfortunately the author does not discuss the "new and peculiar" modes and ideas in any detail.

There is, however, valuable evidence regarding such differences in one branch of mechanics in John Richards' *Treatise on the Construction and Operation of Woodworking Machinery*, published in London in 1872. Richards was a native of Pennsylvania who lived much of his life abroad and was known throughout the world as a designer and builder of all kinds of machinery. As head of the American firm of Richards, London, & Kelley and of the English firm of Richards and Atkinson of Manchester, and as the designer and builder of machinery for the Russian Royal Arsenal, he originated over a thousand different machines and was familiar with contemporary practice in many lands.

Much of his book is of interest only to the specialists for whom it was intended, but there are a number of passages which bear on the development of the vernacular tradition. Richards says, for example, that the distinction between English and American woodworking machinery at that time was perhaps the greatest that had "ever existed in a system of machines both directed to the same, or nearly the same, purposes." Most of the basic machines for wood conversion had been invented at the end of the eighteenth century in England by Samuel Bentham. But from then on the development took place chiefly in the United States, largely because wood was so much more widely used here, not only in building houses, bridges, and ships but even in framing steam engines and in other capacities where iron was used in Europe. In 1844 a number of American machines were imported into England, but—according to Richards—since "the ruling idea in these machines was economy in cost and rapid performance in the hands of skilled men, neither of which elements fitted them for the English market," practically no use was made by English builders of the modifications they might have suggested. It was not until after the Crystal Palace Exhibition in 1851, where the performance of the American machines was amply demonstrated, that English engineers adopted the American improvements.

Necessity, coupled with what Richards called "a strong ingenuity and boldness of plan," had led to the development in America of an entire system of machines for sawing, planing, boring, mortising, and tenoning, plus hundreds of special machines for manufacturing carriages, plows, furniture, joiner's work, bent work, and so on.

What Richards meant by ingenuity and boldness can best be understood by reference to specific machines which he describes. One of these was the reciprocating mortising machine; that is, a machine designed to drive a chisel back and forth into the wood to cut out a square hole. Reciprocating motion in a machine always involves more vibration —and consequent wear—than rotary motion, and at the high speeds required in wood machines the jarring is severe. A skilled engineer, Richards observed, who was conversant with all the principles of the operation and the difficulties to be encountered, would not be inclined to attempt construction of reciprocating mortising machines, and European builders avoided them. But in the United States, "either through an ignorance of the difficulties to be encountered, a greater boldness in such things, or the high price of labour," they were extensively made and generally used.

Another example was the "muley-saw mill," which originated in, and was largely confined to, the Western states. This was an unprecedented device which seemed to defy all the accepted notions about reciprocating—as distinguished from circular—saws. The blades of reciprocating saws had always been operated under tension—that is, tightly stretched between upper and lower frames, which must be strong enough to stand heavy transverse and compressive strain as they moved up and down. The weight of these frames tended to limit the rate of teeth movement of the saw, thereby reducing the saw's efficiency. The muley-saw was simply an expedient to increase the cutting speed of the blade by dispensing with the heavy-tension frame and all possible weight in the reciprocating parts. The blade was left slack, merely guided—above and below the log—by light lateral supports of wood which prevented it from bending. The result was, surprisingly, that the lumber was "cut more true, as to dimensions, than that cut on mills of any other kind; just the opposite of what would be expected from the plan of operating a saw without tension."

Repeatedly through Richards' book one encounters evidence that Americans produced bold and original machines "which upon theoretical deductions would scarcely have been made." This does not, however, mean that all American machinery approached the high level of mechanical perfection which was standard in England. It did not, for a number of reasons. For one thing, European machines were less likely to be improvised than those made in the United States; they were rarely made for the personal use of the designer, or even of the buyer, but rather for a workman employed by the buyer, and this required that they be made to operate as nearly as possible without the intelligence of the workman, even if the original cost was high. In the United States, however, machines were frequently made for the designer's own use, and were usually sold, as Richards noted, *only to those who use them* and understand their use." Most of the early American woodworking machines, for example, were designed and built by carpenters, cabinetmakers, and shipbuilders for their own use. To these men iron was a new material. They had in mind "no constants, or rules for proportions, like an engineer or machinist, but blindly supplied a shaft here, a pulley there, with bolts and framing to support them," very much as they would have made a house or a piece of furniture.

As Richards puts it, the carpenter carried out his architectural ideas in framing his woodworking machines; "the metal was disposed in scrolls and network, and all conceivable forms except those that the strains would indicate, figures of vines and shrubbery, 'pomegranates and lily-work' were raised in relief, the whole was painted in gorgeous hues, and as if to cap the climax, the rough iron surfaces were generally finished off with a coat of transparent varnish." (See Fig. 1.) In ways like this the cultivated tradition in America, acting through the agency of craft techniques, interacted with, and modified, the vernacular. But the influence of the cultivated tradition was largely confined thus to surfaces; the carpenter-builders may have trimmed their woodworking machines with extravagant and uncouth decorations, but the operation of their machines was not open to such criticism. We have it on Richards' authority that nowhere in the world had machines for making doors, sash, and joiner work generally, equaled those made by these carpenter-builders. If they lacked the finish and elaborateness of European machines, that was characteristic of a tradition in which, as Richards said, "the movement and application of the cutting edge was the prime object, everything else unimportant."

Actually, whatever was built or made in the vernacular was likely to be marked by constraint and simplicity. There was no room in such a tradition for diffuseness, there were no resources to spare for the ornate, and it was merely sound sense to design a thing as economically as one could. But in the United States these qualities seem to have become especially characteristic. We had to have machines and tools that would work well in a rough land, would economize labor, and would save the owner from running to far-off shops for repairs. This meant light, simple, tough tools. But as time went on even elaborate machinery took on distinctive qualities. W. F. Durfee, one of the judges at the Centennial, commended the metalworking machines made by Pratt and Whitney of Hartford, Connecticut, for "the admirable character of their general design, which shows the result of careful study and large experience applied to the determination of the proportion and union of parts in the several tools, with the view of eliminating unnecessary details, thus at once cheapening their construction and improving their qualities as working machines."

The great Corliss steam engine in the Centennial's Machinery Hall was a contemporary masterpiece of this tradition in design. The largest and most powerful engine that had ever been built up to that time, it was installed at the exhibition to provide power for all the lathes, grinders, drills, weaving machines, printing presses, and other machinery displayed by the various exhibitors. It weighed altogether 1,700,000 pounds, yet so perfectly was it made that it worked almost as quietly and with as little vibration as a watch.

In large engines of this kind it had long been customary for the designers to strive for architectural or other ornamental effects. Important engines, here and abroad, were usually framed with elaborate Gothic arches or Corinthian columns (see Fig. 2); struts and braces which by every engineering requirement should have been straight lines were often disposed in graceful curves. By contrast with such engines the Corliss design was unequivocally severe, and before the exhibition was opened to the public many commentators, including the editor of the *Scientific American*, thought that it would therefore be disappointing to the general public.

But to anyone who reads the mass of contemporary comment on the exhibition it is obvious that the commentators need not have worried. Even those who, like the correspondent of the *Manufacturer and Builder*, had at first criticized "the undoubted clumsiness of the design," grudgingly admitted after the exhibition opened that the engine looked "much better in motion than it did when standing still."

People said all the fine things that duty required about the pictures and statues in Memorial Hall, but in the presence of the Corliss engine they were exalted. It stood there at the center of the twelve-acre building, towering forty feet above its platform, not an idealization but an unmitigated fact. Yet to the thousands who saw it, it was more than merely the motive power for the miles of shafting which belted their energy to machines throughout the building. (See Fig. 3.)

Consciously or unconsciously, each visitor in his own way testified to its aesthetic impact. Sixty years later the Midwestern poet, Harriet Monroe, remembered being taken from Chicago to Philadelphia to visit the Centennial and recorded that she, at sixteen, was far more impressed by the Corliss engine "turning its great wheels massively" than by any of the art exhibitions. "Josiah Allen's wife," the perennially popular humorist-philosopher of *Samantha at the Centennial* and a dozen later "Samantha" books, had spoken for thousands of ordinary citizens when she wrote that "that great 'Careless Enjun' alone was enough to run anybody's idees up into majestic heights and run 'em round and round into lofty circles and spears of thought they hadn't never thought of runnin' into before." And the French sculptor Bartholdi said in an official report to his government that the engine had "the beauty and almost the grace of the human form." It was such engines which led a London *Times* correspondent to report that "the American mechanizes as an old Greek sculptured, as the Venetian painted." Even the Brahminic *Atlantic Monthly* concluded rhetorically that "surely here, and not in literature, science, or art, is the true evidence of man's creative power; here is Prometheus unbound."

Not often were the technological elements of our environment welded into such a vernacular masterpiece. One could scarcely expect the millennium in the turbulent life of nineteenth-century America. But it is essential to realize that in the very decades which our cultural historians have called the ugliest and bleakest in our history—the years of "chromo-civilization" and the "Gilded Age"—American people had developed skills and knowledge which enabled them to create patterns of clean, organic, and indigenous beauty out of the crude materials of the technological environment.

Most people, of course, failed to recognize in such patterns the substance of art. Inherited notions of beauty and the influences of education interfered with any such recognition. A typical account of the Centennial recorded that "although the first thought would be that no arrangement of axes, hatchets, picks, shovels, etc., could be made that would be pleasing to the eye," an exhibit of such articles was nevertheless "attractive."

Such an attitude inevitably encouraged those attempts to decorate machinery which we have already noted. So prevalent were architectural details in nineteenth-century machinery that it has frequently been assumed that the early designers themselves were originally architects, but there is considerable evidence that this was not the case. Drawings of new machines—other than rough sketches on boards, or chalk marks on the floor—were seldom used in the early years of the nineteenth century. Toward the middle of the century, to be sure, advertisements occasionally appear like that of G. P. Randall, "Architect and Builder," who announced in the pages of a Vermont newspaper in 1846 that he would design not only churches, residences, and bridges, but also "simple and complicated machinery, stoves, etc." But early machines were designed out of the inventor's head, as it were, and changes were made as the work progressed. Since most of these machines were built largely of wood (metal and metal-working facilities being scarce), machine building came into the realm of the cabinetmaker, who had the necessary knowledge and tools. The United States Patent Office for many years required a small-sized working model of an invention instead of the formal drawings required today, and a cabinetmaker usually made the model if the inventor himself did not do so. Since the patterns for the finished machine would closely resemble the model, patternmaking gradually developed as a branch of the cabinetmaker's trade. Accustomed to making furniture, and acquainted with architectural detail through the making of woodwork "trim" for house builders, the skilled craftsman quite naturally embellished the prosaic machine patterns with scrollwork, claw feet, delicately carved legs, and fluted columns.

Opposed to this transferred ornamental habit there was no tradition, no codified grammar, of technological design, but only an intuitive sense of appropriate form. William Sellers, of Philadelphia, for instance (whom the English designer Whitworth is said to have called the greatest mechanical engineer in the world), simply went on the theory that "if a machine was right, it would *look* right." (See Fig. 4.) John Fritz, one of the important figures in the development of the Bessemer process in the United States, was typical of the empirical engineers. One of his favorite remarks after he had finished work on a new machine which he had designed was: "Now, boys, we have got her done, let's start her up and see why she doesn't work." By and large American mechanical engineers adopted original methods of design, taking the problem presented to them and working out the design (as Joseph M. Wilson expressed it) "without any blind adherence to old established forms or precedents."

This empirical attitude was characteristic of almost all early efforts to pattern the technological environment. The men who designed and built the clipper ships of the 1840s and 1850s worked in much the same way as Sellers did in the designing of his machine tools, and the essential characteristics of their designs were the same. Economy of line, lightness, strength, and freedom from meaningless ornament made Donald McKay's *Flying Cloud* and *Sovereign of the Seas* not only two of the swiftest sailing ships of their time but also two of the most beautiful vessels that ever sailed the ocean.

The day of the clippers was brief. During the very years when they were the monarchs of the seas, steamships were being developed and perfected to a point where they would inevitably drive the clippers out of existence. But in steamship design, likewise, the vernacular tradition developed its characteristic qualities.

On the Ohio and Mississippi a distinctive type of vessel

was developed on principles some of which had been worked out by a man whose name scarcely ever appears in the history books: Henry Miller Shreve. Attempts by Robert Fulton and other Easterners to design steamboats for the Western rivers had ended in several costly failures. Shreve had grown up on the rivers, working as bargeman and later as captain of the *Enterprise,* the first steamer that ever ascended the Mississippi to Louisville. He knew what the rivers required, and when he built the *Washington* in 1816 it was in essential respects unlike any other steam vessel then known. Previously, the boilers had always been placed in the hold of the vessel and the cylinders set upright. Shreve set his machinery on the deck, thus permitting the use of flat-bottomed, shallow hulls similar to the keelboats which had long been familiar on Western rivers. Further, he designed and built a high-pressure engine with a cylinder which was horizontal, instead of vertical as in the high-pressure engines of Oliver Evans. And the success of the *Washington* established Shreve's system as the basis of all Western steamboats for many years.

Nevertheless, there were countless variants in the design of American river steamers. In 1838 an English engineer, David Stevenson, reported in his *Sketch of the Civil Engineering of North America* that after minutely examining all the most approved American steamboats he could trace no *general* principles which had served as guides for their construction.

Every American steamboat builder holds opinions of his own [he wrote], which are generally founded, not on theoretical principles, but on deductions drawn from a close examination of the practical effects of the different arrangements and proportions adopted in the construction of different steamboats . . . ; and the natural consequence is, that, even at this day, no two steamboats are alike, and few of them have attained the age of six months without undergoing some material alteration.

In transatlantic navigation, of course, these shallow-draft boats would be useless, and in that field English builders took a quick lead. But even here the vernacular tradition modified the design of American ships. In 1853 Captain Mackinnon of the Royal Navy crossed on the American Collins liner *Baltic*, built by Jacob Bell, of New York, and shortly thereafter published an article comparing the *Baltic's* design and performance with those of English ships. Basically, he found, the American ship was superior. An English vessel would have a heavy bow with a vast bowsprit, "an absolute excrescence," the captain angrily called it, "a bow-plunging, speed-stopping, money-spending, and absurd acquiescence in old-fashioned prejudices about appearance. . . ." But American ships were hampered by no such devotion to traditional design. They had, instead, a long and gently graduated bow without a bowsprit, with the result that they rode the waves gently even in a heavy sea, without shipping water and without the shock and stagger of the blunt-bowed Britishers.

The *Baltic* and the other American steamships of the early fifties were designed and built by the same shipyards that were turning out the famous clippers. Steam clippers and sailing clippers were constructed side by side. Of course the steamships, not being intended to carry an immense spread of canvas, could be much narrower than any sailing vessel that had ever been designed. But the contemporary newspapers in maritime cities throughout the world were full of descriptions of sailing clippers which sound very much like Captain Mackinnon's account of the steamship *Baltic*. The Mauritius *Commercial Gazeteer* (December 7, 1855) said the bow of the *Herald of the Morning*, designed by Samuel Pook, of New York, was "so sharp as to take the form of a razor, the keel forming the edge; there are no rails at the bow, which is quite unencumbered."

The clipper ships, like the Western riverboats, were not any one man's invention. Rather, they were a composite creation, the product of literally scores of keen minds.

McKay himself declared in an interview that before making the model of his *Stag Hound* (1850) he had familiarized himself with "all the celebrated clipper models." The designer did not know how his ship would perform until it was actually put to the test. He borrowed ideas from vessels which were under sail and combined them with his own intuitive sense of the lines which were appropriate to the requirements of the ships he intended to build. George Steers, designer of the schooner-yacht *America* which won the international yacht race in 1851 and brought to this country the prize cup which is still called by its name, was particularly proud of a model he was working on shortly before his death. It tapered so beautifully from the center that the eye could not find the exact center spot—"just like the well-formed leg of a woman," from which, he said, he had borrowed his idea.

Magnificent as these ships were, the railroad locomotive was the dominant symbol of technological progress during the nineteenth century. As would be expected, the design and performance of American locomotives revealed the characteristics of the vernacular tradition and consequently differed considerably from contemporary European engines. We can perhaps get the clearest sense of this difference by referring to accounts of contemporary American civil engineers. These experts profoundly admired English locomotives, as they did all English machinery. United States Commissioner William Anderson, in his official report on railway apparatus exhibited at the Universal Exposition in Paris, 1878, stated that "the locomotives exhibited in the British section were, as may be said of the machinery exhibits of the United Kingdom generally, remarkable for the skill, the directness, the strong common sense, and the faithfulness illustrated in their construction." And Charles Barnard, writing in 1879, flatly asserted that "the finest piece of steam mechanism in the world is undoubtedly the English locomotive engine."

Barnard goes on to describe these engines: a cylindrical

boiler and a capacious firebox, resting upon a massive and rigid frame of iron plates, which in turn was supported by wheels of extraordinary size and strength. In front there might be a pair of smaller wheels, but these like the larger ones were fastened by their axles to the rigid frame which supported the boiler. "One cannot," he wrote, "fail to admire the thoroughly English solidity and stability of the machine. . . . Every part of the mechanism is admirable—strong, accurate, and fitted to its work with marvellous precision."

But the moment the English locomotive was taken from its island lines—relatively straight, and as level as money and labor could make them—and was used in, say, Canada or Australia, it exhibited a number of defects, especially a certain want of pliability. For in those countries, as in the United States, distances were so vast, territory was so thinly populated, capital resources were so limited, and speed of construction was so essential, that the railroads had to negotiate considerable grades and abrupt curves without too much insistence on a straight line or a level roadbed. On such winding and uneven roads the English locomotive was either derailed by the curves, or wrenched and twisted by having only three of its four wheels on the track at one time.

To cope with American roadbeds a very different locomotive was developed which, to anyone accustomed to English engines, would seem a "crazy affair, as loose-jointed as a basket." It had no massive frame. In Barnard's words:

The framework is light and open, and yet strong. The supporting springs that take the weight of the machine from the axles are not secured directly to the frame, but to the levers extending both across and along the engine. . . . The engine is thus hung upon the fulcrums of a system of levers, balanced equally in every direction. Let the road follow its own wayward will, be low here and high there . . . the basket-like flexibility of

the frame and its supports . . . adjusts the engine to
its road at every instant of its journey.

Further, it had a group of small wheels at the front—the
pilot truck, or track feeler—which was designed to carry
the engine around sharp curves. This truck was not only
supported on equalizing bars and levers, as were the driving wheels, but also incorporated an arrangement which
shifted the weight of the engine so that, like a circus rider,
the engine leaned inward on curves to counteract cen-
trifugal force. (See Fig. 5.)

The characteristics of the American locomotive had appeared early. The first really successful railroad locomotive in the world—George Stephenson's *Rocket*—was built
in England in 1829, yet in the very next year H. L. B.
Lewis, of New York, was advertising his invention of a
simple contrivance, consisting of wheels attached to the
front and rear of the engine, "so arranged that they have
a horizontal and lateral motion, so as to admit of their
adapting their position to any curve in the track, or any
inequality on the top sides of the rails." Two years later,
in 1832, Jervis designed the *Brother Jonathan*—the first
locomotive to use the lead-truck principle. Five years later
Garrett and Eastwick built the *Hercules*, the first engine
on which a driving-wheel equalizer invented by Joseph
Harrison, Jr., was used; the weight of the engine rested
upon the center of a separate frame, the driving-wheel
axles being placed in pedestals or supports which allowed
the wheels to adjust to uneven track. In 1842 Eastwick
and Harrison's *Mercury* combined a highly flexible system
of truck suspension with a further development of the
equalized driving-wheel arrangement, and an extremely
light frame. From that point onward, the essential characteristics of the American locomotive rapidly developed.[1]

[1] The difference between American and British locomotives
early in the twentieth century was thus described by the English railroad expert, Vaughan Pendred, in *The Railway Locomotive*, New York, 1908, p. X: "The British locomotive is, above

For about twenty years after 1850, it is true, extraneous attempts were made to apply "art" to the iron horse. As in the large stationary steam engines described earlier, this art consisted, in large measure, in architectural detail, used in constructing the engine cabs which after 1850 became common on American locomotives. Baldwin's eight-wheeled engine of that year had a cab with large decorative panels on the sides, Corinthian columns supporting an ornamental cornice, and Gothic arched windows. As late as 1868 the *Nathaniel McKay*, designed by and named after the son of the clipper-ship designer, Donald McKay, retained the Gothic point in its cab windows. But by 1875 the return of the clean, functional form is reflected in the restrained and attractive design of John C. Davis' engine for the Baltimore and Ohio. (See Fig. 5.)

The characteristics of economy, simplicity, and flexibility which the products of the vernacular displayed so clearly in the United States are closely related to the design of the American system of industrial production itself. There is a clue to this relationship in the comment already quoted from the catalogue of London's Crystal Palace Exhibition in 1851: that productive labor in the United States was "applied with direct reference to increasing the number or quantity of articles suited to the wants of a whole people."

Let us return for a moment to those long-barreled rifles which Washington's frontiersmen demonstrated on Cambridge Common. Each of those rifles was made by hand, and because they were handmade, no two were exactly alike. If more guns were needed, skilled craftsmen had to be found to make them, and each gun that was made had to be shaped and fitted with individual care.

---

all others, simple, strong, and carefully finished. . . . The American locomotive is the incarnate spirit of opportunism. . . . In Europe complication is favored rather than disliked. . . . In all cases the national character appears to stamp itself on machinery of every kind."

As a matter of fact, in 1798, when war with France seemed imminent, the government found itself in need of large quantities of rifles. To meet that need, Eli Whitney, of Connecticut, agreed to manufacture "ten thousand stand of Arms, or Muskets, with Bayonets and Ramrods complete" in two years—an undreamed-of quantity in a land where skilled gunsmiths were rare. To achieve this task Whitney proposed "to substitute correct and effective operations of machinery for that skill of the artist which is acquired only by long experience."

Whitney's part in the development of what came to be called the "American system" of manufacture, employing machine-made, standardized, interchangeable parts, is less well known than his invention of the cotton gin. The gin's more immediate and obvious economic and social effects commanded the historian's interest long before the origins of mass-production seemed important. But interchange-able-parts manufacture, which had been introduced in France by H. Blanc in the 1780s, and which Whitney and the mechanics at the United States Government arsenals developed here in the next two or three decades, is one of the basic constituents of modern civilization. Whitney may not deserve so much credit as he claimed in connection with the introduction and elaboration of the system. Recent investigations by Robert S. Woodbury show that Blanc himself was anticipated by a Swedish maker of clock gears who, fifty years earlier, made parts by machinery so precisely that they were interchangeable. But quite apart from the question of who deserves the credit for inventing such a system, the fact remains that in America it was rapidly developed and was soon applied to a number of manufactures. By the early 1870s it had been applied so extensively to the manufacture of sewing machines, for example, that 600,000 were made and sold in a single year. Firearms, agricultural machinery, watches, and even loco-motives were produced by this so-called American system of manufacture.

There is no need to describe here in detail the development of this system, or how it works in specific cases. The essential point in the present context is that it had collaborated with all the other factors we have considered to strengthen and accentuate the characteristic qualities of the American vernacular tradition. On the one hand, if rifles, reapers, sewing machines, and watches had not already been characterized by simplicity and plainness, it would have been considerably more difficult to apply the new system in the first place; on the other hand, once the system was applied, it inevitably encouraged further simplification and further stripping away of non-essentials. (An American cast-steel plow, as manufactured by the famous Collins Company of Hartford in the early seventies, weighed only forty pounds; whereas a contemporary English wrought-iron plow, which could cut a furrow of equal width and depth, weighed two hundred and fifty pounds.) Furthermore, an industrial structure based upon such a system is pointless unless it turns out large quantities of goods. To some people mass production still seems necessarily to imply inferior products, but there is no technological reason why it should not always produce superior goods. When mass-produced American watches were subjected to comparative tests at the Centennial, only twenty-five years after the new system had been introduced in their manufacture, two different makes surpassed the best performances of fine Swiss watches. There is, to be sure, nothing in the mass-production process which insures that its machines will necessarily be used to turn out the highest-quality products; but the quality can be high if the creators and owners of the machine so desire. Furthermore, the products are uniform and can be made available to more people and at lower prices than is otherwise possible.

The rapidity with which America adopted the new manufacturing procedure, and the relative slowness with which it was accepted in Europe, may well have had some connection with another peculiarity of the American industrial system. Writing in 1841, the English mechanical authority Robert Willis noted that in Great Britain power was transmitted from the prime mover (a steam engine, water wheel, or turbine) to the various machines in different parts of a factory by means of long shafts and toothed gear wheels, but in America by large belts, moving rapidly and quietly. Toothed-wheel transmission is by nature a rigid setup; if the location of the machinery is changed, new shafts and new gears must be arranged. But a system of belts and pulleys is comparatively flexible; the arrangement of machinery can be changed with considerable freedom. It was therefore relatively easy for American manufacturers to rearrange existing factories in a manner appropriate to the new system of interchangeable parts.[2]

Mass production as we know it today, however, depends as much upon mechanical handling of materials as upon interchangeable parts, and the development of mechanical conveyors and their use in an integrated manufacturing procedure can be traced to an even earlier date than Whitney's system. Thirteen years before Whitney set up his armory in New Haven, Oliver Evans built a flour mill in Newcastle County, Delaware, in which he installed belt conveyors, screw conveyors, endless-chain bucket elevators, and, as Joseph W. Roe has noted, nearly all of the modern transporting devices in substantially their present form. A few years later these devices were installed in Thomas Ellicott's mill near Baltimore (see Fig. 6), in which, as Evans wrote, they performed "every necessary movement of the grain and meal, from one part of the mill to another, or from one machine to another, through all the various operations, from the time the grain is emptied from the Wagoner's bag, or from the measure on board the ship, until it is completely manufactured into flour . . . ready for packing into barrels, for sale or ex-

[2] By 1878 the American system of belt and pulley transmission was being adopted in Europe. See William T. Porter, "Machines and Machine Tools," *Reports of the United States Commissioners to the Paris Universal Exposition, 1878*, Washington, 1880, Vol. IV.

portation. All of which is performed by the force of water, without the aid of manual labor, except to set the different machines in motion."

It is this system of mechanical handling plus the system of interchangeable parts which united to make modern mass production, and it is strange that so little attention has been paid to their development by the historians of our civilization. Whitney is usually spoken of only as the inventor of the cotton gin, and Evans—if he is mentioned at all—is referred to as the inventor of an ungainly, amphibious steam carriage called *Eructor Amphibolis*. But it is their contributions to the design of the industrial structure itself, to the fundamental principles of mass production, that command our attention here. For it is to them that we owe the manufacturing system which made the products of technological design available to great numbers of people.

It was Henry Ford, aided by such ingenious technicians as C. W. Avery, William Klann, and Charles E. Sorensen, who finally combined Whitney's system of interchangeable parts and Evans' system of mechanical conveyors to create the modern system of power-driven assembly-line manufacture. When the French engineers, Arnold and Faurote, published their study of *Ford Methods and Ford Shops* in 1915 they described in some detail the Ford system of motor and chassis assembly. Ford practice, they noted, was to place the most suitable component of an assembly on elevated ways or rails, and carry or push it past successive stationary sources of component supply and past successive groups of workmen who fixed the various components to the basic part of the assembly. Since the components were perfectly gauged and absolutely interchangeable, each piece could be affixed in a predetermined time and the whole assembly could be chain-driven along the rails at a uniform rate.

Arnold and Faurote stated that Ford had introduced this system in 1914, and they credited it as "the very first example of chain-driving an assembly in progress of assem-

bling." Ford himself, writing in 1923, said he had installed
the first moving assembly line (for flywheel magnetos)
"along about April 1, 1913." But revolutionary as the Ford
assembly line was, it rested upon a conception which had
long been developing in American industry. For the idea
of conveying a job mechanically past workmen at fixed
stations, each of whom performs a special operation, came
directly from the Chicago meat packers, and the basic procedure in their plants had originated in the hog-slaughter-
ing houses of Cincinnati almost eighty years before Ford
adapted it.

The earliest detailed account of the Cincinnati slaughterhouse procedure seems to be that published in 1861 by
Charles L. Flint. According to Flint, the carcasses of the
hogs were slid from the bleeding platform (where their
throats had been cut) into a long scalding vat, floated
along through it to a lever-operated contrivance which
lifted them out onto the higher end of a long, inclined
table down which they were slid past eight or nine pairs
of men, each of whom had some special job to do in the
process of shaving and cleaning the hog. At the end of
the table the carcass was hung from a hook on the rim
of a huge horizontal wheel, about six feet above the floor,
which revolved around a perpendicular shaft. As soon as
the hog was swung on its hook the wheel turned one
eighth of its circuit, bringing the next hook to the table
to receive its carcass and carrying the first carcass a distance of four feet to the workers who performed the first
operation in the process of gutting it. Successive turns carried the carcass to other workers who in turn performed
their jobs until finally, just before the hook returned to the
table for another hog, the gutted and washed carcass was
lifted off and carried to another part of the building and
hung up to cool.

Sometime in the early sixties the horizontal wheel was
replaced by an overhead railway loop, around which hooks
traveled on pulleys, carrying the carcass past the workers'
stations until, at the end of the loop, they swung off on a

straightaway along which they conveyed it to the cooling chamber. (See Fig. 7.) Thus it was no longer necessary to carry the carcass by hand from the end of the disassembly line to the storage room, as it had been with the wheel conveyor. But in all essential respects the principle of the mechanized assembly line remained unchanged.

Just when the system Flint describes was introduced we do not know, but his account indicates that it was already well established in Cincinnati by 1860, and there is clear evidence that in principle, at least, it originated much earlier. When Harriet Martineau visited Cincinnati in 1835 she was driven about the town by Dr. Daniel Drake (of whom more in a later chapter), who showed her the slaughterhouses on Deer Creek. She did not want to see inside, but the doctor described their method of operation and she recorded what he told her.

One man [she noted] drives into one pen or chamber the reluctant hogs, to be knocked on the head by another whose mallet is for ever going. A third sticks the throats, after which they are *conveyed by some clever device* to the cutting-up room, and thence to the pickling, and thence to the packing and branding. [Italics mine.]

One wishes Miss Martineau had been able to stomach the "reeking carcasses" and had seen and described the clever device which conveyed them from station to station. But whatever it was, a horizontal wheel or other conveyor, it is clear that the basic system must have been essentially the same as that described by Flint.

Our lack of precise knowledge about the origin of the system is an indication of the extent to which we have hitherto neglected the underlying technological factors of our civilization. Up until recently it has frequently been asserted that the system Ford took over from the meat packers and made the core of modern mass-production industry had originated in the seventies or eighties and had thus been a product of the surge of industrialization which is held to have transformed America in the last quarter of the nineteenth century. Siegfried Giedion, in his history of mechanization, dates the system from the late sixties or early seventies, on the basis of patent-office records and such information as he was able to get from Cincinnati's local historians. Yet Miss Martineau's account is pretty conclusive evidence that the industrial system which Giedion justly calls "the dominant principle of the twentieth century" had in all its essentials been put into actual practice more than sixty-five years before that fateful century began. Whatever the precise date may have been, the evidence at hand is sufficient to emphasize that the increasing tempo of industrialization in late nineteenth-century America was a development of technological factors which were already deeply rooted in our national experience during the "agrarian" decades of the thirties and forties. It should effectively remind us that the technology of mass production is as indigenous to the United States as the husking bee.

All this emphasis on mechanical and technological factors in nineteenth-century America may seem to ignore the fact that until 1860 the United States was primarily an agricultural country. But the proportion of people engaged in agriculture, or the relative value of agricultural and manufactured products, is not the most significant index of the role of technology in a nation's life.

Before the American land could be a union in fact as well as in name, the land itself had to be made smaller and more compact than it had been when it took Washington nine days to proceed from Philadelphia to Cambridge to take command of the Revolutionary Army. A number of forces contributed to this contraction and unification of the continent. There were threats from the outside which drove the people to unite in self-protection; there was a vast increase in population to fill the empty spaces; there were the people's common interests in development of new land, in conquest of the wilderness; there was the homesick need of the pioneer to keep in touch with those left behind in the settled regions; there was the invasion of Washington by the frontier in the person of Andrew Jackson; and there was the belief in Union of dynamic idealists like Lincoln. But, as the technological historian Roger Burlingame has said, "without the continuous, inevitable progress of technology—of which, indeed, very few were conscious—all these causes would have failed to operate."

Before the Declaration of Independence there were apparently only two steam engines in the thirteen colonies: one at Passaic, New Jersey, in a copper mine and the other in a Philadelphia distillery. England had forbidden the colonies to engage in most industries, in an effort to keep them dependent on British manufactures. But once the Revolution was achieved, industrial expansion and technological invention proceeded at a rapid rate. As a matter of fact, in the seventeen years between the end of the Revolutionary War (1783) and the end of the century, three major technological achievements had already laid the foundations for future national unification. Whitney's cotton gin unified the South by giving it a new source of wealth—cotton—and a common interest in slavery as a means of exploiting it. Slater's reproduction of English textile machinery in New England began the Industrial Revolution in that section and linked it economically to the South, whose cotton fields supplied the raw materials for the mills. And finally Fitch's steamboats—later promoted by Livingston and Fulton and ingeniously adapted to shallow rivers by Henry Shreve and others—enabled the pioneer to settle the West and at the same time bound him inextricably to the East. McCormick's reaper later made the East and the South dependent on the West for food, and the railroads and other subsequent inventions implemented and strengthened the interdependence of all these diverse regions.

The importance of these factors becomes clear when we remember that the unity of no other nation in history rested to a similar degree upon technological foundations. In the light of that fact the characteristics of the vernacular assume a special significance in the United States. For it is clear that they had inadvertently become *national* in a way that had nothing to do with the naïve nationalism which patriots had self-consciously demanded from our literature and our art.

It was this tradition in which were developed, and kept universally available, certain elements of design and certain principles of structure which were a direct, uninhibited response to the new environment and which finally had decisive influence in the hands of men of skill and vision. This stream of art often failed to create beauty of its own. But its patterns at least reflected actuality, however ugly that actuality often was; and the forms evolved in it were firmly rooted in contemporary experience.

3   Two Traditions in Conflict

It was in the various branches of technology that the ver-
nacular tradition first and most uninhibitedly displayed its
characteristics, and we have therefore attempted to define
it in terms of tools and machines. But even in machine
design, as we have seen, it interacted with the tradition
of cultivated taste which flowed into our national life from
the reservoirs of western European culture. Actually the
two traditions mingle from the beginning in all branches
of the arts; it is in their interpenetration and in their al-
ternate ascendancy in the work of different men and different periods that the history of American art consists.

To make clear the nature of this interaction, let us turn
for a moment to a consideration of the art of building.
Throughout the Western world during the nineteenth century there was a disastrous separation between engineering
and architecture.[1] Academic architecture, swept along on
the flood of classic, Gothic, and Renaissance revivals which
culminated in eclecticism, became more and more archae-
ologically-minded as the century progressed. It was ornament, not construction, that it adopted as its province, and
architects seemed increasingly to share the belief of James
Ferguson—one of the century's most influential writers on
the subject—that "where the engineer leaves off the art of
the architect begins." Given the engineer's structural materials, the architect had merely to arrange them "artisti-
cally," as the phrase was, and then add ornament.

In the United States it was in such academic architecture that the tradition of cultivated taste found expression.
Moreover, it was this tradition that produced some of the
most attractive buildings of the century. Richard Upjohn's

[1] The phrase is Talbot Hamlin's in his magnificent history of
Architecture Through the Ages.

Trinity Church at the head of Wall Street in New York, Minard Lafever's Holy Trinity in Brooklyn, and James Renwick's St. Patrick's Cathedral on Fifth Avenue are all charmingly successful imitations of medieval Gothic forms, and the national Capitol in Washington, with its vast dome, is an impressive echo of classic styles. The very success of such buildings, however, did much to establish in America the dichotomy between architecture and engineering. If Renwick could get away with Gothic nave vaults of papier-mâché painted to look like stone, and if Thomas U. Walter's dome for the Capitol could be so impressive in spite of the structural dishonesty of its iron members, disguised as masonry, why should architecture concern itself with the logic of structural expression?

The development of academic styles necessarily figures largely in the history of the practice of architecture in the United States, and we can learn much about our cultural limitations and aspirations from the way in which we tried to adapt a variety of imported forms and styles to our needs. But, taken by themselves, without reference to the enormous quantity of non-academic and non-professional building which our people produced, these borrowed modes mislead rather than inform us about American civilization, however charming they may be. More significant, from our point of view, are the constructive techniques of the vernacular tradition, which can be seen in their purest form in the technological features of construction—in engineering itself.

National unity, in a land so vast and geographically diverse as ours, could not have been achieved without roads, bridges, canals, railroads, and other means of intercommunication, and farsighted Americans early in our history were well aware that the consolidation and expansion of the nation as a political, social, and economic unit would depend upon technological developments. As early as 1785 Washington was preoccupied with the necessity for developing inland navigation in order to bring the Western settlements in close connection with the Atlantic states. "Without this," he argued, "I can easily conceive they will have different views, separate interests, and other connections." And Thomas Pope, shipbuilder and bridge designer, explicitly stated in his *Treatise on Bridge Architecture* (1811) that no real physical union of the country could take place without "the building of bridges, the digging of canals, and the making of sound turnpike roads."

The speed with which canals and bridges were constructed in America was astonishing to Europeans. With the coming of the canals and railroads it was necessary to span rivers, streams, and chasms cheaply and rapidly, and new techniques were used ingeniously to meet the new needs.[2] David Stevenson, the English civil engineer, traveled widely in this country in the thirties and was struck by the temporary and apparently unfinished state of our canals. "Undressed slopes of cuttings and embankments," he wrote, "roughly built rubble arches, stone parapet-walls coped with timber, and canal locks wholly constructed of that material, everywhere offend the eye accustomed to view European workmanship." But, he added, although the works were wanting in finish, they served their purpose efficiently, and they had the advantage that, as traffic increased, they could be enlarged and improved "without the mortification of destroying expensive and substantial works of masonry." Had some of the Erie barge canal's locks not been originally built of stone, the canal would, he pointed out, have been converted into a ship canal long before. But most construction was of wood, in bridges as well as in canal locks and aqueducts, and all kinds of experiments were tried with it. Most important, the tech-

[2] It was the "ingenious novelty of invention" displayed in American engineering works to which the Englishman, John Weale, hoped to call attention in the illustrated folio he published in London in 1841. See *The Public Works of the United States of America*, edited by William Strickland, Edward Gill, and Henry R. Campbell, London, 1841, with prefatory "Advertisement" by John Weale.

niques developed in wood construction were carried over into later work in more durable materials.

By the seventies, for instance, it had become apparent that the practice of American engineers in iron bridges differed widely from that of their European contemporaries. European bridge builders had always aimed to build structures as strong and safe and durable as possible, cost and speed of construction having been secondary considerations. For hundreds of years before the introduction of iron as a building material, massive stone-arch bridges had been painstakingly erected across European rivers. It had been only natural, therefore, that when in 1793–96 Rowland Burdon built the famous cast-iron bridge at Sunderland, England (based on plans worked out some years before by Thomas Paine, the great propagandist of the American Revolution), he had adapted the methods of stone vaulting to iron construction. The six ribs which formed the 236-foot arch were made up of cast-iron panels which served roughly the same structural function as the wedge-shaped stones in a masonry arch. Even in later bridges European engineers tended to perpetuate in iron the proportions which had been familiar in stonework.

The contrast between European and American practice was made clear in a paper read by Thomas C. Clarke before a meeting of the American Institute of Mining Engineers in 1876. In America the aim of the builders had necessarily been to erect a bridge as rapidly and as cheaply as possible. Lack of capital and the necessity for haste led the early railroad-bridge builder, like the canal builder, to use the most abundant material—wood—and the same influences prompted him to design the bridge so that it could be put together with the utmost rapidity. Hence, as Clarke said, when we began to build our iron bridges, we copied the proportions already established as the most economical in wooden trusses instead of copying the more massive proportions of stone; and rather than rivet the separate parts of the bridge together on the scaffolds (as a mason would cement together the separate stones), we copied the techniques of timber construction—using tenons and sliding joints for the compressive members, and pins and eyebars for those in tension. (See Fig. 8.)

The marked feature of the American method, according to Clarke, was the special use of special machine tools, by which the sizes and lengths of all the parts were fitted with the utmost exactness at the place of manufacture. In other words, the parts of the bridge were prefabricated by machinery and could be rapidly assembled on the spot; whereas in the European system of riveted lattice construction assembly was often tediously slow.

The proportions adopted by American designers and their methods of construction both resulted in great economy of material. The result was that when, for instance, English, continental, and American bridge builders submitted competing designs in 1876 for a bridge over the Minamidic River on the Intercolonial Railway of Canada, the American plans called on the average for roughly half the weight of materials required by their competitors. Similarly, when Roebling had completed the Niagara Suspension Bridge (1851–55)—the first large railroad suspension span in the world—he was able to write in his report to the directors of the company: "The work which you did me the honor to entrust to my charge has cost less than $400,000. The same object accomplished in Europe would have cost four millions without securing a better purpose, or insuring greater safety."

The early builders of wooden-truss bridges, like the early designers of machinery, had worked by rule of thumb. The carpenter-builder had a feel for the strength of timber but no precise knowledge of its capacity to bear loads. Not until 1847—when Squire Whipple, of Utica, New York, published his analysis of bridge building—was there any source of accurate quantitative information on stresses in bridge trusses. The consequence was that some early bridges were uneconomically strong; but the rivalry between the patentees of various wooden trusses in the early days, and the subsequent competition between the various iron-bridge manufacturing companies (like Keystone, Phoenix, and Baltimore) constantly encouraged economy of materials and standardization of design.

In the realm of house building, as in bridge building, the prevalence of wood construction in America as opposed to the stone or brick construction of Europe led to significant differences in architectural fundamentals.

In the twenty-five years immediately preceding the Revolutionary War the tide of Adam's and Chambers' classic revival architecture, which had already swept Gothic, Tudor, and Jacobean ideas out of favor in Britain, reached its height in the American colonies. Almost all the early classic revival buildings in England had been of stone or of brick faced with stucco. But in America the plentifulness of wood had resulted in the development of more skilled carpenters than masons; so the New England builder usually approximated in wood the stonework details he found illustrated in the English books he imported. But modifications of the original designs began to appear almost immediately. Cornices became smaller and more delicate, mantels became daintier, and all the decorative details took on more and more the essential characteristics of wood.

But far more important than these modifications of borrowed forms was the way in which wood construction cooperated with the social system to undermine the cultivated tradition and develop new and more flexible forms. As would be expected, the cultivated classes regarded wood as an inferior material. For one thing it was perishable, and subject to the dangers of storm and fire. But from the earliest days of the Republic there were other and weightier arguments in favor of brick and stone. The article on architecture in *The New and Complete American Encyclopaedia* (New York, 1805) baldly put it thus:

Considered politically, there is this good attending brick buildings: from durable habitations, in which more money has been spent, and more of the refined tastes gratified, an affection for the soil is increased. . . . But the last and highest consideration which strikes us is that emigration would be less easy, and not so common amongst us, were a finer spirit of building to prevail. The facility with which we *may* move, is a strong incentive to that love of change which it particularly interests us to repress in our citizens.

But change was irresistible under democratic political institutions. Ruskin might appropriately argue in Britain that the right to have a house express one's character and history belonged to its first builder and should be respected by his children. But among the majority of Americans there were few who would have agreed with him that it was "an evil sign" when a people built their houses to last for one generation only. A farmer neighbor of Emerson's, who had been reading the Report of the Agricultural Survey of Massachusetts in 1840, had small respect for the Report's recommendation of stone houses. "They are not so cheap," he said, "not so dry, and not so fit for us. Our roads are always changing their direction, and after a man has built at great cost a stone house, a new road is opened, and he finds himself a mile or two from the highway. Then our people are not stationary, like those of old countries, but always alert to better themselves, and will remove from town as a new market opens or a better farm is to be had, and do not wish to spend too much on their buildings." It was inevitable that in the United States the facility of wood construction would be exploited.

Technologically, the most important contribution in building was the anonymous development of the so-called balloon frame, a revolutionary method of wood construction which appeared early in the nineteenth century in the vernacular realm of utilitarian architecture. No historian of our architecture considered this invention worthy of notice until Siegfried Giedion, in the Norton Lectures at Harvard in 1939, emphasized its importance as marking the point at which industrialization began to penetrate housing. But despite the refusal of academic architecture to concern itself with such a utilitarian development, there are a number of sources for information about the role it played in American life.

For hundreds of years men had made wood frames for houses out of heavy timbers (often a foot or more thick) which were joined together by cutting down the end of one timber to form a tenon which could be fitted into a hole, or mortise, which had been cut out of the other timber. If the joint had to support a pull, rather than a thrust, the two pieces were fastened together with a wooden peg driven through auger holes.

With the invention of nail-making machinery early in the nineteenth century, and the resulting availability of cheap nails, the way was open to the development in the United States of a new construction which soon replaced the old type and which has been used throughout the country ever since. This was the balloon frame (so nicknamed, in contempt for its lightness, by traditional carpenters and builders), which the mid-century builders G. E. and F. W. Woodward described as characterized by light sticks, which did not require laborious mortising and tenoning, and (in language very reminiscent of that used in contemporary descriptions of American locomotives) by "a close basket-like manner of construction." The balloon-frame house is nailed together with light studs only two inches by four inches, but is so tied and strengthened that every nail holds to its utmost strength. (See Fig. 9.)

Credit for the invention apparently belongs to a carpenter-builder named Augustine Deodat Taylor, who in 1833 built St. Mary's Catholic Church in Chicago—the first balloon-frame building ever built. Giedion and others have credited it to another Chicagoan, but the researches of Walker Field, first published in 1942, seem to establish Taylor as the real originator. Throughout the nineteenth century, however, the new construction developed anonymously.

The first professional architect who recognized its importance, so far as I have discovered, was Gervase Wheeler, an Englishman who came to the States to practice in the 1840s. His book, *Homes for the People* (published in 1855), was the first architectural publication to quote the description of balloon framing which Solon Robinson had given at a meeting of the American Institute and which had been reported in the New York *Tribune*, January 18, 1855. Robinson himself, who was apparently the first person to describe the new system of construction, was a farmer who had migrated from Connecticut to Indiana in 1834, and he had seen how these lightly framed buildings, erected on the open wind-swept prairies, stood as firm as any of the old frames of New England with posts and beams sixteen inches square. How long they might endure he did not know, but for all practical purposes they were substantial enough to meet the needs of those who were building towns in the wilderness. When another member of the Institute expressed doubts about the long-term durability of the balloon-frame structures, in spite of their admitted strength, Robinson replied: "Sir, we are Christians, you know, and therefore we take no thought for the morrow."

Yet, in spite of Gervase Wheeler's interest in the new method of construction, it was generally ignored by professional architects. As one of the most successful of them put it in 1879:

It sometimes happens, in localities remote from large cities or large towns, that persons are obliged to do with make-shifts, to get a home at all. It was such a condition of things that led the well-disposed pioneer of the West to adopt the method called "Balloon framing", which is really no framing at all. . . .

It was the carpenter-builders and the farmers who developed it, and its role in American life was best understood by men like Robinson and one of the anonymous authors of *The Great Industries of the United States* (published in Hartford in 1873), who hailed it as "the most important contribution to our domestic architecture which the spirit of economy, and a scientific adaptation of means to ends, have given the modern world." There was, he thought, hardly a better evidence of the American spirit than the prompt adaptation to new conditions reflected in the introduction of this new method of building. And he demonstrated his understanding of its relationship with other aspects of technological advance when he added that "our methods of construction, like our means of transportation, have passed into the railroad phase of development."

Here, then, were the roots of the vernacular tradition in building. Here were the same characteristics which we have already traced in technological design: simplicity, lightness, flexibility, and wide availability.

These balloon-frame buildings were often designed and constructed without reference to any requirements other than those of utility, and they were often appallingly unattractive. Professional architects usually regarded them with horror. To Calvert Vaux, for instance, who, like Gervase Wheeler, had come to the United States with the best available English training and had devoted his life to the realization in this country of his ideals of his art, such houses seemed to have been constructed without any sense of proportion or the slightest apparent desire to make them agreeable objects in the landscape. These "bare, bald white cubes," as he called them in 1857, struck him as monotonous evidence of a life spent "with little or no cultivation of the higher natural perceptions." And like many of his cultivated contemporaries, he set about doing his best to educate the American people in sifting, testing, and improving all suitable architectural forms and modes of the past. He recommends, for instance, Moorish arcades and verandas and Chinese balconies and trellises added to what he calls the "irregular Italian" or to the "later modifications of the Gothic."

But Vaux, again like a number of his contemporaries, was at least vaguely aware of the basic problem represented by the conflict between the cultivated academic tradition and the square boxes which were springing up in every direction. Republicanism, he argued, "tacitly, but none the less practically, demanded of art to thrive in the open air, in all weathers, for the benefit of all, if it was worth anything, and if not, to perish as a troublesome encumbrance." The balloon-frame houses might trouble him because of their builders' apparent lack of capacity for enjoying what is really desirable in life, but he nevertheless recognized that they were rooted in the lives of the people, "simply and unceremoniously" reflecting both the migratory, independent spirit which pervaded Americans and the economic opportunity which made it possible for almost every storekeeper and mechanic to build his own home.

Vaux was typical, in a sense, of a whole group of professionals to whom it was obvious that the forms and modes of the past could not be slavishly copied in this country. The past, they proclaimed, should be regarded as a servant, not as a master. Yet no matter how devoutly they professed, as William M. Woollett did, that "architectural effect should be obtained by the natural combinations and workings of the constructive portions of the structure, and not by adding or planting on of these features," they nevertheless were capable of the kind of alteration of old houses illustrated in the accompanying plates from Woollett's book. (See Fig. 10.) Calvert Vaux was willing enough to quote Emerson's exhortation to the American architect to "study with hope and love the precise thing to be done by him, considering the climate, the soil, the length of the day, the wants of the people, the habit and form of government." Indeed, many professionals felt in a vague sort of way that American architecture would develop some distinctive characteristics, but they generally agreed with Vaux that whatever these characteristics might ultimately turn out to be, they could "hardly be expected to depend much on the employment of really new forms."

Clearly it could not be from men so disposed and so bound to tradition that fundamental innovations would come. Those would continue to develop anonymously in haphazard response to social necessity, as did balloon-framing. But as the anonymous and revolutionary contributions of the vernacular tradition became established in building construction, they inevitably influenced and modified, and were modified by, the ideas and practice of the professional architects. There is no more charming evidence of the interaction of the two traditions than the carpenter-Gothic houses (like the "Lace House" in Black-hawk, Colorado, Fig. 11), built in all parts of the country during the middle decades of the century. The fanciful and sometimes highly elaborate scrollwork overlies a balloon-frame structure in much the same way that the carpenter's scrollwork overlay the bold, simple mechanism of many American woodworking machines.

The essential point, however, is that through all the various revivals which were borrowed from Europe by the professional architects in the United States—whether it were Asher Benjamin's Greek style, Alexander Jackson Davis' and Upjohn's Gothic, or Vaux's Italian—certain characteristics recur which distinguish the American examples from their European contemporaries; and these characteristics clearly reflect the recurring influence of the vernacular tradition.

One of these characteristics is the plane surface—the flat wall of wood, or brick, or stone. The simple clapboard wall, for instance, which was evolved in response to the lack of lime in the colonies, has dominated American wood construction for three centuries. There have been, of course, numerous instances in the United States of cluttered and elaborate wall surfaces, in wood as well as in other materials. But in general, even in the worst moments of nineteenth-century eclecticism, American buildings differed from those of England, Germany, or France in being less given to surface richness. Similarly, early in the century, when classic styles had been revived, in Europe it was chiefly the magnificence of Roman forms which had been imitated, while in the United States (except momentarily in a few urban centers in the East) it was the serenity and severity of Greek forms which had appeared in churches, houses, and courthouses throughout the country.

Newspapers, farm journals, family magazines, and many books of the period offer ample evidence of the attitude which is expressed in the buildings themselves. There is a whole literature, for example, on the general subject of rural architecture, some of it by trained architects but much of it simply by farmers or "friends of agriculture" who had enough ingenuity and good sense to plan houses which met practical needs. Almost all of this literature expresses pragmatic contempt for "Gothic castles with piecrust battlements," "fantastical and puerile 'bird cages' with gewgaw carvings," and other follies which, as D. J. Browne told his fellow farmers at an American Institute meeting in the forties, were at variance with the simplicity of our manners, with our climate, and with reason and sound taste.

Nowhere did the interaction of the vernacular and the cultivated tradition find clearer expression than in the popular books on architecture which appeared in the middle of the century. One of the most amusing and enlightening of these was Lewis F. Allen's *Rural Architecture,* originally published in New York in 1852 and reissued several times in the sixties and seventies, a forgotten volume which did more to shape the course of ordinary house building than many a more pretentious and less salty book. Allen was a farmer in western New York State (and an uncle, incidentally, of Grover Cleveland) who had no formal training as an architect, and whose contempt for the professionals sprang from a conviction that they showed no understanding of the purposes to which a rural home should be adapted. He therefore took it upon himself to instruct his neighbors in the fundamentals of house building, so that they would have their own notions about it, "and not be subject to the caprice and government of such as profess to exclusive knowledge." He was concerned, he said, only with the shape, arrangement, and accommodation of the building, not with modes and styles of exterior finish. The latter, so long as they suited those who adopted them, were of little consequence, he felt, and could therefore safely be left to the architects.

The fundamental principles which Allen keeps reiterating throughout his book—whether in connection with farmhouses themselves, or barns, or poultry houses, or rabbit hutches—are all summed up in his definition of good taste. It is a definition which in our day may sound commonplace enough, but which most academic architects of his day overlooked. Good taste, Allen believed, demanded both a fitness to the purpose for which a thing was intended and a harmony between the various parts. Any product of good taste would be both "pleasing to the eye, as addressed to the sense, and satisfactory to the mind, as appropriate to the object for which it is required." No style of architecture or finish could be really *bad*, he insisted, if utility were duly consulted and complied with. Provided there was a harmony amongst them even the meanest buildings on a farm derived a dignity from "the character of utility or necessity which they maintain."

Planting himself on these convictions, he mercilessly attacked the meaningless current styles which the architects of the cultivated tradition were exploiting. At the slightest excuse he laid into "the ambitious cottage, with its covert expression of humility" such as those which men like Vaux and Downing were building. "What," he asks, "are the benefits of a parcel of needless gables and peaked windows, running up like owls ears above the eaves of a house, except to create expense, and invite leakage and decay?" He detested all the "gewgawgery" of the haberdasher-built houses of his time and maintained stoutly that all buildings should show for themselves what they were built of, rather than masquerade as something else.

Being altogether untutored in draftsmanship, Allen had to employ a Buffalo architect to draw up the elevations and plans of his houses for illustrations in his book, and—as might be imagined—the results were not satisfactory. Throughout the text Allen snipes at the architect's renderings. For instance, he objects to the diamond-paned windows with which the draftsman dressed up his design for a poultry house; "but," he sourly remarks, "as he had, no doubt, an eye to the 'picturesque,' we let it pass, only remarking that if we were building the house on our own account, there should be no such nonsense about it." (See Fig. 12.)

But the significance of his book is not confined to its attacks upon frippery and pretense. Its positive contribution is that all the plans for buildings which it offers have their origin in the life to be lived, or the jobs to be done, within them. The layout of buildings, arrangement of rooms, provision for light and ventilation—all are managed with an eye to the comfort, convenience, and pleasure of actual farm living rather than to stylistic design.

Another book which should be better known to students of American architecture is Orson S. Fowler's *A Home for All, or, The Gravel Wall and Octagon Mode of Building,* originally published in New York in 1849. Fowler was, in a way, typical of the reformer-enthusiasts who flourished in the forties and fifties. For a generation he and his brother Lorenzo were the most active boosters of phrenology—the "science" based on the belief that mental faculties and character traits are revealed by the conformation of the skull—and he traveled throughout the country lecturing and selling copies of the books and magazines which he and his brother wrote and published.

It was on one of his Western trips that Fowler came across a method of building which, combined with certain phrenological conceptions of his own, produced a system of building examples of which can still be seen in many

Hudson Valley towns and elsewhere. Fowler was convinced that, from all points of view, an octagonal form was the ideal one for a home. For one thing it provided considerably more enclosed space than a square or rectangle of the same circumference, and hence was economically superior. Furthermore, it permitted floor plans which, he argued persuasively, were phrenologically sound and which made housekeeping less of a burden than it had to be in houses of other shapes. The trouble was, simply, that its obtuse angles were harder to frame than the right angles of conventional houses.

The solution to this problem he found, however, when he saw houses near Janesville, Wisconsin, built of lime, gravel, and sand. But let him tell it in his own words:

I visited Milton [Wisconsin], to examine the house put up by Mr. Goodrich, the original discoverer of this mode of building, and found his walls as hard as stone itself, and harder than brick walls. I pounded them with the hammer, and examined them thoroughly, till fully satisfied as to their solidity and strength. Mr. Goodrich offered to allow me to strike with a sledge, as hard as I pleased, upon the inside of his parlor walls for six cents per blow, which he said would repair all damages. He said in making his discovery he reasoned thus: Has nature not provided some other building material on these prairies but wood, which is scarce? . . . Let me see what we have. Lime abounds on them everywhere. So does coarse gravel. Will they not do? I will try. He first built an academy not larger than a school house. . . . It stood; it hardened with age. He erected a blacksmith's shop, and finally a block of stores and dwellings; and his plan was copied extensively. And he deserves to be immortalized, for the superiority of his plan must revolutionize building, and especially enable poor men to build their own houses.

Here was a method of construction (in reality an empirical rediscovery of Roman concrete, and one of the earliest uses of this material for domestic architecture in modern times) which was easily adapted to octagonal houses, and Fowler at once set out to sell the idea to his countrymen. His own house at Fishkill, New York, was a sightseers' objective for many years, until seepage from a cesspool made it a typhoid breeder and broke the old man's heart. In the meantime, however, hundreds of houses had been built according to his proposals, and his book did a great deal to promote a method of construction which, quite apart from his octagonal plan, had a share in the development of what later became ferro-concrete architecture.

Like Lewis F. Allen, Fowler had no use for fancy trimmings, and one of the things he liked about his "gravel walls" was the plain surfaces they presented. Nature, he reminded his readers, "never puts on anything *exclusively* for ornament *as such*. She appends only what is useful, and even absolutely *necessary*," and that should be the law of design.

This brings us to another recurring characteristic which —like the plane surface—distinguishes American domestic architecture from its European counterpart: flexibility of ground plan. This flexibility may be traced from its origins in the early eighteenth-century practice of adding ells and lean-tos to the central-chimney houses on up through the nineteenth-century development of sliding doors which came into American house design with the Greek revival in the late 1820s and were extensively used thereafter. Yet to Wilhelm Bode, the German critic, these sliding doors seemed a novelty at the end of the century, when he visited the Chicago World's Fair in 1893.

Openness and flexibility have been characteristic of American house plans for three hundred years, and have to a great extent resulted from the influence of the vernacular tradition. An 1872 book of plans, each of which is designed "to afford an easy opportunity of adding to it in the future without interfering with the construction already in use," was the work of an architect named C. P. Dwyer who in his preface claimed "years of residence in the Great

West" and "a knowledge of the various modes of cheap construction" in Europe as well as in America, "where necessity is the superintending architect." It is possible to trace a part of the development in the records of academic architecture, especially in summer cottages and country homes where architect and client felt relatively free to develop independent solutions. But for many of the most daring innovations one must turn to such unlikely and neglected sources as, for example, a volume produced in the sixties by Catherine Beecher and her more eminent sister, Harriet Beecher Stowe. Here, in *The American Woman's Home* (New York, 1869), these worthy and earnest ladies laid down the specifications for what they called "a Christian house; that is, a house contrived [notice the verb] for the express purpose of enabling every member of a family to labor with the hands for the common good, and by modes at once healthful, economical, and tasteful." The house they contrived is a remarkable job. They planned it for mass use, and deliberately acknowledged the industrial environment by arguing that, owing to the railroads, men working in cities could build such a house and rear families in the country. The over-all plan, and every detail, aims—in Miss Beecher's words—at "economizing time, labor, and expense by the close packing of conveniences." (See Fig. 13.)

As in Frank Lloyd Wright's Suntop Homes at Ardmore seventy years later, all the heating, plumbing, and storage facilities are concentrated in a central unit—at the darkest part of the house—leaving the well-lighted outer parts free for family life. The kitchen and stove room, the arrangement of which the authors liken to a cook's galley on a steamship (from which, indeed, they probably got the idea) are an extraordinarily advanced piece of compact, functional planning. The glazed sliding doors between stove room and kitchen serve to shut out heat and smells and to let in light. The whole house is artificially ventilated by a system of flues connected with the stove; the stove warms the air in the flues, thus setting up a current in them, which both draws off the heat and smells of the kitchen (and of the water-closet room on the second floor) and draws fresh air from outdoors to supply all the rooms of the house.

Particularly interesting, since it seems to be the earliest recorded use of a movable partition in an American house, is the screen on rollers by means of which the large room to the left of the entrance could serve as a big, airy sleeping room at night; then in the morning, when the screen is rolled to the middle of the room, as a sitting room on one side of the screen and a breakfast room on the other; and finally, through the day, a large parlor on the front side and a sewing room behind. By means of this movable partition (which, incidentally, was also a "storage wall," with shelves and compartments built in to economize space), and the compact kitchen and stove room, the useless spaces usually devoted to kitchen, entries, hall, back stairs, pantry, etc., would all be eliminated. It is, on the whole, a radical interior plan, broadly prophetic of features of the best twentieth-century design. But the ladies got nowhere with the exterior; that remained strictly conventional. Working from the inside out, they—like Allen and other nameless exponents of the vernacular tradition —did not have the requisite experience and training to evolve a suitable exterior shell for their creation. The chances are, indeed, that they were not much concerned about relating the exterior to the interior. Even among professional designers it was assumed that although the ground plans of a house should be made to conform to the necessities and requirements of those who were to occupy it, those plans did not, as the architect S. B. Reed said, "decide, or even indicate, the style, character, or expense of the outside dress that may be put upon them."

But it was the gradual pressure of flexible and open plans, co-operating with the freedom and facility of the vernacular balloon-frame construction, which encouraged a few architects to abandon the stagnation of academic traditions and to evolve new solutions to the problems of house building.

A writer in *Putnam's Magazine* in 1854 declared that splendors of architecture were not to be looked for in America (except in the shape of bridges and aqueducts) until such time as we learned that twenty or thirty families might live in a palace by pooling their wealth and building one capacious dwelling, while if each built separately they would be compelled to live in inconvenient and unattractive houses. The problem which the writer was facing was one which is still much agitated: how can we provide adequate housing for the masses of our people? As a matter of fact his suggested solution (an idea which he caught from the vast hotels of his pre-apartment-house period) is basically the same as the one which Lewis Mumford and others have advocated in our time: dividing up the expense of major installations, such as heating units and water mains, among a number of families to reduce the per capita investment. But the other approach to the problem—mass-produced portable and prefabricated housing—about which we hear even more today, goes back at least as far.

Balloon-frame construction, as we have seen, early in the last century made substantial houses much more widely available than they had been before. But maximum availability could be achieved only when the building industry adopted mass-production techniques similar to those developed in the manufacture of firearms, machinery, and watches. In recent years, particularly as a result of the war-stimulated demand for emergency housing of workers, we have learned a great deal about prefabrication of houses and about portable and demountable buildings. One gathers from present-day writers on architecture and construction that these are almost exclusively twentieth-century developments. (The John B. Pierce Foundation, for example, published in 1943 a *History of Prefabrication*, by Alfred Bruce and Harold Sandbank, which men-

tions no case of precut or sectional buildings before 1892.)
Certainly many important features of modern technique
are of recent origin, but the theory of prefabrication itself, and its pioneer practice, go back well into the nineteenth century. The frames of hewn-timber houses and
buildings were shipped ready-cut to all parts of the world
in the late seventeen hundreds, as we know from early
records. The old Seamen's Chapel, or Mission House, in
Honolulu, was sent, disassembled, from Boston around
Cape Horn in a whaling ship in 1820.

Even some of the most revolutionary current methods
were proposed more than a hundred years ago by a weird
Pittsburgh genius named John Adolphus Etzler. He described them at considerable length in a long memorial to
Congress and in a book called *The Paradise within the
Reach of All Men, without Labor, by Powers of Nature
and Machinery,* first published in this country in 1833,
reissued a number of times in England, and rather scornfully reviewed by Henry Thoreau in the leading article of
the *Democratic Review* for November 1843. Etzler described, for instance, how wood, if "cut and ground to
dust and then cemented with a liquor," could be molded
into any shape and dried so as to become a solid, consistent substance which could be dyed and polished. Thus,
he announced, "we may mould and bake any form of any
size, entire walls, floors, ceilings, roofs, . . . furnitures,
. . . kitchen utensils, pieces of machineries." He proposed
the construction of huge, air-conditioned apartment buildings, to be made of "large solid masses, baked or cast in
one piece . . . so as to join and hook into each other
firmly."

Apparently Etzler's schemes never came to anything
much, and the man himself was so completely lost sight
of that a popular American writer of the seventies—confused by the numerous English editions of the book—
referred to him as "Mr. Etzler, of England." But prefabrication on a less ambitious scale managed to make considerable headway during the next few years. "Barnard's

Portable Patent Houses" were exhibited and sold in St. Louis, Missouri in 1847, and were described in the St. Louis *Daily New Era* (June 26, 1847) as "made in single or double sections, . . . suitable for dwellings, stores, offices, shops, &c., . . . of various sizes with one or more rooms, and can at any time be taken down and removed to any part of the town or country at small expense." Thomas P. Kettell observed in 1861 that "the settler on the new lands of the West is now not always required to plunge into the wilderness and rear his first shelter from logs, but may have his house sent from Chicago or other cities by railroad, and put up to await his coming." By 1873 an anonymous writer was able to say that with the opening of the West, with the new methods of transportation, and with the application of machinery to lessening the expenditure of labor, domestic architecture had "partaken fully" of the spirit of the age; the Western prairies, he said, were dotted over with houses which had been "shipped there all made, and the various pieces numbered, so that they could be put up complete, by anyone."

One of the most interesting of the United States exhibits at the Paris Universal Exposition of 1867 was a balloon-frame farmhouse which had been shipped in sections by its manufacturer, Colonel Lyman Bridges, of Chicago, and assembled at the exposition. Bridges had, for a number of years, been in the business of supplying settlers in the West with portable, prefabricated buildings of this type. According to his own testimony at the time, the majority of his customers ordered houses of from two to four rooms, which cost from two hundred to six hundred dollars, but about one out of seven bought more pretentious houses which sold at prices up to a thousand dollars. Schoolhouses, also, were supplied to pioneer villages (usually of a standardized 24' × 36' floor plan—costing a thousand dollars), and stores of various styles and sizes could be had at prices ranging from five hundred to two thousand dollars. It was the colonel's firm, no doubt, which James Parton described (in the chapter on Chicago in his *Triumphs of Enterprise,* 1872) as "happy to furnish cottages, villas, schoolhouses, stores, taverns, churches, courthouses, or towns, wholesale and retail, and to forward them, securely packed, to any part of the country." Similarly, D. N. Skillings and D. B. Flint manufactured and sold in Boston and New York in the early sixties farmhouses, barns, hospitals and barracks for the Union armies, depots for the Adams Express Company, all made in sections, any one of which could be applied to any building of their make (on the general principle of interchangeable parts).

It is difficult to trace the development of prefabrication. Source material for such history (such as catalogues and advertisements) is ephemeral, and no one thus far seems to have bothered to collect the available scraps. But by the seventies the system was well established. Derrom's Ready-Made Houses were widely advertised in 1876. (See Fig. 14.) The Ducker Portable House Company, of New York, published an extensive catalogue of buildings made up of strong, light, wood-framed sections—covered with an indurated, waterproof fiber—which locked together without the use of nails, screws, or any other appliance. William H. Wahl, writing in the eighties, said that the manufacture of portable houses had become an important industry in the United States. According to his account, they were extensively used by builders of such public works as railroads and canals; by the Army (as barracks, hospitals, etc.); and by miners, sportsmen, photographers, and others. Railway stations, storehouses, bathing houses, pavilions, fruit stands, summer kitchens, and outbuildings of every description were available, and one could buy substantial summer cottages "of many styles and as elaborately finished outside and inside as may be wished." By 1897, when the Klondike gold rush began, a New York company immediately shipped a large number of houses overland, and began loading a vessel to carry more of them to Seattle via Cape Horn, all of them ready-made in sections so that they could be carried easily in boats up the Yukon or packed on sleds.

Unfortunately these early experiments with prefabricated houses did not lead to a thoroughgoing modernization of the building industry. For one thing carpenters and builders early organized to resist the adoption of a house-manufacturing method which threatened to deprive many of them of jobs. Perhaps equally important, the architects must have quietly done all they could to discourage people from buying the mass-produced products which threatened not only to deprive their profession of work, but also to standardize architectural forms and characteristics which seemed to them incompatible with good taste. We have seen how the vernacular tradition in purely technological design ran afoul of the cultivated tradition during the early days of machine design when inventors had to turn to cabinetmakers and architects for patternmaking. But that was simply the result of the inevitable fumbling for methods and techniques which characterizes early procedure in any new field. House design was quite a different matter; it was not a new field, and it had long been the province of the architects—who had the weight and prestige of the cultivated tradition behind them.

Here, then, and in the development of balloon-framing, were the makings for a showdown between the two traditions. The inevitable clash was marked by all the features which we have come to recognize as misfortunes in the social and artistic history of the United States. On the one hand, the emergent vernacular tradition—neglected as it was by the architects—was free to evolve solutions for problems inherent in the new civilization's environment; but its freedom was bought at the cost of losing all contact with the humane tradition of western European art. On the other hand, the cultivated tradition, refusing to adapt itself to the new environment, turned in upon itself—marrying itself to its own past; and the more it did so, the more anemic and impotent it became. The results of this conflict, at the worst, were on the one hand the

bare, unimaginative, depressing houses which stalked both
sides of Main Street in Western manufacturing and mining towns, and on the other hand the pointlessly men-
dacious pseudo-classical and pseudo-Renaissance public
buildings which were pompously erected in the proudest
cities of the land.

Yet, however much weight the cultivated tradition had,
it was a dead weight. In the long run the vernacular, with
its creative vitality, was certain to exert increasing influence wherever it appeared—in the United States or abroad.
At first, of course, this influence was felt almost exclusively in those areas where the new civilization was least
subject to the restraining influence of the older culture. In
geographical terms this meant the new industrial centers,
particularly in the Midwest and West; in social terms it
meant the fields of inexpensive housing and of commercial
and industrial structures. It was precisely in these sub-
artistic areas that balloon-frame construction and prefabrication of buildings were developed (both of them, apparently, first in Chicago, and both of them for the
satisfaction of plain people's needs); and it was largely in
such utilitarian structures as factories, grain elevators, and
warehouses that a tradition was developed of direct, un-
embarrassed simplicity and common-sense adaptation of
form to function.

In these areas also there emerged yet another major
achievement of the vernacular: the expressive use of the
iron or steel skeleton. In order to understand the relationship of this architectural advance to the vernacular tradition as a whole, we must turn for a moment to an even
earlier development: the use of iron as a building material.

The first building in which iron columns replaced the
masonry of the outer walls as the support of the various
floors was a five-story factory erected by James Bogardus
in New York in 1848–49. Boulton and Watt in England
had used cast-iron beams and columns in interior construction forty-seven years earlier, but Bogardus was the first

to employ exterior iron columns as supports in place of
brick or stone columns or walls. From 1850 on he designed
and built a great number of buildings of this type, using
prefabrication techniques much like those which we have
already mentioned in the discussion of the construction of
American iron bridges. (See Fig. 15.)

The discovery of gold in California gave the necessary
impetus for the development of Bogardus' invention. Previously he had been unable to persuade American or English capitalists to invest in his project, but when the rush
to California set in there was suddenly a huge market.
Wrought-iron parts for buildings which were shipped to
San Francisco by his English competitors required a month
to assemble, but the buildings Bogardus sent out by the
shipload could be put up in a day.

Throughout the next thirty years iron was widely used
in the United States; but in spite of the fact that Bogardus
had hoped from the start to introduce it in domestic architecture, its use (other than in hidden or disguised structural members—as, for instance, in the dome of the Capitol
at Washington) was largely confined to warehouses, office
buildings, and other structures which were often regarded
as beneath the notice of official architecture. Iron, as iron,
was suspect.[3]

To the custodians of the cultivated tradition the new
material offered nothing. Ruskin, after all, had made it
clear that "true architecture does not admit iron as a constructive material" because the sense of proportion and

[3] The professional architect's attitude toward iron as a structural material is plainly revealed in Minard Lafever's *The
Architectural Instructor*, New York, 1856, pp. 405–07. Iron,
Lafever wrote, was suitable for "warehouses, crystal palaces,
banks, and printing establishments" and also "for the interior
structure and decoration" of other buildings where fireproof
construction was desirable and where floors and galleries required strong support with a minimum of material. For such
decorative details as window pediments and cornices, he
pointed out, iron when painted and sanded "has the ornate
and massive appearance almost of carved stone."

the laws of structure had always been based on the use of clay, wood, and stone; a metallic framework would inevitably create a flimsy appearance. Indeed, such works as the cast-iron central spire of Rouen Cathedral and the roofs and pillars of iron railroad stations were, he flatly asserted, "not architecture at all." In 1869 the editors of *Appleton's Journal*, one of the most influential of all the magazines which were trying to improve America's taste in the arts, announced that the use of iron in architecture was "utterly destructive to its dignity." Seven years later Richard Morris Hunt, architect of a number of Fifth Avenue châteaux and Newport villas, and a staunch advocate of "art education for the masses," echoed Ruskin in his official report on the architecture of the Centennial Exhibition when he said that because the main building was built of glass and iron there was "a total absence of anything like monumental grandeur or even apparent substantiality" about it. The author of *Gems of the Centennial Exhibition* (1877) went even further, asserting that there was an "utter lack of beauty and picturesqueness in all iron-frame buildings," and that iron columns and girders, filled in with plate glass, could only produce an inartistic effect.

But to those who, like the authors of *The Great Industries of the United States*, had living contact with the everyday world of machines and trade about them, the use of iron seemed "one of the chief improvements of modern times." It was clear enough to them, to be sure, that the architects of the sixties and seventies had not yet evolved a satisfactory treatment of the new material; but they knew that it had potentialities which should not be neglected. They saw that London's Crystal Palace of 1851 had pointed the way toward exciting new architectural forms and methods of treatment. Here, they wrote, was a material whose tensile strength permitted its use in slender pillars and thin sheets, allowing "an unprecedented proportion of space for windows"; a material which was cheap, handy, strong, safe, and easily movable. No sentimental, Ruskinish objections could, in their view, prevent the increased use of a material with such advantages, and the time would surely come when increased knowledge would lead to its scientific use.

Meanwhile, however, the chief recommendation of iron as an architectural material was the ease with which it could "embody any architectural design." From the architectural rather than the engineering point of view, it was the "iron front" rather than the iron frame that was most interesting, and huge factories were built in Baltimore, New York, Chicago, and other cities to make iron fronts for buildings throughout the country. (See Fig. 16.) Little attention has been paid to this aspect of our architectural history, and the available information has never been collected. Casual research reveals, however, that twenty iron-front buildings, all designed by the architects Van Osdel and Bauman, were built in Chicago in the year 1856, the iron fronts for all but two of which were made (if not designed) by D. D. Badger & Co. of New York. The other two, one of which was a bank, were made by Stone, Boomer, and Bouton of Chicago.

A few fine, intelligently handled examples of iron buildings were built anonymously during the third quarter of the century, such as the warehouses which were torn down to make room for the Jefferson Memorial Park on the old St. Louis waterfront. But most architects who used iron at all continued to treat it as nearly as possible as if it were stone, casting it in Corinthian columns and Romanesque or Gothic arches. (See Fig. 17.) In cities like Chicago and Baltimore there were by 1870 many buildings with iron fronts which were modeled as nearly as possible in the forms and proportions of stone, with only such modifications as the nature of iron made necessary. Such imitation of old forms in new materials is apparently an inevitable stage of development. When sheets of galvanized steel were used to cover the fronts of wooden-frame buildings in the eighties, they were stamped in patterns resembling stone and brick and iron. (See Fig. 18.) Worse still, when Chicago was rebuilt after the fire of 1871, and stone was reintroduced in place of the iron which had melted and buckled so quickly in the fire, the forms which had themselves been modified metal imitations of stone construction were now in turn imitated in masonry which was painted to look exactly like cast iron.

Nevertheless, the essential scheme of a metal frame was becoming firmly established, and the way was being prepared for the development of the steel-skeleton architecture which—in skyscrapers and great factories—later appeared as one of the most distinctive achievements of American art. With the increasing use of steel during the seventies and eighties, new techniques of construction had been evolved. In 1874 James B. Eads completed the famous steel-arch bridge across the Mississippi at St. Louis—the first bridge in the world in which steel was extensively used, and a structure which served as an important stimulus to the development of the Chicago School of Architecture in the eighties and nineties. The engineering problems presented by Eads' design and solved by him in carrying it out, and the honesty and majesty of the finished structure, marked it at once as a monument in the history of bridge building. But it was more than that. From this bridge Louis Sullivan, the greatest of the Chicago architects of the end of the century, caught his vision of the power of the creative dreamer—"he who possessed the power of vision needed to harness the intellect, to make science do his will, to make the emotions serve him."

One of the first buildings in which the steel skeleton was used without any self-supporting walls was William Le-Baron Jenney's second Leiter Building (1889) at the corner of Van Buren and State streets, Chicago. Unlike Jenney's earlier Home Insurance Company Building (1883–85), which was the first "skyscraper" actually erected, the Leiter Building displays practically no reminiscences of academic architectural styles; as in Jenney's proposed building for the Hercules Manufacturing Company, the huge squares of the steel skeleton give shape and form to the exterior. Wide areas of glass screen the interior from the weather, and there is so little ornament that the eye is not distracted from the clean, strong shape of the building. To many critics it was of no account as architecture, but the anonymous author of *Industrial Chicago* (1891) admired its light, airy, yet substantial appearance and astutely observed that it was constructed "with the same science and all the careful inspection" that would be used in the construction of a steel bridge of the first order.

It would be wrong to give the impression that engineering construction in the United States surpassed the achievements of contemporary Europe. As in the case of machine building, the truth seems to be quite the contrary. According to Giedion, French engineers achieved the most audacious and brilliant constructions during the period from 1855 to 1900, Cottancin's and Dutert's Galerie des Machines and the Eiffel Tower at the Paris Exhibition of 1889 marking the climax and conclusion of a long development. But it was in the United States, and specifically in Chicago during the eighties and nineties, that the science of the engineer and the creative genius of the artist combined to produce a new urban architecture: the clearcut, open skyscrapers of Jenney, of Burnham and Root, and of Adler and Sullivan.

While emphasizing the engineers' role in developing new techniques and forms we should not, however, lose sight of the fact that architecture, rightly conceived, has always concerned itself with more than mere construction, and that the engineers had by no means taken over the large-scale humanizing and planning functions of the architect. The result inevitably was that whenever vernacular forms were in competition with the work of the best cultivated architects people were likely to prefer the latter. So, for example, the success of the vernacular in Chicago's business district during the eighties and early nineties was for a time almost completely obscured by the academic brilliance of the cultivated tradition as displayed at the Chicago World's Fair of 1893. Returning to the classic forms which had dominated our official architecture in the first decades of the century, the architects erected an impressive group of buildings which, according to the glowing tribute of Hubert H. Bancroft, the Western historian, were "a triumph of the aesthetical." It has often been said that the Chicago Fair set back American architecture thirty years; and in a sense it did. Certainly there was more originality of design in Sullivan's Transportation Building than in the scholarly classic revival buildings which dominated the exhibition. But in another sense the fair was a significant achievement. Never before had Americans seen a group of buildings so skillfully harmonized; nowhere else had they been able to wander down one apparently endless vista of beautifully correlated façades, then turn a corner and face another, and never encounter a discordant detail. It was this over-all planning, this total effect, which made the borrowed, academic style so impressive to the thousands who visited the fair. So long as the fine achievements of the vernacular remained isolated and unrelated phenomena, they inevitably failed to capture the public imagination on so vast a scale.

The century ended with academic architecture in the ascendancy, and with McKim, Mead, and White as the leading practitioners of the art. But despite the elegance and echoed charm of such buildings as the Boston Public Library (1887–95) and New York's Pennsylvania Railroad Station (1906–10), the work of men like McKim, who operated in the cultivated tradition, had less relation to the vital contemporary forces of American life, and to its future, than even the crudest, least ingratiating examples of small-town dwellings or the most materialistically functional office buildings. And meanwhile, however thoroughly Louis Sullivan's work was eclipsed by his Eastern contemporaries, he for one had fused the vital impulses of the vernacular into what he liked to describe as *organic* architecture (a word which he loved for its sense of "a ten-fingered grasp of reality"). The vision he had caught from the great Eads bridge at St. Louis was given concrete expression in his buildings. "With me," he wrote to Claude Bragdon, "architecture is not an art, but a religion, and that religion but a part of the greater religion of Democracy." Here, close to the vernacular roots, was the first flowering of an architecture indigenous to modern civilization.

4 The Practical and the Aesthetic

It is neither necessary nor possible in this book to analyze in detail the interaction of the cultivated and vernacular traditions in nineteenth-century architecture. Enough has been said to suggest the limitations of a historical or critical approach which confines its attention to the development in the United States of the western European tradition, and to indicate that wherever modern civilization has been freely accepted the characteristics of the vernacular tradition have appeared in whatever patterns people have created.

It is not a question of which examples of architecture (or painting, or literature) are "best" or "finest"; such absolute qualitative judgments are meaningless unless they are made in relation to specific criteria of judgment. By the standards of the academic tradition Memorial Hall at the Centennial Exhibition (now the Pennsylvania Museum in Fairmount Park) was a "finer" building than others which, by the standards of good facilities for exhibiting things, were far finer than it was. A striking instance of the latter was the Pomological Annex, a temporary structure which has been neglected in all discussions of the Centennial's architecture and of which only one picture seems to have been made, but which deserves attention for the striking way in which its form and spirit prefigure those of many modern buildings. (See Fig. 19.) The only description of it which has come to light speaks apologetically of the fact that it was designed without any effort at ornamentation, for purely utilitarian purposes. The walls rose solid to a height convenient for purposes of display, but above that point they were simply glass screens of continuous sash. The interior was light, airy, and cheerful, painted white, with a roof supported by plain joists and girders. In short, the annex was an intelligently designed structure, without any of the pretense that infected the other exhibition buildings. Even the Main Building and Machinery Hall, for all that they were competent engineering designs in iron, were dressed up in meretricious ornament copied from stone and wood forms.

Indeed, in the United States, as throughout the Western world, one of the most characteristic features of the interaction of the two traditions in the industrial and plastic arts was the way in which the materials and methods of technology were employed to perpetuate the forms and modes of craftsmanship. Nothing could be more marked, for instance, than the contrast which frequently existed between the clean, functional design of nineteenth-century machines and the unreasonable fussiness of the objects they were used to manufacture. Industrialization has often been accused of cheapening everything it touched, but the case was often precisely the opposite. Manufacturers in Europe and in America often went to a great deal of extra trouble and expense in order to satisfy cultivated taste by turning out machine-made lighting fixtures, hardware, mantel decorations, furniture, and other ornamental objects which were designed to be beautiful in the same way that handicraft objects were beautiful. (See Fig. 20.) It was not until the twentieth century that the custodians of culture acquired any confidence in the aesthetic merit of forms which were appropriate to machine manufacture. And by that time they faced the tremendous task of undoing the work of their predecessors who had so diligently labored to undermine popular esteem for the vernacular. Schools and museums and books and magazines had so long and so arduously taught people to despise the indigenous products of their environment that it was difficult to persuade them to cherish suddenly what they had so long ignored. Many Americans were—and for that matter are—timid or indifferent in their relationships with the so-called fine arts; it is only in those areas which are outside the scope of the cultivated tradition that they universally felt—and feel—themselves to be on sure ground. As one of our art historians has said, the dealer who put on the market an automobile as inept and clumsy in design as nine out of ten public monuments would be unable to sell it. But this fact is noted as an indication only of the average American's lack of artistic sense, the historian clearly assuming that a beautiful monument is inherently more artistic than a beautiful automobile. Elsewhere in the same volume, for example, it is admitted that automobiles, airplanes, and locomotives are perhaps "the most satisfying aesthetically" of all modern products, but they are excluded from consideration on the grounds that they are in the realm of industrial design, not art.

This exclusive doctrine of art's domain is closely allied to another doctrine which has had considerable vogue in one form or another for many years. This is the doctrine, alluded to earlier in this book, which maintains that art cannot exist except in the neighborhood of a wealthy and aristocratic class. As applied to the post-Civil War period, for instance, the theory is that the newly rich, "fired with the innate human passion for conspicuous waste," surrounded themselves with luxury and patronized art. Being alien to the aristocratic tradition, the theory continues, they did these things crudely; and yet the collections of Mr. Morgan, Mr. Altman, and Mrs. Gardner, for example, are nevertheless held to have "greatly enriched American cultural resources." This, it seems to me, is a weird mismarriage of Veblen and snobbery! It is hard to believe that those who hold such a theory have any basic objection either to conspicuous waste or to the idea that the artist is by nature a sponge to absorb such waste. One suspects that the thing they are interested in is whether the particular sponges they happen to like are doing the absorbing.

The doctrine of artistic exclusiveness has a sturdy history. In J. L. Blake's *Family Encyclopedia* (1834) the orthodox view is bluntly revealed in the statement that "a

general love of coarse pleasures" distinguishes the multitude from the more polite classes, and "the inferior orders
of society are therefore disqualified from deciding upon
the merits of the fine arts." That was the cant phrase of a
camp follower of the cultivated tradition. But less than ten
years later the vernacular found its first important defender.

Horatio Greenough (1805–52) has been known almost
exclusively as the sculptor of a vast, almost naked Washington which horrified his contemporaries. All of his completed work was sentimentally imitative of classical sculpture; one could scarcely find an American artist whose
work more clearly reflected the impotence of creative talent working in alien but admired forms. But in recent
years it has become clear that Greenough's place in the
history of art in the United States has little relation to his
statues. It is his life, and his ideas, which now seem important.

Discouraged by the popular reaction to the statue of
Washington which he had brought over from his studio
in Florence in November 1842 ("A grand martial Magog,"
Philip Hone called it, "undressed, with a napkin lying in
his lap"), and disappointed by the inadequate setting provided for it, Greenough nevertheless was a staunch and
loyal democrat. He wrote to his brother Henry from Wilmington, Delaware, in the spring of '43: "If I succeed in
placing my Washington in a good light, I may dissolve my
connection with the Government. I have enjoyed as much
as any artist ever enjoyed in my profession. . . . My heart
will always yearn after America." Having gone to Rome
to study sculpture directly after finishing his studies at
Harvard in 1825, he spent most of his time abroad (chiefly
at Florence) until 1851, making only occasional trips to
the United States. Italy appealed to him, as to all our early
sculptors, because skilled marble workers were available
there. But Europe was never his home, and he missed what
he called the "world of living and acting men." In Liverpool, for instance, he spoke of the contrast between Englishmen and Americans and how the former had "a kind

of groomed neatness which seems to be the result of police interference,—an expression of respectable servitude." Again, in Vienna he noted "the sort of military view taken of life" which "sweetens subordination to all classes. . . . I believe that we found our institutions upon hope, they upon experience. We hoist the sail and are seasick; they anchor and dance." Although, as he wrote shortly before he died in 1852, he had been inoculated to some extent during his travels with the various ways of thinking of men of different races, creeds, and forms of civilization, he had nevertheless retained "nearly the same proportion of original Yankee conviction to afterthought that you will find of matrix to pebbles in the puddingstones of Roxbury, Mass."

In 1851 political troubles in Florence had led him to give up his studio there and return with his family to the United States. Here he was caught up immediately by the spirit of active power which seemed to him the characteristic feature of American life. And he began work on a book which appeared in incomplete form in 1852 (the year of his death).

This extraordinary little volume—*The Travels, Observations, and Experience of a Yankee Stonecutter*—included several essays and lectures which Greenough had written some years earlier during visits to America, and which had been published in periodicals.

Writing in the *Democratic Review* for July 1843, Greenough had early declared his impatience with the doctrine of exclusiveness in art. Just as the British aristocracy had come to regard the masses as "a flock to be fed, and defended, and cherished, for the sake of their mutton," he wrote, so also the Academies of Fine Arts in Europe had made "a band of educandi the basis of a hierarchy." But Greenough could not accept such dogma. "It is the great multitude for whom all really great things are done and said and suffered," he maintained. And he added, with a humility rare in men whose own work has been damned: "The great multitude desires the best of

everything, and in the long run is the best judge of it."
And again: "The monuments, the pictures, the statues of
the republic will represent what the people love and wish
for,—not what they can be made to accept. . . ."

Despite the recent revival of interest in Greenough's
ideas, his writings have never been reprinted in their en-
tirety and copies of his book are available in only a very
few libraries.[1] It will be necessary, therefore, to quote here
those passages which will convey some notion of the alert-
ness of his observation and the flavor of his genius; for
this neglected writer was possessed of one of the wisest
and most farseeing critical talents in American literature.

The subjects of his various chapters seem strangely assorted at first glance: "Chastity," "American Art," "Social
Theories," "Aesthetics at Washington," "American Architecture." Yet all the essays are essentially related to one
another; they are all, as he said of his book, meant to be
signs that he, for one, "born by the grace of God in this
land, found life a cheerful thing, and not that sad and
dreadful task with whose prospect they scared my youth."

Living in an age of transcendentalists and social vision-
aries, he clung stoutly to the actual. "For these reasons,"
he wrote in his essay on Fourier and the other social re-
formers of Europe and America, "do I mistrust the theorist.
Nine times in ten hath he no wholesome, working, organic
relation with God's ground or with his fellow-men. . . .
Nine times in ten doth he sit perched upon an income
which is a dead branch of the living tree of industry, and
with his belly distended by the east wind, and his heart
sour with the ambition that hath struck inward, doth he
spout generalities." The real test of Fourier's theoretical
writings, Greenough felt, would be to read them in a German beerhouse in New York, or amid throngs of low-
browed and big-jawed Hibernians, stepping here on shore
with vast appetite and a faith that removes mountains.

[1] Some of his best essays were reprinted early in 1948 in a
small collection entitled *Form and Function,* edited by Harold
A. Small and published by the University of California Press.

"I love the concrete, my brother! and I can look Sir Isaac Newton in the eye without flinching; I kneel to Willy Shakespeare, who guessed to a drop how much oil goes to a Lombard's salad. Give me the man who, seated in that fog bank between the North Sea and the Irish Channel, held horses at the playhouse and found it in his head to teach kings how to wear a crown! . . . That's the mind that I will follow, not only because he is substantial, hath an *avoirdupois*, a perfume and a taste, but because he is multiform, elastic, not procrustean, not monomaniacal."

With an elaborate (and not altogether successful) figure of speech in this same essay Greenough probes once more for the heart of his belief. The fruit of the tree of civilization, he says, is knowledge, or science, and the seeds within it are wisdom; but the fruit must be plucked from the tree and consigned to "that earth which we all despise so truly—the hearts and heads of common men; there must it find the soil and moisture, blood and tears, which burst its rind and evolve the godhead within."

Greenough was bound by no reverence for the conventional view of any subject. He denounces the notion of chastity, for instance, as any but a negative and relative virtue. "I know that it comes from very far east and is very old—I am, however, from very far west, and . . . disposed to look narrowly into the matter."

As for architecture, Greenough felt that Americans had mauled and misused Gothic and Greek and Roman and, even where we had succeeded in actually copying, had produced something which was only a make-believe. The number and variety of our experiments with architectural styles was a witness of our dissatisfaction with them; their expense, a witness of the strength of our desire for excellence. And the talents and abilities of the men employed were an indication that the failure to create a satisfactory architecture lay in the system, not in the men.

The Mint in Philadelphia, for instance, was in reality built to house vast engines and printing and coining machines, and the furnaces to operate them. Its Chestnut

Street front, however, was a "maimed quotation of a passage of Greek eloquence, relating to something else," while in the rear rose a huge brick chimney, talking everyday English and warning you that the façade was to be taken with some grains of allowance.

However, let us turn, says Greenough, to a structure of our own, one which by its nature and uses commands us to reject authority:

Observe a ship at sea! What Academy of Design, what research of connoisseurship, what imitation of the Greeks produced this marvel of construction? Here is the result of the study of man upon the great deep, where Nature spake of the laws of building . . . in wind and waves, and he bent all his mind to hear and to obey. . . . If this anatomic connection and proportion has been attained in ships, in machines, and, in spite of false principles, in such buildings as make a departure from it fatal, as in bridges and in scaffolding, why should we fear its use in all construction!

Greenough looked about him with eyes unclouded by the cant and conventions of aesthetic tradition.

The men who have reduced locomotion to its simplest elements, in the trotting wagon and the yacht America, are nearer to Athens at this moment than they who would bend the Greek temple to every use. I contend for Greek principles, not Greek things. If a flat sail goes nearest the wind, a bellying sail, though picturesque, must be given up. The slender harness, and tall gaunt wheels, are not only effective, they are beautiful for they respect the beauty of a horse, and do not uselessly tax him.

Looking at the skeletons and skins of animals, birds, and fish, he found a variety and a beauty which led him to observe that there is "no arbitrary law of proportion, no

unbending model of form in them. It is neither the presence nor the absence of this or that part or shape or color
that wins our eye in natural objects; it is the consistency
and harmony of the parts juxtaposed, the subordination
of details to masses, and of masses to the whole." And
from these direct, unborrowed observations of the world
around him he deduced a theory which anticipates—even
in its phrasing—the famous theory of which Louis Sullivan
became the apostle a half century later: "If there be any
principle of structure more plainly inculcated in the works
of the Creator than all others, it is the principle of un-
flinching adaptation of forms to function."

In all structures which are by their nature purely scientific—such as fortifications, bridges, and ships—we had, as
Greenough saw it, been emancipated from the authority
of tradition "by the stern organic requirements of the
works." If an artist would compare American vehicles and
ships with those of England, he maintained, he would see
that "the mechanics of the United States had outstripped
the artists." In the American trotting wagon he would see
the old-fashioned and pompous coach dealt with "as the
old-fashioned palatial display must yet be dealt with in
this land. . . . The redundant must be pared down, the
superfluous dropped, the necessary itself reduced to its
simplest expression. . . ."

The quality which Greenough admired in the work of
American mechanics was quite the opposite of that which
appeared in "art-manufacture"; he made it perfectly clear
that it was not to be confused with the crude plagiarisms
of "steam artisans." Nor was it the cheap product of mere
naïve materialism; for the style the mechanics had achieved
was really the dearest of all styles. "It costs the thought
of men," he wrote, "much, very much thought, untiring
investigation, ceaseless experiment. Its simplicity is not the
simplicity of emptiness or of poverty: its simplicity is that
of justness, I had almost said, of justice."

The simplicity Greenough admired was the simplicity
which resulted from knowledge and understanding, from

science. Embellishment of any kind was to him the product of ignorance or superstition, and was hence to be avoided even at the risk of nakedness; for in nakedness he recognized "the majesty of the essential, without the trappings of pretension."

Greenough never elaborated a theory of aesthetics to bolster his judgments, but he did state his position briefly, and far more cogently than he has been given credit for. In essence his idea was this: man is not gifted, as brutes are, with an instinctive sense of completeness. Being aware, through his *senses*, that there is a rhythm and harmony in the universe beyond any adaptation of means to ends which his *reason* can measure, man seeks to perfect his own approximation to the essential by crowning it with a wreath of measured and musical, yet non-rational (or as he put it, "non-demonstrable") additions of ornament. In other words man applies embellishment to the products of his rational and scientific designing, hoping thereby to make them more *beautiful,* more in keeping with the many-sided and full and rich harmony which he senses but does not understand in nature. But, says Greenough, this many-sided harmony in nature is in reality a many-sided response to the call for many functions, not an aesthetical utterance of the Godhead. If we find an apparent embellishment in nature, we can assume that it appears to be such only because we do not yet know enough to understand the function to which it is adapted.

"I base my opinion of embellishment," he wrote, "upon the hypothesis that there is not one truth in religion, another in the mathematics, and a third in physics and in art; but that there is one truth even as one God, and that organization is his utterance." Here, then, was the basis for his admiration of the functional forms achieved by mechanics and engineers, and for his distrust of all those theories which asserted that this or that form or color was beautiful *per se*—theories which, he maintained, could be held only by those who arrogate to themselves godship; and to one with Greenough's faith in democracy it seemed clear that "once that false step is taken, human-godship or tyranny is inevitable." Here, too, was the first reasoned defense of the vernacular in the arts.

Few of Greenough's articulate contemporaries shared his interest in and enthusiasm for the aesthetic qualities of the forms of the emerging vernacular. There were, of course, striking analogies between his ideas about American art and those of some of the great writers of his time. Emerson, especially, was hospitable to his ideas; "when one has once got his thought," he wrote to William Emerson, "it will stick by you." And Greenough's admiration for Emerson is indicated by the fact that he sought his opinion of the material to be included in *The Travels, Observations, and Experience of a Yankee Stonecutter*, saying that he would publish nothing till he had Emerson's advice. But the only mid-century art critic who came anywhere near Greenough's discovery of the new art forms was James Jackson Jarves, who in 1864 published *The Art Idea: Sculpture, Painting, and Architecture in America*. Jarves had traveled a great deal (he established the first newspaper in the Hawaiian Islands in 1840), and had studied and collected Italian art. Toward the close of his book, which surveys the history of art, he concludes that were the Americans annihilated tomorrow, "nothing could be learned of us, as a distinctive race" from our architecture, for example. But if "the mechanical features" of our civilization were left to tell the national story, our "ocean-clippers, river-steamers, and industrial machines" would reveal "an enterprise, invention, and development of the practical arts" which would proclaim us to have been a remarkable people. In this respect his vision approached Greenough's (and may have been influenced by it). But Jarves's appreciation of vernacular forms was confined to those around which some aura of nostalgia had begun to collect. By 1864 the ocean clippers and paddlewheel steamers were disappearing and being replaced by propeller-driven steamers and by railroad locomotives "about which," Jarves mournfully asserts, "human affections scarce can cluster, and which art has yet to learn how to dignify and adorn." To Greenough in the forties, the clippers and machines were beautiful in themselves, here and now; to Jarves in the sixties they were beautiful because they had begun to be bathed in a retrospective haze that blurred their functional meaning. He is back to art as adornment again.

For the most part, Jarves and his contemporaries who wrote about the arts inevitably thought in terms of the cultivated tradition. Art, in that tradition, was centuries old; its products were housed in the public and private museums and libraries of Europe and America; its history had been explored and recorded by devoted scholars; great writers from Vasari to Ruskin had interpreted it to the world; and schools and academies had codified and institutionalized its patterns and forms. The vernacular, on the other hand, was only beginning to take shape. Its characteristics were not established; its products were scattered and impromptu; it had no textbooks or histories.

In the United States, as in Europe, those whose innate responsiveness to patterns of shape, sound, texture, color, or ideas developed into a literate, self-conscious interest quite naturally turned for education to the libraries, the museums, the galleries, and the schools of the cultivated tradition.

The consequence was that the more interested in art Americans became, the more firmly they (like their counterparts abroad) subjugated themselves to a tradition which not only was alien to the seminal forces in modern civilization but which also tended to discourage any appreciation of the emergent indigenous forms and patterns. They came to feel that American civilization and art were mutually incompatible. In fact their lack of firsthand contact with the heritage of Western art often seems to have made them even more humble in the face of its prestige and authority than were their European brethren, who could in effect take that heritage more or less for granted, as a natural right. They came to feel that American civilization, lacking as it did those survivals of an older culture which in Europe tempered and diluted the raw realities of democracy and technology, was incompatible with "art." Writing late in the seventies, George Parsons Lathrop (one of the *Atlantic Monthly's* editors, a son-in-law of Hawthorne, who helped Walter Damrosch convert *The Scarlet Letter* into an opera, of all things, and was himself converted to Catholicism), declared that America's "practical" civilization had "imperilled the higher development of the aesthetic," and that in the United States the museums of fine arts were defending art against what he scornfully called "an enlightened age" just as the monasteries had once protected it from the Dark Ages. And Henry T. Tuckerman, whose *American Artist Life* (1870) was an early and sympathetic study of our artistic progress, came to the conclusion that even if the adverse influences of our civilization did not altogether extinguish the love of art, or quell the talent for it, they did at least limit the development of both among us.

Yet even the most ardent apostles of the cultivated tradition recognized what Lathrop called the American's "inborn responsiveness to the artistic." Tuckerman, surveying the American scene at the beginning of the Gilded Age, noted that there were pianos in wilderness log cabins; daguerreotypes, photographs, engravings, and lithographs everywhere; stereoscopes in every parlor. Singers and instrumentalists drew a large box office in towns and cities throughout the land; vast quantities of sheet music were sold; art exhibits drew crowds; and art unions, picture raffles, art clubs, and art journals were ubiquitous. To play the piano with "superficial dexterity," to sketch from nature, to own "a tolerable landscape or engraving," and to read Ruskin, were all common social phenomena. The level of all this artistic activity was very mediocre, Tuckerman thought, but even so it represented "a somewhat remarkable interest in the subject."

This interest the custodians of the cultivated tradition

tried (as they still do) in many ways to foster. To them, for instance, the Centennial Exhibition of 1876 offered no hint of that emerging vernacular whose characteristics appear in retrospect to have been so clearly illustrated in the Corliss engine; they saw it only as a chance for Americans to absorb—from the foreign exhibit of fine arts and art manufacture—the splendors and charms of the European tradition. Here at last was the opportunity demanded by Eugene Benson in *Appleton's Journal* six years earlier, to replace the "common, pretentious, and ugly objects of our everyday life" by those from abroad which would "soften manners and counteract the now unmitigated exercise and influence of mere industrialism." There was, of course, industrialism to counteract in Europe too. But there, at least, it was not unmitigated.

Robert Underwood Johnson, writing in 1923, remembered that not only he and his wife but the whole country got their "first bent toward the aesthetic" from the Centennial, and William H. Ellsworth in his recollections of *A Golden Age of Authors* (1919) recalled that the Centennial had not only "implanted an appreciation of art which was new to the American people," but had also stimulated a whole generation of new artists.

There is evidence enough to support these claims. E. A. Abbey acknowledged the debt he owed to the foreign contemporary paintings which he saw there—particularly those in the English section. Many of his young contemporaries were correspondingly impressed by the work of the Paris and Munich schools; in the fall of 1876 Dwight William Tryon auctioned off all his unsold pictures and sketches, made two thousand dollars, and set out for Paris to study with a pupil of Ingres. A number of American painters had, of course, been deeply influenced by contemporary European styles long before the Centennial. William Merritt Chase and other American students had met regularly with Frank Duveneck in the smoke-filled rooms of the Max Emanuel Café in Munich in the early seventies to discuss art over huge flagons of beer; both Inness and W. M. Hunt had long shown the influence of French painting, and Saint-Gaudens and Olin Warner had studied at the École des Beaux-Arts. But never before the Centennial had so many American artists been so overwhelmed by the work of their European contemporaries.

Three years later S. G. W. Benjamin was reporting that there was everywhere apparent "a deeper appreciation of the supreme importance of the ideal in art, and a gathering of forces for a new advance against the strongholds of the materialism that wars against the culture of the ideal." For one thing, a widespread interest in decorative art had been excited at Philadelphia by the exhibits of tiles, furniture, textiles, and decorative objects by William Morris, De Morgan, and Alma-Tadema, and by the work of the Kensington School of Design. A number of our ablest artists—including Abbey, Saint-Gaudens, Elihu Vedder, and Stanford White—founded the famous Tile Club the year after the exhibition (at which Minton tiles had been the rage), and in the following decade a number of schools of industrial art and normal schools for training art teachers were established throughout the country.

There was a great deal of talk about "applied art"; and "art" *was* applied, with a vengeance—to everything the culture collectors could get their hands on. *Harper's Bazaar* (in its leading article for the issue of July 1, 1876) urged its fair readers to clip poems out of periodicals, paste them in "a pretty scrap album for the library table," and then "stick on all sorts of little ornaments . . . monograms, little gilt devices cut from envelope bands, flowers—anything at all that is pretty." Bric-a-brac and fretwork, in George W. Curtis' phrase, became "a consolation and joy beyond music or poetry" to many people, and two years after the Centennial the sale of jig-saw blades had leaped from a few thousand a year to about five hundred thousand a month.

Even before the Centennial the progress of art manufacture in the United States had been encouraging to those whose hatred of the ugliness of early machine civilization led them, like Morris and Ruskin in England, to attempt to revive and perpetuate the forms and the spirit of handicraft. When foreign exhibitors at Philadelphia sent only their less ornate products, because they thought Americans would prefer the plainer things, some of our commentators were bitterly offended. "Even gorgeous articles of luxury," as Walter Smith smugly recorded, "such as only princes in Europe could purchase, were sold to wealthy persons here." And he was borne out by the French critic Simonin, who warned his countrymen, in an article about the Centennial which appeared in the *Revue des Deux Mondes*, that the Americans were continually borrowing the methods and skilled processes of continental workmen and were already producing *bijouterie*, artistic bronzes, luxurious furniture, gold and silver ware, and artificial flowers which had "the veritable stamp of solidity and good taste." Nor was Simonin the last Frenchman to worry about these matters. In 1884 Monsieur Lourdelet, vice-president of the Society of Commercial Geography in Paris, excitedly urged his compatriots to abandon their inefficient craft techniques in making bronzes, furniture, and artificial flowers and adopt the system he had seen in America, where they used "elevators" to move materials from one floor to another in factories, and where "nearly everything is done by steam, even the carving." To be sure, he added, "the taste, perhaps, is not perfect . . . ; it is not, perhaps, the best expression of art"; but American manufacturers, he warned, were sending designers to Europe all the time in search of "purer" ideas, and their products were cutting heavily into the French market in South America as well as the United States.

As an example of this American work we may take a brass corona chandelier made by Mitchell, Vance and Company of New York. (See Fig. 21.) Here, according to Walter Smith's survey of the masterpieces of the Centennial, was an example of American industrial art workmanship which Europeans might look at with pleasure and profit. Smith never tired of repeating the Kensington doctrine that good design calls for "honesty in construction, fitness of ornament to material, and decorative subordination"; and it was these very qualities, he said, which made this chandelier thoroughly satisfactory. Similarly he declared that the beauty of musical instruments should always lie rather in their shape and adaptation to their purpose than in the richness of their ornamentation, and as an example of an instrument "free from all the abortions in the shape of ornament with which many pretentious instruments are disfigured" he selected the Mason & Hamlin organ which is illustrated in Fig. 22.

Nothing could show more vividly than these comments the difference between the Kensingtonian doctrine of "subordinating decoration to use" and Greenough's doctrine of functionalism. Nowhere better than in such examples of art manufacture can we see the fruits of that tradition which had dedicated itself to persuading the Americans that they were a "raw and noisy and obtrusive people" who could be saved only by placing themselves under the influence of the past and reverently studying specimens of the arts of luxury from Europe. This is what happens when, as Howells said, "the mass of common men have been afraid to apply their own simplicity, naturalness, and honesty to the appreciation of the beautiful. They have cast about for the instruction of someone who professed to know better, and who browbeat wholesome commonsense into the self-distrust that ends in sophistication."

5   The Figure in the Carpet

It was only in areas from which the propaganda of cul-
ture was completely excluded that the vernacular aesthetic
of the machine was wholeheartedly accepted. The present-
day interest in Shaker crafts and architecture, no matter
how carelessly the antique collectors and folk-art en-
thusiasts may lump them with the quaint survivals of an
agrarian era, is essentially a recognition of the vitality and
strength of vernacular forms evolved without any reference
to the cultivated tradition. The Shakers had no fear of the
machine. Their communities actually seem to have produced more mechanics and inventors per capita than most
other towns and villages of comparable size. In the Shaker
laundry and dairy at Canterbury, New Hampshire, at
least as early as 1868 there was a stationary steam engine
that did "all the work of lifting, lowering, turning, wash-
ing, ironing, drying, churning, etc."—which indicates a degree of mechanization not achieved in commercial laun-
dries for some years thereafter. Indeed it is a noteworthy
fact that the mechanical and inventive faculties which have
so long been claimed as the peculiar virtue of rugged individualism turn out on inspection to have been a distinctive characteristic not only of the Shakers but of a number
of other nineteenth-century socialist communities as well.
Charles Nordhoff traveled across the country in the early
1870s, visiting and collecting data on the Shakers, Perfectionists, Rappists, and others, and reported his findings
in *The Communistic Societies of the United States* (1875).
No one, he says, who visited a society which had been
for some time in existence could fail to be struck with "the
amount of ingenuity, inventive skill, and business talent
developed among men from whom, in the outer world, one
would not expect such qualities."

At the Shaker colony in New Gloucester, Maine, Elder Hewitt Chandler was the inventor of a mowing machine which was manufactured by the society, and of other machines which were used in making oak staves for molasses hogsheads. At the Oneida community the Perfectionists had contrived all the machines for making traps, including a very ingenious one for making the links for the chains, machines for measuring silk thread as it was wound on spools, and machines for testing the strength of thread. The severity and stripped utility of all Shaker objects (their furniture is never decorated with stencils or painted designs as are chairs and chests made in a true folk tradition like that of the Pennsylvania Dutch) was in perfect harmony with machine work. But its plain forms—though admired by "outsiders" for their utility—could scarcely have seemed beautiful to people who were accustomed to the ornamental design of the cultivated tradition. When Nordhoff, for instance, visited the Shaker settlement at New Lebanon, he was depressed by what seemed to him to be the homeliness of the buildings, which struck him as "mere factories or human hives." He asked Elder Frederick Evans whether, if they were to build anew, they could not "aim at some architectural effect, some beauty of design." Evans' reply was a direct, though negative, statement of the deliberate rejection of embellishment which Greenough had achieved in theory and the Shakers in practice. "No," he replied with great positiveness. "The beautiful, as you call it, is absurd and abnormal. It has no business with us. The divine has no right to waste money upon what you would call beauty, in his house or his daily life." If they built anew, he added, they would design their buildings with an eye to "more light, a more equal distribution of heat, and a more general care for protection and comfort, because these things tend to health and long life. But no beauty."

Shaker art was thus much more closely identified with the vernacular than with what the antiquaries call the folk arts. In its simplicity, lightness, linear clarity, and mechanical ingenuity it was sensitive to the technological environment, and its social aims were in harmony with equalitarian democracy. It had a share in molding the new tradition.

But the tradition was certainly not appreciated or understood by those in Elder Evans' time who were interested in encouraging an American style of decorative art. To be sure, Emerson's essays and lectures were quite widely known among the cultivated classes, and Emerson had expressed some ideas about art which had a touch of Greenough in them. In *The Conduct of Life* (1860), for instance, he had said, in the essay on "Beauty," that "outside embellishment is deformity. . . . Hence our taste in building rejects paint, and all shifts, and shows the original grain of the wood . . . ," and had pronounced it as "a rule of widest application, true in plant, true in a loaf of bread, that in the construction of any fabric or organism, any real increase of fitness to its end, is an increase of beauty." But few, if any, of Emerson's readers then were free enough from cultivated preconceptions about design to grasp the literal truth of his idea. One may doubt, indeed, whether Emerson himself, in spite of his fondness for a man who liked a good barn as well as a great tragedy, would have been able to see in the New Lebanon buildings the application of his own rule. That perception had to wait for another sixty years, and for the intuitive grasp of a painter like Charles Sheeler, working in a medium for which Emerson had little use.

In the meantime culture-conscious Americans, in their search for suitable decorative arts, as in their search for a suitable architecture, overlooked the products of the vernacular. Just as Washington Irving had filled his pseudo-Gothic Sunnyside with furnishings many of which were pure Georgian, people everywhere tried to adapt assorted available styles to their everyday requirements. Far from being plain, the various fads and fashions which were encouraged by our cultural teachers—from A. J. Downing's Elizabethan and Gothic hybrids to the Eastlake-Morris styles which were so well advertised at the Centennial—were elaborate and ornate. It was left to industrial commercial folk to appreciate the plywood (or, as it was then called, "pressed-work") furniture, made out of thin sheets of wood glued together and then heated and pressed in molds, which in the seventies was replacing the old-fashioned solid, high-backed chairs and ponderous tables. It was one of the anonymous authors of *The Great Industries of the United States* who pointed out the relationship between these "lighter articles and more graceful forms" and the lightness and strength of balloon-frame construction.

No one in the mid-century had a greater influence on American taste in architecture and decoration than Downing. He published a number of books which sold widely, and his influence was further spread through the work of disciples like Calvert Vaux and Frederick Law Olmstead, the designer of New York's Central Park. On the whole his influence was healthy, and he did much to encourage the formation of what he liked to call a free and manly school of republican tastes and manners as opposed to transplanting "the meaningless conventionalities of the realms of foreign caste." But he was aware that to many people memory is dearer than hope, and he instinctively shared the tastes of these "natural conservatives," as he called them, "whom Providence has wisely distributed, even in the most democratic governments, to steady the otherwise too impetuous and unsteady onward movements of those who, in their love for progress, would obliterate the past, even in its hold on the feelings and imaginations of our race." He was happy to assure such people that they were under no obligation to be interested in an architecture related to their own time. They were quite free, he said, to surround themselves with the "forms and symbols" of some former age.

Downing was not unaware of the importance of the purely functional elements in design, but he was not prepared to follow Greenough (or the Shakers) into a rejection of all embellishment.

> A head of grain [he insisted], one of the most useful of vegetable forms, is not so beautiful as a rose; an ass, one of the most useful of animals, is not so beautiful as a gazelle; a cotton-mill, one of the most useful of modern structures, is not so beautiful as the temple of Vesta. . . .

Therefore it was an undeniable truth, he argued, that the beautiful was intrinsically something distinct from the useful, and it was consequently inevitable that many people would be unsatisfied with mere utilitarian design and would "yearn, with an instinct as strong as for life itself, for the manifestation of a higher attribute of matter." With the result in Downing's own case, for example, that though he lays it down as a general law of design that "the material should *appear* to be what it is," when he gets down to cases he nevertheless specifies that woodwork should be "oak or other dark wood, varnished, *or it should be painted and grained to resemble it.*" (Italics mine.)

Downing and his followers all opposed the brightness which was characteristic of American interiors. "Soft and delicate tints," "cool and sober tones," "fawn or neutral shades"—these are the recurrent phrases in their prescriptions for wallpapers, drapery, and carpets. They agreed with Edgar Allan Poe, who had told the readers of *Burton's Gentleman's Magazine* in 1840 that "glare is a leading error in the philosophy of American household decoration," and had lamented that no one here, least of all the money aristocracy, understood "the spirituality of a British *boudoir.*"

Poe's article about house furnishings suggests some interesting points about the relationship between the vernacular tradition and popular taste in interior decoration. It reminds us that the very concept of decoration, whatever its nature, is incompatible with the vernacular's unembellished utility. There could not be any such thing as vernacular decoration, in the sense which we have here attributed to that term. But the democratic-technological environment which determined the characteristics of vernacular design also imposed certain qualities upon decorative patterns wherever they occurred.

Take the matter of carpets, for example. According to Poe, whose taste in these matters was molded altogether by his affinity for a romantic if decadent aristocracy, the soul of every room is the carpet. From it should be deduced not only the hues but the forms of all other objects.

> Everyone knows [he went on] that a large floor *may* have a covering of large figures, and that a small one *must* have a covering of small—yet this is not all the knowledge in the world. As regards texture, the Saxony is alone admissible. . . . In brief, distinct grounds and vivid circular or cycloid figures, *of no meaning,* are here Median laws. The abomination of flowers, or representations of well-known objects of any kind, should not be endured within the limits of Christendom. . . . As for those antique floor-cloths still occasionally seen in the dwellings of the rabble—cloths of huge, sprawling and radiating devices, stripe-interspersed, and glorious with all hues, among which no ground is intelligible—these are but the wicked invention of a race of time-servers and money-lovers—children of Baal and worshippers of Mammon—Benthams, who, to spare thought and economize fancy, first cruelly invented the Kaleidoscope, and then established joint-stock companies to twirl it by steam.

Everyone, it seems, who wanted to "improve" American taste in decoration—in Poe's time and for many years thereafter—tried to discourage the popular taste for bright light, cheerful color, and for realistic forms in ornamental design. In *High Life in New York* (1854), Mrs. Ann S. Stephens ridiculed the fashionable dining room where "everything glittered and shone so it fairly took away my appetite," and the parlor whose carpet was "the brightest and softest thing I ever did see . . . enough to make a feller stun blind to look at it, the figgers on it were so allfired gaudy." And in the seventies cultivated writers were still objecting to flower patterns in carpets and to rugs which were "the best imitation of landscape painting that can be woven in dyed wool."

In this opposition to realism in fabric design, cultivated Americans were reflecting the opinion of the most respectable English authorities. They were fond of quoting, for example, from Sir Matthew Digby Wyatt, Slade professor of fine arts at Cambridge and author of a learned volume on *Industrial Arts of the Nineteenth Century* (1853). Sir Digby thus put the case against floral designs in upholstery and carpets in his painfully academic prose:

> The moment one is impressed with the idea of walking or sitting upon what no person in his senses would think of walking or sitting on, a painful sense of impropriety is experienced, proportioned in intensity to the vivacity with which this misappropriation of judicious design is expressed in the fabric.

But in spite of all cultivated objections, realistic representations of natural forms continued to suit the popular taste. If carpets were to be colorful, people in general shared Walt Whitman's preference for figures closely imitated from nature: the deep and pale reds of autumn leaves, the green of pines, the bright yellow of hickory. "How much better," Whitman had written in 1862, "than the tasteless, meaningless, and every way inartistical diagrams that we walk over, now, in the most fashionably carpeted parlors."

Similarly, people continued to be "violently enamored of gas and of glass" in spite of Poe's or anyone else's objections. At the Centennial the furnished rooms exhibited

by American firms were full of glass (one New York manufacturer exhibited furniture all made of mirrors), and
looked, as one disapproving observer remarked, like the
bridal chambers of hotels or the saloons of steamboats.
Indeed, it may well be that the popular ideal of interior
decoration found its most accessible symbol in the cabins
of the Mississippi steamboats which Mark Twain delighted
to describe. The subdued tones and the air of repose encouraged by Downing, Vaux, and their successors had no
place in the "snow-white cabin; porcelain knob and oil-
picture on every stateroom door; curving patterns of
filigree-work touched up with gilding . . . ; big chande-
liers every little way, each an April shower of glittering
glass-drops"; nor, for that matter, in the ladies' cabin, with
its "pink and white Wilton carpet, as soft as mush, and
glorified with a ravishing pattern of gigantic flowers."

Marietta Holley's "Samantha Allen" had a carpet in her
parlor in Jonesville which would have perfectly suited
Whitman's taste and have horrified Poe. In affectionate
detail she describes its "green ground work that looks just
like moss, with clusters of leaves all scattered over it, crim-
son and gold colored and russet brown, that look for all
the world as if they might have fell offen the maple trees
out in the yard in the fall of the year." Here is the same
insistence upon meaningful design and the realistic representation of natural forms which we will later encounter
as an important characteristic of the vernacular attitude
toward painting.

The Centennial brought to America an impressive display of English decorative arts. The *Illustrated London
News* had told its readers that Great Britain certainly
would carry off the prizes in the departments of art furniture and ceramics. And so, indeed, she did. For a decade
and more thereafter, America had her share of conscience-
smitten women (to use the phrase of a later female authority on decoration) who went in for "art" wallpaper,
"art" furniture, and "art" textiles. But it wasn't many years
before Eastlake and Morris were forgotten, and the floral

wallpaper, floral carpets, and floral upholstery against which they had inveighed were back in fashion.

Some light on this is shed in an essay by Mary Gay Humphreys on "The Progress of American Decorative Art," which appeared in the London *Art Journal* in 1893. Faced, at the close of the century, with the same popular preferences which had been opposed from the beginning by various exponents of cultivated taste, she concluded that since we were short on museums, private collections, noble houses, and other "depositories of accumulated treasures of Art," and since our "foraging-ground" for such materials was across many thousand miles of water, we had been thrown more or less on our own resources. Our designers had been driven to seek their inspirations in natural forms and had thus contracted an "allegiance to nature," as Miss Humphreys called it, "which the most determined theorist on the subject of conventional decoration" could not overcome. The consequence, she admitted, was that "in purely American work the boundaries between realism and conventionality are far less rigidly defined than elsewhere."

In this area of the arts, as in the others we have looked at, the vernacular and the cultivated traditions interacted. Even in a curtain designed by the painter John La Farge, appliqué and embroidery were used to define a realistic perspective landscape. But by the end of the century we had gone a long way toward accumulating on this side of the Atlantic enough "treasures of art" to threaten to suffocate not only the patterns which had evolved in the vernacular tradition but even the popular taste for realistic decorative designs. Too many of us, convinced that the useful and the aesthetic were antithetical and that our genius lay with the former, had comfortably decided—like the editor of *Harper's Magazine* in 1859—that "what is fine in the buildings of the old countries we can borrow; their statues and their pictures we will be able in good time to buy." Borrow and buy we did, filling our homes as well as our museums with the plunder, and sending generations

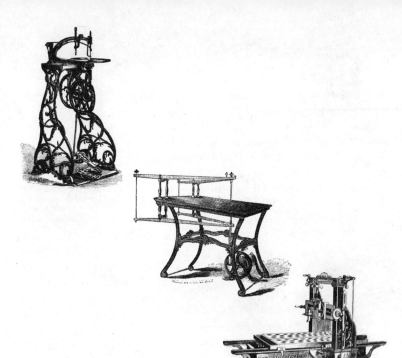

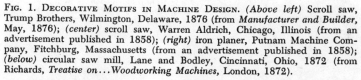

FIG. 1. DECORATIVE MOTIFS IN MACHINE DESIGN. *(Above left)* Scroll saw, Trump Brothers, Wilmington, Delaware, 1876 (from *Manufacturer and Builder*, May, 1876); *(center)* scroll saw, Warren Aldrich, Chicago, Illinois (from an advertisement published in 1858); *(right)* iron planer, Putnam Machine Company, Fitchburg, Massachusetts (from an advertisement published in 1858); *(below)* circular saw mill, Lane and Bodley, Cincinnati, Ohio, 1872 (from Richards, *Treatise on...Woodworking Machines*, London, 1872).

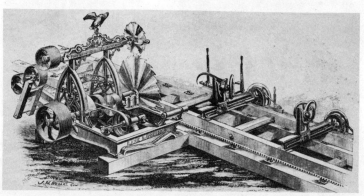

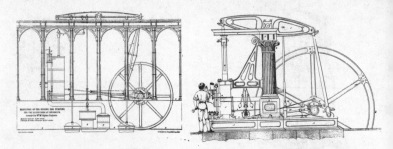

FIG. 2. ARCHITECTURAL ELEMENTS IN MACHINE DESIGN. *(Left)* Gothic frame of steam engine designed by William McAlpine for U.S. Drydock at Brooklyn; *(right)* Corinthian frame of steam engine designed by J. T. Sutton and Co. (from Oliver Byrne, *The American Engineer, Draftsman, and Machinist's Assistant,* Philadelphia, 1853).

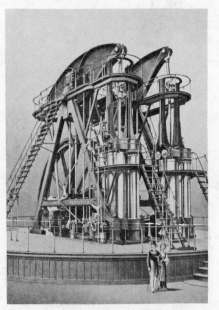

FIG. 3. THE CORLISS ENGINE AT THE CENTENNIAL EXHIBITION, 1876. This vast steam engine, designed without any concessions to contemporary notions of ornament and decoration, was the dominant feature of the exhibits in Machinery Hall. This picture, never before reproduced, is taken from a choromo-lithograph published in *Treasures of Art, Industry and Manufacture Represented in the American Centennial Exhibition at Philadelphia, 1876,* Buffalo, New York, 1877.

FIG. 4. VERNACULAR MACHINE DESIGN. *(Left)* Portable riveting machine, and *(right)* carwheel boring mill, both designed by William Sellers (from *The Masterpieces of the Centennial International Exhibition,* Philadelphia, 1877).

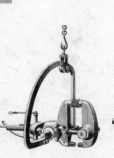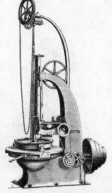

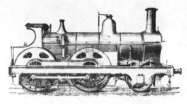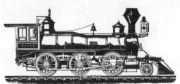

FIG. 5. ENGLISH AND AMERICAN LOCOMOTIVES, 1875. *(Left)* The express passenger engine, built for the Midland Railway, typifies the massive and rigid construction of English locomotives of the period (from *The Scientific American Supplement*, No. 27, July 1, 1876); *(right)* the Baltimore and Ohio express engine, designed by John C. Davis, master machinist, is typical of the light and flexible locomotives developed in America (from *The Railway Journal*, November 17, 1876).

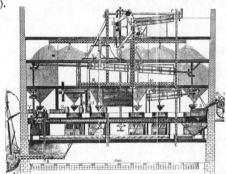

FIG. 6. OLIVER EVANS' AUTOMATIC CONVEYORS, 1785. A diagrammatic drawing of Thomas Ellicott's grain mill, near Baltimore, in which automatic machine production was achieved by the use of the conveyors, elevators, hopper-boys, and descenders invented by Oliver Evans (from Evans' *The Young Mill-Wright and Miller's Guide*, Philadelphia, 1795).

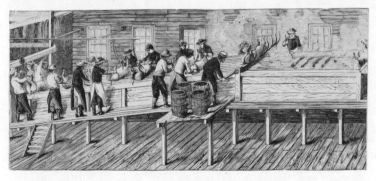

FIG. 7. ORIGIN OF THE ASSEMBLY LINE—HOG SLAUGHTERING IN 1860s. Interior of Cincinnati slaughterhouse showing line production and mechanical handling of materials (from *One Hundred Years Progress of the United States*, Hartford, 1872; an earlier but less detailed picture of the overhead-rail conveyor was published in *Harper's Weekly*, January 11, 1868).

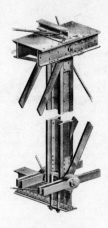

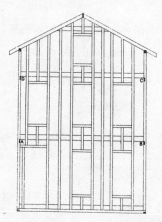

FIG. 8. DETAIL OF IRON BRIDGE CONSTRUCTION. The Point Bridge, Pittsburgh, built by the American Bridge Company, 1875 (from *The Masterpieces of the Centennial International Exhibition*, Philadelphia, 1877).

FIG. 9. BALLOON FRAME AND TRADITIONAL FRAME. (*Above right*) Framing plan of two-story balloon-frame house, with 2″ x 4″ studs and corner posts of two 2″ x 4″'s nailed together (from James H. Monckton's *The National Carpenter and Builder*, New York, 1873); (*below right*) framing plan for "English style" cottage, with 4″ x 8″ beams and 4″ x 6″ and 3″ x 6″ studs, mortise and tenon joints (from William H. Ranlett, *The Architect, A Series of Original Designs*, New York, 1847).

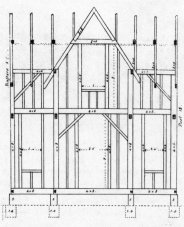

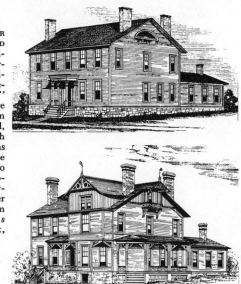

FIG. 10. THE VERNACULAR SUCCUMBS TO CULTIVATED TASTE. According to William M. Woollett, the architect who did the remodeling, "the not very attractive-looking structure" shown in the upper picture was in first-class condition and was "withal a good, comfortable house in which to live." The alterations shown in the lower picture were designed merely "to slightly improve its appearance without destroying the date and character of the building" (from Woollett's *Old Homes Made New*, New York, 1878).

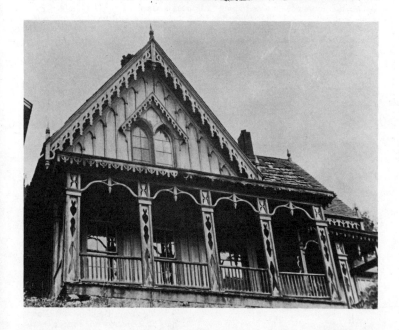

FIG. 11. CARPENTER GOTHIC. The "Lace House" on Main Street, opposite the railroad station, Blackhawk, Colorado. Built by Frederick Fiske (photograph reproduced by courtesy of the Denver Public Library, Western History Collection).

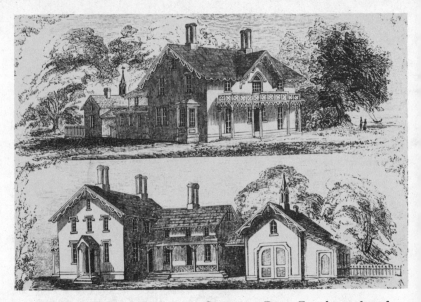

FIG. 12. VERNACULAR BUILDINGS IN CULTIVATED DRESS. Farm house planned by Lewis F. Allen, as rendered by Otis and Brown, architects, of Buffalo. As usual, the architects insisted upon fashionable decoration. The design, Allen remarked in his book, "is rather florid . . . but the cut and moulded trimmings may be left off by those who prefer a plain finish. Such, indeed, is our own taste" (from Allen's *Rural Architecture*, New York, 1852).

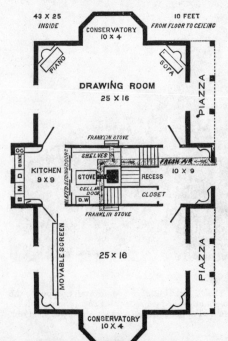

FIG. 13. FLEXIBLE AND COMPACT FLOOR PLAN. Floor plan of house designed by Catherine Beecher and Harriet Beecher Stowe. Note movable screen partition in room to left of entrance and the compact kitchen and stove-room unit. The counter-height working surface in the kitchen included a breadboard (B), molding board and meatboard (M), and drainboard (D). Beneath this continuous work surface were bins, drawers, and cupboards for flour, meal, towels, and utensils; above it were open shelves extending to the ceiling (from Beecher and Stowe, *The American Woman's Home*, New York, 1869).

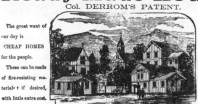

FIG. 14. PREFABRICATED HOUSES AS ADVERTISED IN 1876 (from *The Manufacturer and Builder*, February, 1876).

FIG. 15. THE SUN IRON BUILDING, BALTIMORE. Designed by James Bogardus (from G. W. Howard, *The Monumental City, Its Past History and Present Resources*, Baltimore, 1873).

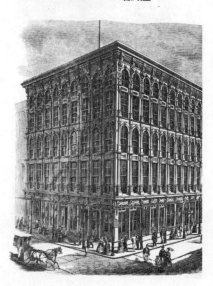

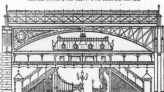

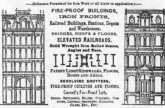

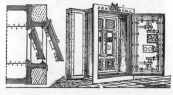

FIG. 16. IRON FRONTS TO ORDER (from advertisement in *The Vermont Business Directory*, Boston, 1881).

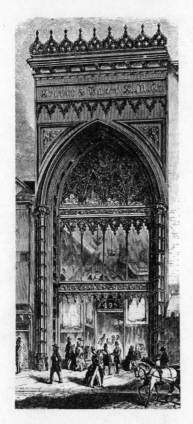

FIG. 17. GOTHIC TRACERY IN IRON
AND GLASS. The Grover and Baker
Sewing Machine Company's building
at 495 Broadway, New York (from the
New York Illustrated News, August
25, 1860).

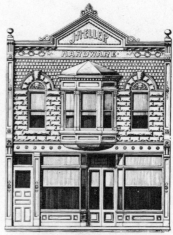

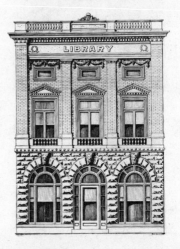

FIG. 18. STAMPED METAL FRONTS—
CIRCA 1890 (from *General Catalogue
No. 24,* The Eller Manufacturing Company, Canton, Ohio. Reproduced with
permission of the Milcor Steel Company, Cleveland, Ohio).

of our children to school to study the uprooted masterpieces of another civilization. In that cultural climate
Emerson's essay on "Art" must have seemed like pure
vapor. Perhaps only in our own time, when the achievements of the vernacular have begun to be recognized, has
that strange essay found its audience. At all events, these
paragraphs provide a fitting postscript to this chapter:

> The old tragic Necessity, which lowers on the brows
> even of the Venuses and Cupids of the antique . . .
> —namely that they were inevitable; that the artist was
> drunk with a passion for form which he could not resist,
> and which vented itself in these fine extravagances—
> no longer dignifies the chisel or the pencil. But the artist
> and connoisseur now seek in art the exhibition of their
> talent, or an asylum from the evils of life. Men are
> not well pleased with the figure they make in their own
> imaginations, and they flee to art, and convey their bet-
> ter sense in an oratorio, a statue, or a picture. Art makes
> the same effort which a sensual prosperity makes;
> namely to detach the beautiful from the useful, to do
> up the work as unavoidable, and, hating it, to pass on
> to enjoyment.

> Now men do not see nature to be beautiful, and they
> go to make a statue which shall be. They abhor men
> as tasteless, dull, and unconvertible, and console them-
> selves with color bags and blocks of marble. They reject
> life as prosaic, and create a death which they call
> poetic. . . . Beauty must come back to the useful arts,
> and the distinction between the fine and the useful arts
> be forgotten. . . . In nature all is useful, all is beautiful.
> It is therefore beautiful because it is alive, moving,
> reproductive; it is therefore useful because it is sym-
> metrical and fair.

> Beauty will not come at the call of a legislature, nor will
> it repeat in England or America its history in Greece.
> . . . It is in vain that we look for genius to reiterate its

miracles in the old arts; it is its instinct to find beauty and holiness in new and necessary facts, in the field and roadside, in the shop and mill.

Emerson wrote these words a generation before the Corliss engine or the Eads bridge were built. Indeed, it was to be several years before Emerson's friend Greenough identified specific manifestations of the vernacular, in the clipper ships, for example, and in machines and scaffolding. But by a characteristically perceptive insight Emerson grasped the inevitability of a new tradition in art. He faced the stubborn fact that art could never be at home in the new civilization if it clung to forms which were no longer alive and reproductive.

6   To Make All Things New

Throughout the nineteenth century, as we have already observed, both writers and readers had been actively interested in the creation of an American literature. Longfellow had made a plea for a native American poetry as early as 1825, but like many others he had thought chiefly in terms of substituting native New England birds for the skylarks and nightingales of English poetry, and he soon perceived the futility of that kind of superficial nationalism. Other writers followed William Gilmore Simms in the belief that "to be *national* in literature, one must needs be *sectional.*" But as Melville said in the mid-century, the usual mistake of those Americans who looked forward to the coming of a literary genius among us was that "they somehow fancy he will come· in the costume of Queen Elizabeth's day."

However popular these fallacies may once have been, they need not concern us here. They had, after all, no influence except among second- and third-rate authors. We can learn more from another and more enduring attitude toward the problem, namely faith in "the West" as the source of the distinctively American element in character and therefore in literature. It was truly a national faith, shared by many who otherwise had little in common. In *Israel Potter,* written four years after *Moby Dick,* Melville ascribed the peculiarly American quality of Ethan Allen to his "essentially Western" spirit, that spirit which "is, or will be (for no other is, or can be), the true American one." When Thoreau went out for a walk he found that, though he turned round and round irresolute, his instinct inevitably led him to walk southwest or west. "Eastward I go only by force; but westward I go free. . . . I must walk toward Oregon, and not toward Europe. And that way the nation is moving. . . ." And Whitman saw in "the grandeur and superb monotony" of the Western prairies the home of America's "distinctive ideas and distinctive realities."

One of the most interesting expressions of the typical popular confidence in the West appeared in an article by J. Milton Mackie called "Forty Days in a Western Hotel" which was published anonymously in *Putnam's Magazine* in December 1854. It pulls together so many of the threads of the vernacular tradition as we have defined it, and weaves them so skillfully into the fabric of the Western faith, that it is worth quoting here at some length.

> I saw in the West [Mackie wrote], no signs of quiet enjoyment of life as it passes. . . . At present the inhabitants are hewing wood and drawing water—laying the foundations of a civilization which is yet to be, and such as has never been before. . . . Though men do not write books there, or paint pictures, there is no lack, in our western world, of mind. The genius of this new country is necessarily mechanical. Our greatest thinkers are not in the library, nor the capitol, but in the machine shop. . . . The youth of this country are learning the sciences, not as theories, but with reference to their applications to the arts. . . . Even literature is cultivated for its jobs; and the fine arts are followed as a trade. . . .

> The American mind will be brought to maturity along the chain of the great lakes, the banks of the Mississippi, the Missouri, and their tributaries in the far northwest. There, on the rolling plains, will be formed a republic of letters which, not governed like that on our seaboard by the great literary powers of Europe, shall be free indeed.

This is a quite different attitude from that of Thoreau, for example, to whom the West was really only another name for the wild, for the forests and savage wilderness from which civilization could draw nourishment and renewed vigor. It suggests, rather, an aspect of the West which should be sharply distinguished from the frontier as it was defined so effectively by Frederick Jackson Turner. Turner's theory, first presented in 1893, dealt with the effects upon our history of the area of free land, moving westward as the wilderness was settled, where savagery and civilization were continually in tension. His book, *The Frontier in American History,* was a tremendously fruitful one and much of the best recent historical work has owed a great deal to its insights and suggestions. But the frontier has since come to be thought of chiefly as Thoreau thought of it—as geographical wilderness; it is this conception of the West which has underlain most of the recent analyses of the significance of the frontier in our history and literature.

Mackie, a graduate of Brown, who had gone on to tutor there from 1835 to 1838, and had since traveled extensively in Europe and the West Indies as well as in the United States, sees the West in a less romantic perspective. He fastens on the Westerner's utilitarian attitude toward the arts and sciences, his mechanical bent, and his freedom from European influence. In Boston or Charleston it was easy enough for a writer to agree with Longfellow's brother-in-law, Tom Appleton, that Europe was "the home of his protoplasm." But beyond the centers of cultivation and good breeding—and not just on the advancing frontier either—men were to a considerable extent free from European precedents and forces. The man of the industrial town, the man in the machine shop, had placed himself as completely as Turner's frontiersman "under influences destructive to many of the gains of civilization" and looked at things just as independently and with as little regard or appreciation for the best Old World experience. The new environment was the product of both frontier democracy and machine civilization, and from it inevitably emerged new attitudes toward writing, and new themes which would interweave to make a fabric whose texture would seem harsh and garish to those who were familiar with the great tradition of English literature.

Anyone who reads widely in American nineteenth-century literature must be struck with the reiteration, in a variety of terms and in many different contexts, of an attitude which was foreshadowed by William Ellery Channing in 1830. The aristocratic institutions of the Old World, Channing declared, had all tended to throw obscurity over "what we most need to know, and that is the worth and claims of a human being." But in America, he thought, man was not hidden from us by so many disguises as in Europe, and he therefore hoped that our literature would explore and develop that consciousness of our own nature which teaches us at once self-respect and respect for others.

Channing knew well enough that his prosperous Boston contemporaries were fearful of the political power of "the labouring classes," and he also knew that their fear was justified in so far as the masses could be used as tools. He insisted nevertheless that it was the vices of the prosperous which bring about a community's downfall, and he denounced those who used the French Revolution as a horrible example of what happens when the mob has power. The saddest aspect of the age, he said in 1840, "is that which undoubtedly contributes to social order. . . . It is the selfish prudence which is never tired of the labour of accumulation, and which keeps men steady, regular, respectable drudges from morning to night."

It may well be true (as has been argued by Arthur M. Schlesinger, Jr.) that Channing in the long run sabotaged the liberal principles of his day by urging reform only in ways in which it could not practically be achieved. Certainly his talk about "the Elevation of the Soul" in the *Lectures on the Elevation of the Labouring Portion of the Community* (1840) is either complacent or naïve. But he was not frightened or dismayed by the outcropping of

violent revolutionary activity in Europe in the forties, and
it would be unfair to assume that it was only because the
ocean separated his world from the world of violence that
he could hail it as "the dawning of that great principle,
that the individual is not made to be the instrument of
others . . . ; and that he belongs to himself and to God,
and to no human superior."

It has been fashionable in recent years to emphasize
the economic rather than the moral and religious elements
in democratic thought, and criticism has therefore tended
to ignore one of the basic motives in American life and
literature. Channing's Unitarian liberalism was only one
manifestation of an impulse which recurs in many different forms. The socialist communities and religious sects of
the nineteenth century frequently gave expression to related attitudes. Among the Campbellites and their followers in western Pennsylvania and Ohio, for instance, it
led to a belief in democratic America as the new Jerusalem, "a new political heaven and a new political earth,"
where each man would interpret the Bible for himself
and sectarianism would be dissolved into divine unity. One
of the leading Campbellites was a man named Walter
Scott, described by a fellow preacher as one of the first
on this continent "who took the old field-notes of the
apostles and run [sic] the original survey, beginning at
Jerusalem." Scott's most important book, *The Messiahship,*
was published in Cincinnati in 1860, and salted down
amid its arguments touching baptism, the symbolism of
the scriptures, and other theological matters, there are repeated evidences of the democratic faith. "Everything in
old society nearly, that is truly desirable," Scott wrote, "is
royal or aristocratic; the people cannot reach it; it belongs,
if it is good, to the rich; if bad, to the poor." But Luther
and Washington had given us "a *new* religion and a *new*
society in a *new* world."

Among our writers this attitude produced a widespread
interest in reaching a large audience rather than a select
few. On one level it prompted Catharine Maria Sedgwick's

pious query, "If the poet and painter cannot bring down their arts to the level of the poor, are there none to be God's interpreters to them?" On quite a different level it led Melville, in his enthusiasm for Hawthorne's *Mosses*, to call upon America to recognize those of her writers "who breathe that unshackled, democratic spirit of Christianity in all things, which now takes the practical lead in this world." And in still another form—and one which reflected little enthusiasm for democracy—it found expression in Poe's defense of the short prose tale as the form which, next to lyric poetry, "should best fulfill the demands of high genius." The tale, he pointed out, permitted the writer a vast variety of modes or inflections of thought and expression in a form "more appreciable by the mass of mankind" than any other. Similarly, in a letter to Charles Anthon, written in June 1844, Poe outlined his interest in establishing a magazine of his own which would satisfy the contemporary demand for "the curt, the terse, the well-timed, the readily-diffused, in preference to the old forms of the verbose and ponderous and the inaccessible."

Forty years later elements of the same basic attitude found expression in Mark Twain's famous letter to Andrew Lang. "I have never tried in even one single instance," he wrote in 1889, "to help cultivate the cultivated classes. I was not equipped for it, either by native gifts or training. And I never had any ambition in that direction, but always hunted for bigger game—the masses." He had his fling, too, at the critics who assumed that if a book didn't meet the standards of the cultivated class it was valueless. If a critic should start a religion, he went on, it would not have any object but to convert angels, and where was the use of that? The thin top crust of humanity—the cultivated —were worth pacifying and coddling and nourishing with delicacies, to be sure, but for himself Mark Twain could see no satisfaction in feeding the overfed. He was only half in jest when he argued that "It is not that little minority who are already saved that are best worth trying to uplift, I should think, but the mighty mass of the uncultivated who are underneath." His friend, William Dean Howells, meant something very similar when he said two years later that art must make friends with need, or perish. It would be a suicidal mistake, he insisted, for art to take itself from the many and give itself to the few, for "the art which . . . disdains the office of teacher is one of the last refuges of the aristocratic spirit which is disappearing from politics and society, and is now seeking to shelter itself in aesthetics." The same basic attitude is still current in our own time, as when Upton Sinclair, defending his novels against an academic review in the *Atlantic Monthly,* retorted that "somebody has to write for the masses and not just for the Harvard professors."

This concern with the ethical uses of the arts in a democratic society had, of course, received its most explicit statement in the works of Emerson and Whitman. "Art," said Emerson, "has not yet come to its maturity if it do not put itself abreast with the most potent influences of the world, if it is not practical and moral, if it do not stand in connection with the conscience, if it do not make the poor and uncultivated feel that it addresses them with a voice of lofty cheer." And Whitman, rebelling against everything represented by the popular conception of culture, had demanded "a programme . . . drawn out, not for a single class alone, or for the parlors or lecture-rooms, but with an eye to practical life, the West, the working-man, the facts of farms and jack-planes and engineers. . . . I should demand of this programme or theory a scope generous enough to include the widest human area."

The aesthetic problems involved in this attitude need not be elaborated here. For the moment it is necessary only to indicate that over a period of many years concern with the availability of the arts and with the ethical and (in the non-sectarian, even anti-church sense) religious purposes of literature was shared by so many American writers. The opposite tendency also existed, to be sure. There were always people who wanted to preserve the arts inviolate from contact with the vulgar masses. (*Apple-*

ton's in 1869 dismissed scornfully any and all arguments in favor of what it called "the multiplication of poor copies of inferior pictures by means of chromolithography," just as the aesthetic snobs of our own day refuse to countenance even the best contemporary color reproductions of paintings.) There were always some who acknowledged no connection between art and use. But through all the changes in literary fashion, among the so-called romanticists equally with the realists, and in all sections of the country, American writers—with a few notable exceptions—would have agreed with the doctrine which Orestes Brownson had expounded in 1843: that the literature of America should breathe a free, noble, and generous spirit, give expression to the love of man as man, and impart to all who came under its influence "the needed wisdom to labor for the moral, the religious, the intellectual, and the physical well-being of all men."

As one would expect, this attitude toward the functions of the arts was reflected in the subject matter with which our writers concerned themselves. At its worst it led to the attempt to sugar-coat useful knowledge and to insinuate all sorts of dry erudition and historical lore into fictional form. It was this sort of thing which led *Appleton's Journal* to protest that Harriet Beecher Stowe's *Oldtown Folks* was a sample of what it unhappily admitted was a distinctively American kind of fiction which gave expression to the utilitarianism of the people. At its best, however, it led to a realization of the importance of everyday life, to a stalwart reckoning with the actualities of our civilization.

"Give me insight into today," Emerson had said in his Phi Beta Kappa address at Harvard in 1837, "and you may have the antique and future worlds. What would we really know the meaning of? The meal in the firkin; the milk in the pan; the ballad in the street; the news of the boat; the glance of the eye; the form and gait of the body. . . ." And ten years later, in the essay on "The Poet" he cast his belief into the form of a challenge which has become a landmark in our cultural history:

> Time and nature yield us many gifts, but not yet the timely man, the new religion, the reconciler, whom all things await. . . . We have yet had no genius in America, with tyrannous eye, which knew the incomparable value of our materials, and saw in the barbarism and materialism of our times, another carnival of the same gods whose picture he so much admires in Homer; then in the Middle Age; then in Calvinism. Banks and tariffs, the newspaper and caucus, Methodism and Unitarianism, are flat and dull to dull people, but rest on the same foundations of wonder as the town of Troy and the temple of Delphi, and are as swiftly passing away. Our log-rolling, our stumps and their politics, our fisheries, our Negroes and Indians, our boats and our repudiations, the wrath of rogues and the pusillanimity of honest men, the northern trade, the southern planting, the western clearing, Oregon and Texas, are yet unsung.

It was left to Walt Whitman to take up Emerson's challenge and explore the full range of his conception of a poet. But American writers both before and after Emerson were preoccupied with the actualities of everyday life and tried, with whatever limitations of understanding, to know their meaning. Our first professional novelist, Charles Brockden Brown, announced himself as "one of those who would rather travel into the mind of a ploughman than into the interior of Africa." Margaret Fuller, during her term as book reviewer for Horace Greeley's *Tribune* in the mid-forties, chanced on an anonymous novel called *Ellen* which, though coarsely written, she fastened upon as a genuine example of an increasingly common type of fiction. It was, she observed, a transcript of the "crimes, calumnies, excitements, half-blind love of right, and honest indignation" which were characteristic of the uncultivated classes. Further, it gave a picture of the kind of life which

Cooper or Miss Sedgwick "might see, as the writer did, but could hardly believe in enough to speak of it with such fidelity." Yet even Miss Sedgwick, for all her sentimental fondness for uplift, understood something of the intrinsic dignity of the human being. In one of her contributions to the *Token* she stated a belief (to which many of her novels and tales bore witness) that every family, however insignificant in the stranger's eye, has a world of its own which offers a richer field for exploring the infinite story of human relations than the deeds of gods and heroes. And thirty years later, out of a very different background, we have Edward Eggleston's declaration, in the preface to *The Circuit Rider* (1874)—a landmark in the realistic representation of the lawless frontier—that no man is worthy to be called a novelist "who does not endeavor with his whole soul to produce the higher form of history, by writing truly of men as they are, and dispassionately of those forms of life that come within his scope. . . . The story of any true life is wholesome, if only the writer will tell it simply. . . ."

Much has been made by both social and literary historians of the sentimental rot—the "pure Cinderella with a touch of Bluebeard," as Della T. Lutes defined it—which has formed such a large part of the reading matter of the American people. But this emphasis on the trashy melodramatic novels and stories which have been written and read in such numbers from the days of *Charlotte Temple* and Mrs. E. D. E. N. Southworth to the present has tended to obscure the fact that an opposite tendency has also existed, much of it outside the limits of what is commonly regarded as literature even in its broad sense.

Constance Rourke was the first to point out that the long delay in the development of the novel as a literary form in America may have resulted in part at least from the fact that its function was fulfilled by other forms of reading matter. She called attention in her essay on the Shakers to the controversial literature which sprang up between members of the communities and their critics in the

"outside world." As an example she used the pamphlets
written by Mary Dyer and her husband during their controversy over the children and property which he took with
him when he joined the Shaker community at New Lebanon. Both husband and wife, as Miss Rourke noted, had
the gift for portraying concrete instances that good novelists possess, and both frequently quoted sworn testimony
of neighbors and friends who likewise had an eye for
specific details and a sense of narrative pace. The Dyers
and the Shakers were the center of all these events and
episodes, but their story emerged against a three-dimen-
sional background built up out of domestic habits, the rise
of errant personalities, and vivid discussion of sexual relationships revealing considerable psychological insight.
Indeed, Miss Rourke was quite accurate in saying that in
these pamphlets the very substance of the novel was exhibited "with far more candor than in any English novel
of the period or indeed of the entire nineteenth century.
Only Fielding or Smollett could have matched it."

From the earliest times there have been personal narratives of life in the new country, vivid records of individual adaptations to new environments. There were the
narratives of Indian captivity, of which Mrs. Mary Jemison's was perhaps the most widely read, full of high and
terrible adventure and loaded with specific details about
how to get along in the wilderness and about the charms
and miseries of savage life. There were the minute psychological revelations of the innumerable religious autobiographies and biographies, well represented by those
collected in Jonathan Edwards' *Faithful Narrative of the
Surprising Work of God* (1737) and later in the camp-
meeting testimonies of the saved and damned. There were
the wild and bloody narratives of border violence like
Virgil Stewart's *History of the Detection, Conviction, Life,
and Designs of John A. Murel* (1835).

At every stage in our history there have been conflicts
and conquests—religious, political, and economic—out of
which have come such personal narratives, set against a

lively background of social struggle and development. The "anti-rent" agitation in New York in the 1840s, the abolitionist movement of the pre-Civil War years, the Mormon controversy, the populist movement, and the exploration and settlement of the West all furnished materials for pamphlets, newspaper articles, and books by the men and women who participated in them. *Pat Crowe, His Story, Confession and Reformation,* a paper-bound booklet published in 1906, is set against the background of popular resentment against the beef trust at the end of the century, and is typical of the best of these personal narratives. Crowe had kidnaped Eddie Cudahy, son of the Omaha packer, in 1900—the very year in which the trust succeeded in eliminating competition in buying, so as to fix prices—and he had demanded and collected twenty-five thousand dollars' ransom. The first part of the paper-bound booklet contains Crowe's own direct, undramatized narrative of the affair ("I want to start right by confessing in plain English that I was guilty of the kidnapping"); a reprint of a magazine article by W. H. Hodge, claiming that the Omaha jury which acquitted Crowe didn't consider the question of guilt but only the question "Isn't it all right to rob a member of the beef trust if you can?"; and Crowe's reply, defending the verdict as "the most popular ever returned in Nebraska." But the most interesting part of the book is the full text of the "Address to the Jury" by which Crowe's attorney, Albert S. Ritchie, had swayed the jurors to acquit a guilty man. There is a dramatic immediacy about it, a sense of social forces shaping the lives of the individuals present in the courtroom at that very moment, which surpasses any scenes in the plays or novels of the period. "Much as I admire my friend, the county attorney here, who shows so much enthusiasm and warmth for Mr. Cudahy and for the State, so mingled that you cannot distinguish them . . ." Ritchie begins, thrusting his words deep down into the popular resentment against the rising power of industrial monopoly; and as he speaks the courtroom scene comes alive, and the popular attitudes are clear. "If you will give me a million dollars," he continued, "and make me a vice-president of the Cudahy Packing Company, I can pretty near move the social world in the City of Omaha." It becomes plain as the drama unfolds that the jury's vote was not to acquit Crowe but to indict monopoly.

Such narratives were, however, only one of the many kinds of writing which our literary histories have neglected but which have performed the double function of satisfying the demands of the reading public and at the same time exploring the techniques for coping with new ways of life in a new environment. The almanacs which hung on a nail in almost every kitchen evolved a pattern of anecdote, comment, and humor with a distinctly native flavor. Melville had grown up on Webster's *Albany Almanacs* in the thirties and rediscovered them years later with relish. And Hamlin Garland was only one of thousands of Americans who in the sixties, seventies, and eighties pored over the testimonials in the almanacs distributed by the makers of Hostetter's Bitters and Allen's Cherry Pectoral, dwelling on their realistic accounts of the aches and pains of humankind and their heartening statements of cures.

Something of this same clinical interest attached to the "doctor books" and collections of recipes which were as universally owned as the Bible and far more widely read. But these books have another and greater importance to us. The most famous was probably *Dr. Chase's Recipes; or, Information for Everybody*, which was first published in 1863 and in the next thirteen years sold over seven hundred thousand copies. The author, A. W. Chase, of Ann Arbor, Michigan, had been in the drug and grocery business for a number of years when he decided to study medicine. Thereupon he put together a pamphlet containing recipes he had learned in his business, and for seven years traveled "between New York and Iowa" selling the pamphlets and pumping everyone he met for useful information in every practical field. The material thus collected made up the book, divided into departments for

merchants and grocers, tanners and harness makers, painters, blacksmiths, gunsmiths, home bakers and cooks, and
others.

Apparently the recipes gave satisfaction; the book contains innumerable testimonials from professors at the University of Michigan and other worthy citizens. But the
clue to its universal popularity is contained in a review
of it which appeared in the Syracuse (New York) *Journal.*
For, as the paper said, the eight hundred recipes were "in-
terspersed with sufficient wit and wisdom to make it interesting as a general reading book, besides the fact that
it embraces only such subjects as have a practical adaptability to 'Everybody's' everyday use." It is not an incon-
siderable social phenomenon that three quarters of a million Americans of the Gilded Age paid out a dollar and a
quarter for a "reading book" dealing solely with such matters of everyday usefulness as how Byron Rose, of Madi-
son, Ohio, tanned and finished horsehides for harness
leather, how elm bark made a horrendous tapeworm
"come away" from the daughter of Mr. E. Fish, of Beards-
town, Illinois, and how C. Keller, gunsmith, of Evansville,
Indiana, browned his gun barrels.

The public welcomed any useful and informative book,
and Dr. Chase had many rivals in the race to supply the
demand. One of the most successful was Thomas E. Hill,
of Aurora, Illinois, an industrious and enthusiastic pen-
manship teacher who became publisher and editor of the
local newspaper, mayor of the town, and author of *Hill's
Manual of Social and Business Forms,* which went through
thirty-nine editions in the ten years following its publication
in 1873. Hill subtitled his book "A Guide to Correct Writing" and dedicated it to "the millions who would, and
may, easily and gracefully express the right thought." It
is also a bible of decorous social deportment and correct
business and legal procedures, combined with a guide to
the refinements of culture. But it is more than merely another of that vast number of books which appeared in
England and America during the nineteenth century, de-

signed to feed the middle-class appetite for self-improve-
ment and self-culture. Hill devised a distinctive formula
which fitted into the native American interest in specific
detail. The models he offers as guides—to the mother writing to a teacher to excuse her child from school, the inventor applying for a patent, and the man who wants to
mortgage the family farm—are in all cases apparently genuine letters or documents, most of them bearing the names
of actual people and places. The man who wanted to
write his will could model it on that of Warren P. Holden,
of Bennington, Vermont. The young man on his travels
could get ideas for his letter home from one written by
Alfred T. Weeks, during a visit to the "old home" in
Cambridge, New York, to his family in the West. The boy
who wanted to become an apprentice could study the
agreement made between fourteen-year-old Allan Ellis, of
Pittsburgh, and the blacksmith Marcus Moran. And the
pioneer settler who wanted to encourage a friend in the
East to emigrate could be guided by the letter Martin
Fuller, of Big Stranger, Kansas, wrote to Chas. W. Can-
field of Toledo, Ohio.

These letters and documents still retain something of the
fascination they must have had for the men and women
who dog-eared and almost wore out their copies of the
Manual. The book offered, in effect, a vast panorama of
the nation at work and at play, settling new country,
building towns and factories, burying the dead, giving
parties, courting, organizing village lyceums and "protec-
tive associations" against horse thieves, with real people
—your own neighbors—as the actors. In Hill's section on
"How the United States Are Governed" the operations of
legislatures are illustrated by a detailed and stubbornly
realistic narrative of a freshman congressman's schooling in
the techniques of introducing a bill, pushing it through
committee by lobbying and by deals with other congress-
men, and finally bringing it to a vote. There is no more
vivid and unvarnished picture of American politics in our
literature than Hill's straightforward, saltily satirical ac-

count of how Representative Smith of the Tenth District of Wisconsin got a federal appropriation for a dam across a non-navigable stream on which he wanted to operate a steamship line.

One of the most significant features of such books as those by Chase and Hill is that they achieved national scope by radiating outward from a Midwestern center and localizing themselves in so many specific places, and that they comprehended such a diversity of activities and occupations in terms of concrete events in the lives of individual citizens. It was a vernacular technique to which the cultivated literary tradition made no contribution but from which—as Whitman demonstrated—it could draw vitality.

It is high time these vernacular sources were fully explored in other fields. Years before Chase and Hill, for example, and five years before *Leaves of Grass* itself, a frontier physician named Daniel Drake had published a book which should be recognized as a landmark in our literary history. It bore the ungainly title, *A Systematic Treatise, Historical, Etiological, and Practical, on the Principal Diseases of the Interior Valley of North America,* and it was first published in Cincinnati in 1850. Drake was a crusty, indefatigable doctor, born and raised in a Kentucky frontier settlement. During the academic year he quarreled with his fellow professors on the staff of the medical college he had helped to establish, and in the summers, for thirty years, pursued evidence out of which to build his theory of the relationship of disease to climate, geography, and social environment. On horseback and on foot if there were no other means of transportation he traveled more than thirty thousand miles from the Great Lakes to the Gulf, and from the Alleghenies to the Rockies, talking with every physician he met, mingling with all kinds of people, making notes on climate, soil, and wind, employing topographical engineers and draftsmen to make plans of the localities noted for specific diseases, recording the occupations, habits, racial and social backgrounds of the people, and relating all this to the incidence of yellow fever, pneumonia, intermittent fever, and other diseases.

His work is one of the monuments in the development of American medical science, but that is not what concerns us here. The point is that Drake's book played a part in the development of techniques for recording the sprawling divergences of American life in concrete, local, and factual terms.

In contrast with the tradition of actuality which was developed in these non-literary forms, there were, of course, quite different tendencies in much of the fiction and poetry which was most popular with American readers. The "Choice Selections from the Poets" which Hill included in his *Manual* offer a fair sample of the kind of thing his readers wanted as a relief from the frequently harsh realities of life in booming towns and cities and on lonely farms. "How dear to this heart are the scenes of my childhood" was in this sense the theme song of the century. It appeared over and over again, in Whittier's

> *God pity them both! and pity us all*
> *Who vainly the dreams of youth recall;*

and in Florence Percy's

> *Backward, turn backward, O Time, in your flight,*
> *Make me a child again, just for tonight.*

Looking back to youth, for many Americans, meant looking eastward—either to some longer-settled region in this country, or to Europe itself. Time-past did not extend downward into a wealth of accumulated experience on the ground where you stood but stretched backward across plains and mountains and perhaps the sea. In youth, and in his buoyant moods, the American faced west. The boys Hamlin Garland grew up with during the sixties and seventies in the lumber town at the mouth of the Black River

in Wisconsin and on the prairies of Iowa all talked of
Colorado, never of New England, and his father's favorite
song was "Freedom's Star":

> *Then o'er the hills in legions, boys,*
> *Fair freedom's star*
> *Points to the sunset regions, boys,*
> *Ha, ha, ha-ha!*

But to Garland's mother, as to many pioneer women, moving West meant "not so much the acquisition of a new
home as the loss of all her friends and relatives." And
even his father in some moods talked nostalgically of the
East while refusing to revisit it—proudly saying "I never
take the back trail." There were moods in every American
which required him to hold onto the elastic threads con-
necting him with the cultivated tradition, however thin
they had been stretched.

It was these moods that were exploited by the pub-
lishers who brought out editions of the English novelists
and poets and to which many minor American writers
gave expression. Ralph L. Rusk, in his definitive study
of *The Literature of the Middle Western Frontier*, has
pointed out that although there were few people on the
frontier in the thirties who read about any subject but
politics, there was nevertheless a good market in the more
settled communities for the work of the English romantic
sentimentalists like Felicia Hemans and Thomas Moore,
and that both Scott and Byron enjoyed an unparalleled
popularity. By 1840, indeed, there were steamboats on the
Ohio and Mississippi which bore such names as *Lady
of the Lake*, *Marmion*, *Corsair*, and *Mazeppa*—a rather
touching evidence of the compelling need somehow to relate the vernacular environment to the cultivated tradition,
even if only by such a superficial device as a label.

The sentimental novels which formed such a large part
of nineteenth-century reading matter both in England and
America offer some instructive evidence of the divergence

between English and American attitudes. The most notable trend in their development during the seventy years after the founding of the federal government was the increasing tendency to make fiction out of what exists, rather than out of things wished for and dreamed of. The stock figures of the early American novels in this class were the seduced maiden, the captivating libertine, the mercenary parents, and the reformed rake—all borrowed straight from Richardson's *Pamela, Clarissa,* and *Sir Charles Grandison.* The heroines were delicate, full of sensibility, devoted to the thankless task of refining and spiritualizing man, winning, if successful, an adoring and reclaimed husband, but ready otherwise to reclaim the sinner by an uncomplaining, lingering decline which would "teach how innocence should die." By mid-century, however, the heroines were typified by Mrs. C. L. Hentz's Rena, who was "very fond of the poetry of the kitchen, such as the beating the whites of eggs," and the novels themselves frequently revolved —like Elizabeth Wetherell's *Queechy*—around plain domestic duties and hard work.[1]

In some measure this change was the result of the conscious effort of a number of women writers "to do good," as Sarah Josepha Hale put it, "especially to and for our sex." Mrs. Hale was for forty years the editor of *Godey's Lady's Book,* and month after month she hammered home to her feminine readers the message which Ola E. Winslow summarized thus: "You have a mind; cultivate it. Home is woman's proper sphere; stay in it. Woman's influence is profound; exercise it." As Miss Winslow says, women like Mrs. Hale and Catharine Maria Sedgwick did what the women's rights leaders, or idealists like Emerson and Whitman couldn't possibly have done for the same audience, stripping off layer after layer of romance and moonlight from the literature of the average woman reader, and helping her to plant her feet solidly on the American earth.

[1] For a fascinating survey of these books see the volume by Herbert R. Brown cited in the bibliography.

But the trend toward reality in the novels, and the emergence of the heroine who had two hands and knew how to use them, probably owed even more to the tradition which was developed in the non-literary personal narratives which were referred to earlier in this chapter—to Mrs. Jemison's story, for instance, or to such narratives as that of Deborah Sampson, published in 1797 under the title *The Female Review: or, The Memoirs of an American Young Lady*. Deborah had disguised herself as a man and served as a soldier in the Continental Army for more than two years, during which time, as the book assures us, "she performed the duties of every department and preserved her chastity inviolate."

What was true of the sentimental novels was also true of the sensational fiction of dark and gruesome texture which was so widely read, especially by young men. In the novels of George Lippard, for example, this sensational matter took on characteristics directly related to the kind of social drama illustrated in Pat Crowe's confessions. Lippard, who was a friend of Poe's and whose work may possibly have influenced him, wrote a number of melodramatic tales of vice in large cities and in 1850 founded a semisocialist "Brotherhood of the Union" which aimed to wipe out the sources of poverty and crime. *New York: Its Upper Ten and Lower Millions* (Cincinnati, 1854) is a loosely organized narrative dealing with the fulfillment of the terms of an eccentric will left by a wealthy New Yorker who committed suicide in 1823. The plot evolves through a series of episodes involving sex crimes, murders, robberies, kidnaping, and political intrigue, and the settings include brothels, slums, gambling dens, and the palaces of the rich. But through all this there is woven a thread of flamboyant yet effective preaching of Lippard's romantic socialism, with savage attacks on ministers and priests who preach a clockwork gospel "invented some years ago for the purpose of supplying the masses with *something to believe* and themselves with a good salary" while ignoring "the true Word . . . which enjoins the establishment of

the kingdom of God, *on earth,* in the physical and intellectual welfare of the greatest portion of mankind."

The hero of the book (if it has a single hero) is Arthur
Dermoyne, intelligent shoemaker who refuses to enter a
profession because, as he says, "I cannot separate myself
from that nine-tenths of the human family who seem to
have been born to work and die." His dream is to lead a
group of workmen out of the city shops to the West where
they can build a community in which "every man will
have a place to work and every one will receive the fruits
of his labor," and where, without priest or monopolist or
slaveholder, they can worship "that Christ who was himself a workman, even as he is now the workman's God."
But the most interesting point is that when one of the
other characters charges Dermoyne with having absorbed
the doctrines of the French school (presumably those of
Fourier, whose socialist theories were widely known in
America at the time), he replies that they were the ideas
of his Pennsylvania-Dutch forebears who had emigrated
from Germany to William Penn's colony a hundred and
fifty years before. It was an assertion of Lippard's consciousness of the native roots of his faith.

Of all the strands which are woven into the fabric of
vernacular American writing, humor might seem to have
least connection with the religious faith in democracy
which motivated so many of our writers. Yet the two are
closely related. In her book on *American Humor* (1931),
Miss Rourke showed, for instance, how the comic spirit
co-operated "to fulfill the biblical cry running through
much of the revivalism of the time: 'to make all things
new.'" Humor, especially the frontier variety, served as a
leveling agent, deflating lofty notions and tossing aside all
alien traditions, partly out of sheer delight in destruction
but also as a part of the necessary process of clearing the
ground for new growth. As one of the burlesque writers
of the sixties said, the thing he and his fellow humorists
were doing for literature was "simplifying matters—strip-

ping them of their excrescences," the very thing that American mechanics and builders were doing in machine design and house construction.

Miss Rourke has pointed out that the central figures in the humorous writing of the period of national expansion were the representatives of racial or regional elements of the new society—the Yankee, the backwoodsman, the Negro—broadly drawn types which emerged from and belonged to the mass of the people and to the insurgent and revolutionary class. They formed a "comic trio," each member of which took on coloring from the other two as the types developed, though they never blended into a single symbol. Each represented a class which had been torn from all roots in an established culture and which willingly or unwillingly had become wanderers. And as their world is created—in the monologues of Yankee Hill, the sayings of Seba Smith's Major Jack Downing, the tall tales of the Crockett almanacs, Johnson J. Hooper's "campaign biography" of Captain Simon Suggs, and the Negro minstrelsy of Jim Crow, Zip Coon, and Dan Tucker—it takes form as a richly detailed panorama of the raw realities of American life which provides a setting for repeated comic triumphs of sharp wit or outlandish rascality, frequently operating in terms of the wildest fantasy.

Much of this humorous writing had its sources in oral tales—the stories about legendary figures like Davy Crockett and Mike Fink and the tall stories which were swapped around campfires in the wilderness, in country stores and taverns, on steamboats and trains. And these tales were often grotesque and humorous handlings of the same everyday materials which we have encountered in other vernacular forms. An Englishman riding in a stagecoach between Wheeling and Zanesville in the forties, for example, listened to his fellow passengers swapping yarns which blended outrageous and exuberant fantasy with the same class of factual material which Daniel Drake was amassing for his monumental treatise. "The unhealthy condition of some of the Western rivers, the Illinois in particular, was the subject of their discourse," he recorded.

> One asserted that he had known a man to be so dreadfully affected with the ague, from sleeping in the fall on its banks, that he shook . . . all the teeth out of his head. This was matched by another, who said there was a man from his State, who had gone to Illinois to settle, and the ague seized him so terribly hard that he shook off all his clothes . . . and could not keep a garment whole, for it unravelled the very web, thread by thread, till it was all destroyed.

And the climax was capped by still a third who told of a friend of his who got the ague so bad that he shook his whole house down about his ears and buried himself in the ruins.

Similarly the humorous writings, like other forms of the vernacular, all have panoramic sweep. The inclusive realism of the backgrounds against which the sagas of Simon Suggs, Sut Lovingood, and the others are set is another manifestation of the same impulse to encompass and localize the diversities of the American environment which we have traced in the "doctor books" and in Hill's famous *Manual*. Like Dr. Drake, and Dr. Chase too, for that matter, the authors of the humorous classics of the frontier were peripatetic. A. B. Longstreet, the author of *Georgia Scenes*, and Johnson Hooper were both lawyers who had traveled the circuit in their regions. George W. Harris, creator of Sut Lovingood, had learned to know Tennessee as a jeweler's apprentice, river-boat captain, silversmith, postmaster, hunter, journalist, and inventor. It is no wonder that their books reveal every aspect of the life of the frontier.

Much has been made of the quality of wild exaggeration in these humorous narratives. Exaggeration has, indeed, been repeatedly specified as the significant element in all characteristically American humor. And it does form

a large part of our humorous tradition. On that famous
January morning when it was so all screwen cold that the
very daybreak froze fast as it was trying to dawn, Davy
Crockett (as the 1854 Crockett Almanac tells us) decided
something must be done or creation itself would be done
for. So he took up a fresh bear and beat the animal against
the ice "till the hot ile began to walk out on him at all
sides."

> I then took an' held him over the airth's axes [Davy
> recounted] an' squeezed him till I'd thawed 'em loose,
> poured out about a ton on't over the sun's face, give
> the airth's cogwheel one kick backward till I got the
> sun loose—whistled "Push along, keep movin'!" an' in
> about fifteen seconds the airth gave a grunt, an' began
> movin'. The sun walked up beautiful, salutin' me with
> sich a wind o' gratitude that it made me sneeze. I lit
> my pipe by the blaze o' his top-knot, shouldered my
> bear, an' walked home, introducin' people to the fresh
> daylight with a piece of sunrise in my pocket.

Something of this same quality has appeared in less
genuinely poetic form in much of our oratory, and has
always provided our humorists with grist. As far back as
the middle of the eighteenth century Mather Byles, the
grandson of old Increase Mather, had created a satirical
portrait of Richard Stentor, who was "moderately speaking, Nine Foot high, and Four in Diameter," and who delivered an oration in praise of Beacon Hill, hailing it as
"so pompous, magnificent, illustrious, and lofty-towering,
that, as I twirle around my Arm with the artful Flourish
of an Orator, I seem to feel my Knuckles rebound from
the blew vault of Heaven. . . ." And the tradition of oratorical bombast was still fair game for the humorists a
century and a quarter later when Orpheus C. Kerr trav-
estied their technique in his delightfully anticlimactic:
"The sun rushed up the eastern sky in a state of patriotic
combustion, and as the dew fell upon the grassy hillsides,
the mountains lifted their heads and were rather green."

But in all the grandiose oratory which democratic politics produced, and in all the non-literary humorous writings, there was an expansive gusto, an inventive and nervy handling of language, and a bold contempt for ordered forms which offered a healthy contrast to the sterile decorousness of most of the cultivated literature of the period. It was from such sources that Mark Twain drew, and it is to them that we can trace many of those elements in his style and manner which made him the first writer of international stature who is thoroughly and completely American.

These Western and frontier elements of vernacular literature were of great importance, as many of our historians and critics have realized. But they were not the sole elements of the tradition. We should not let the brilliance of Turner's theory blind us to other aspects of the emerging cultural patterns. Yet even H. L. Mencken, whose historical and critical study of the American language has been one of the most stimulating achievements of recent scholarship, seems to have pursued his investigations chiefly along the trails lighted by the Western star. It is to the influence of "the great open spaces" that he assigns the credit for the distinctive characteristics of American speech in the nineteenth century. To be sure, he acknowledges that "the slums of the great Eastern cities" continued to provide what could be called frontier conditions even after the frontier had vanished at the end of the century, and in another place he urges intensive studies of American slang and of "American trade argots" as well as further investigation "of the novelties introduced into the language by the great movement into the West." But throughout his books the emphasis is placed upon the frontier as the source of the American elements in our language.

And so it is, if you focus your interest on the flashier neologisms like *sockdolager, hornswoggle,* or *absquatulate.* But many of the frontier words were more startling than useful, and their total contribution to the American language as it is now used has probably been overemphasized. At all events, when Mencken draws up a list of words to illustrate the current, twentieth-century differences between American and English usage on the level of everyday speech, remarkably few of the American words appear to have had their origins on the frontier. Most of them, on the contrary, come from technological and industrial sources—as in the case of such railroad terms as *caboose, freight car,* and *roundhouse* (in English usage, *brake-van, goods wagon,* and *running shed*)—or from the world of trades and commerce, as with *ashman, clapboard,* and *truck farmer* (in England, *dustman, weatherboard,* and *market gardener*). Even a casual search through lists of American words and phrases will turn up a number which are plainly of vernacular origin in the special sense that we have applied to that term. For example: *to know the ropes* (from sailing ships), *to pan out* (from mining), *single-track mind, jerk-water,* and *to clear the track* (from railroads), *claw hammer* (slang for full-dress tailcoat, from carpenter's tool). It is amusing to note, furthermore, that many political terms of American origin are borrowings from technology: we speak of political organizations as *machines,* and politics is full of such terms as *steering committee, logrolling, pump priming, to steamroller,* and *to engineer.*

The romantic glamour of the frontier has apparently bewitched even the iconoclastic sage of Baltimore into neglecting a lead which was suggested by a British observer of our language more than a hundred years ago. For in 1837, as Mencken himself has noted, Captain Marryat remarked on the tendency in America for technical words and phrases to enter into general speech by metaphor, as an example of which he offered the transformation of "straining at a gnat and swallowing a camel" into "straining at a gate and swallowing a sawmill." Elsewhere Mencken quotes a specimen of frontier brag which illustrates the same phenomenon: "I'm the ginewine article, a real double-acting engine, and I can out-run, out-jump, etc., etc." Perhaps after all Howells was right when he said that American writers would find the sources of a vital native language not only in the great open spaces but in both "the shops and fields."

Granted the purposes which were so much a part of the vernacular tradition and granted the universal appeal of its subject matter, it was inevitable that—side by side with the development of new oral and written forms for handling its materials—there would be a corresponding development of techniques for distribution of its products. The plays and variety shows in which the figures of the comic trio were developed were taken by traveling theatrical troupes into the remotest settlements. P. T. Barnum's "Grand Scientific and Musical Theater," his first traveling show, toured the Southern states in two wagons, and from the earliest days similar troupes gave performances on canalboats and flatboats, and later on the elaborate showboats which plied the Western rivers. The characteristics of oral literature, its personal and anecdotal flavor, its racy and colloquial style, were developed in the Lyceum lecture circuits established by such men as Josiah Holbrook and James Redpath and later in the Chautauqua camps and tent shows. Almost all the prominent writers of the period from 1830 to 1924 had traveled across the country at least once, lecturing at village Lyceums or at Chautauquas. Never before in history had so many authors had firsthand contact with such vast audiences in so many diverse communities.

In book publishing also there were significant developments. Both Dr. Chase and Thomas E. Hill, for example, set up their own special printing and publishing establishments to handle their books, and neither was satisfied with the conventional process of distribution through bookstores. As Chase announced in his preface, his book was sold "only by Travelling Agents, that all may have a chance to purchase; for if left at the bookstores, or by advertisement only, not one in fifty would ever see it."

Subscription publishing, as this method was called, was an important development in the latter half of the century.

It is described in *The Great Industries of the United States* (1873) as a fairly new branch of the book business, which was becoming more popular every year because it was the best, if not the only, means of introducing books to a large circle of readers, "especially in interior towns which are remote from book-publishing and book-selling centers." Essentially it was simply an industrialized extension of the earlier system (described in 1841 by S. G. Goodrich, the bookseller and publisher) whereby peddlers—mostly from Connecticut, apparently—bought books and almanacs wholesale from some supplier like the Pearl Street Bookstore in New York, and then traveled by horse and wagon through the Southern and Western states, selling them at any house where they could find "a sucker." But in subscription publishing the traveling agents carried with them samples only, taking orders for later delivery.

That the new method was successful, and that it was admirably suited to the vernacular forms, is indicated by the fact that it was a subscription publisher who brought out all Mark Twain's early books. Not long after *The Innocents Abroad* was published by the American Publishing Company in Hartford, Twain wrote to its proprietor, Elisha Bliss, that everywhere he went on his lecture tours he found that an agent had been there before him and many people had read the book. "It is easy to see, when one travels around," he added, "that one must be endowed with a deal of genuine generalship in order to maneuver a publication whose line of battle stretches from end to end of a great continent, and whose foragers and skirmishers invest every hamlet and besiege every village hidden away in all the vast space between."

Important as all these factors were in the development of the vernacular, the most serviceable vehicle of all was journalism. No literary vehicle is more flexible than the newspaper, and none responds more directly to the tastes and preferences of its readers. Many of the writers who have figured in the development of a distinctively American literature—Whitman and Mark Twain among them—

have at some time been newspapermen or newspaper contributors.

It is a notable fact that the essential feature of the success of cheap journalism in England and America, first exploited in the United States by Benjamin H. Day's New York *Sun* (1833) and the other penny dailies of the thirties, turned out to be human-interest stories: non-political local news about people who were—or might be—known to the reader. It was the same principle which Chase and Hill were later to rely on in their books. It was precisely what Mark Twain, out in Virginia City in the mad mining days, had in mind when he wrote to his sister in St. Louis that she would never make a good reporter because she didn't appreciate the interest that attaches to names. "An item is of no use," he told her, "unless it speaks of some *person*, and not then, unless that person's *name* is distinctly mentioned. The most interesting letter . . . is one that treats of *persons* . . . rather than the public events of the day." American journalism from the beginning has demonstrated that we are more interested in what local individuals do, and what they say about politics, than we are in what goes on in the rest of the world, or what really happens in politics. From Ben Franklin's *Dogood Papers* to Finley Dunne's *Mr. Dooley* and on down to Will Rogers and thence to Winchell, Pegler, and Eleanor Roosevelt, Americans have been specialists in personal journalism.

So we have come full circle and are back again to the individual human being whose worth, Channing had said, it should be the function of our literature to show. We have seen how, in a variety of subliterary ways, the vernacular tradition improvised techniques to tear away the disguises from men living under democratic institutions in a machine age. But the search for new forms and techniques was by no means confined to these subliterary areas.

Think, for a moment, of the eminent American writers of the nineteenth century and notice how many of them are difficult to classify in terms of the literary forms in which they worked. Was Melville a novelist? Certainly not in the sense that Thackeray, Flaubert, or even Tolstoy were novelists. *Typee, Omoo,* and *Mardi* are not novels by any definition, and *Moby Dick* itself is—in form—altogether unlike any other book ever written, a compound of tragic drama, treatise on whaling technology, allegory, philosophical speculations, adventure narrative, and seamanship manual. Were Emerson and Thoreau essayists and poets? But Emerson's essays are really oral lectures, and his stature as a writer depends fully as much on the *Journals* as upon the essays; it is the *Journals* after all which come closest to being the kind of "Montaigne's book" he wanted, "full of fun, poetry, business, divinity, philosophy, anecdote, smut." Thoreau's masterpiece, *Walden,* is part poetic record of a personal adventure, part a philosophy of rebellion against social conformity, and part the record of a reporter-naturalist. For years Whitman's *Leaves of Grass* was only reluctantly admitted to be poetry. ("Confused, inarticulate, and surging in a mad kind of rhythm which sounds as if hexameters were trying to bubble through sewage," Professor Barrett Wendell of Harvard's English department called it in his *Literary History of America* in 1900.) The author of *Huckleberry Finn, Life on the Mississippi, Personal Recollections of Joan of Arc,* and *Roughing It* is hard to label in terms of the forms he worked in. Even Hawthorne and Poe, who on first thought are easily classified as writers of fiction, were the creators of a new form: the modern short story.

The influence of vernacular elements is notable in the work of all these writers. Charles Olson called attention to the fact that the whaling ship, which Melville wrote about in *Moby Dick,* was one of the most highly developed industrial machines of its time, and it is significant that it was in writing this book that Melville for the first and only time succeeded in fusing the techniques of reporting and of allegory, which, as Professor Matthiessen has said, were his two contrasting methods of dealing with material.

The vernacular elements in Emerson's writing are no less important for being less obvious. Constance Rourke was the first to call attention to the relationship between his lectures and the oral and communal dialogues of the humorists, the lyrical strain which had sounded in the midst of Jack Downing's Yankee lingo, "the air of wonder, the rhapsodic speech" of Western tall talk. But the relationship had been sensed in Emerson's own time. Two newspaper accounts of his lectures were included, side by side with samples of Down East and frontier humor, in *Yankee Smith's American Broad Grins,* one of innumerable such collections brought out in the fifties and sixties. One of the accounts, in spite of its self-consciously arty journalism, moves very close to the rhapsodic boasting of the frontier demigods, in its picture of the gentle Yankee speaker as "a spiritual shuttle, vibrating between the unheard of and the unutterable."

> Like a child he shakes his rattle over the edge of chaos, and swings on the gates of the past, and sits like a nightingale in a golden ring, suspended by a silver cord from a nail driven into the zenith.

One is reminded of Lowell's less ebullient description of Emerson's lectures as "a chaos full of shooting stars, a jumble of creative forces."

Emerson learned his techniques the hard way, in small towns and villages all over the land where he gave Lyceum lectures. In spite of his shy and withdrawn nature and his predilection for contemplation rather than action he never lost his conviction that his audience must include the great mass of people who "understand what's what as well as the little mass." He had scathing contempt for the "pert gentlemen" who assumed that the whole object was "to manage 'the great mass' and they, forsooth, are behind the curtain with the Deity and mean to help manage."

Emerson's lectures—like the published essays which were based upon them—were loosely organized as compared

with the formal prose of a contemporary like Lowell. But
they had a vitality and flexibility which his oral medium
required. His friend Carlyle objected that his paragraphs
were square bags of duck shot rather than beaten ingots,
and he himself seems to have felt occasionally that his
essays should have had more continuity. But fundamentally Emerson cared little for the purely literary values.
He put his writing to different tests, measuring it against
values inherent in the vernacular environment.

Out in Beloit, Wisconsin, for instance, on a January day
in 1856 when the temperature was down somewhere between twenty and thirty degrees below zero, he made this
entry in his journal:

> This climate and people are a new test for the wares of a
> man of letters. All his thin, watery matter freezes; 'tis
> only the smallest portion of alcohol that remains good.
> At the lyceum, the stout Illinoian, after a short trial,
> walks out of the hall. The Committee tell you that the
> people want a hearty laugh. . . . Well, I think with
> Governor Reynolds, the people are always right (in a
> sense), and that the man of letters is to say, These are
> the new conditions to which I must conform. The archi-
> tect who is asked to build a house to go upon the sea,
> must not build a Parthenon, or a square house, but a
> ship. And Shakespeare, or Franklin, or Aesop, coming
> to Illinois, would say, I must give my wisdom a comic
> form, instead of tragics or elegiacs, and well I know to
> do it, and he is no master who cannot vary his forms,
> and carry his own end triumphantly through the most
> difficult.

That is a typically Emersonian passage not only in the
freshness of its imagery but also in its modesty and honesty.
The Illinoian walked out on him, and the Illinoian was the
very man he was after. The Illinoian wanted a laugh. Very
well, then, that was a fact which genius should accept and
turn to its own account.

To be sure, Emerson was never able to give comic form to his own genius—as Mark Twain was later to do in the same vernacular medium of the platform lecture. But, as he said of the sailor preacher, Father Taylor, he did succeed in making abstractions "accessible and effectual" to hearers who were not much given to reading philosophical essays, and in the process of doing so he created a personal idiom more instant and supple than any in our literature before him. What matter if he could not meet the cultivated tradition's standard of polished and finished prose? "Only that good profits which we can taste with all doors open, and which serves all men."

Whitman, too, drew on vernacular oral techniques in evolving a form suited to his purposes. Faced with the vast panorama of American life, the poet, he insisted, must abandon conventional poetic form and rhyme and seek a more flexible, more eligible medium of expression, "enlarging, adapting itself to comprehend the size of the whole people." The form of expression which had most powerfully moved him and which contributed most to his own style was the "passionate unstudied oratory" of men like the Quaker preacher Elias Hicks, to whom he had listened as a boy on Long Island, and Emerson's friend Father Taylor. Dilating confidently in the oratorical rhythms of a language which, as Emerson described it, was compounded from the *Bhagvat-Geeta* and the New York *Herald,* Whitman sometimes lapsed into such unconscious burlesque as the exclamatory line from "Night on the Prairie":

How plenteous! how spiritual! how resumé!

But at its rare best the instrument he had created was the most flexible and powerful medium yet created for expressing the American scene. Even in the much-deprecated "catalogue passages" there are such visually and emotionally concise, reportorial lines as these from Section 15 of "Song of Myself":

> *The carpenter dresses his plank, the tongue of his*
> *foreplane whistles its wild ascending lisp. . . .*
> *The jour printer with gray head and gaunt jaws*
> *works at his case,*
> *He turns his quid of tobacco while his eyes blur*
> *with the manuscript;*
> *The malformed limbs are tied to the surgeon's*
> *table,*
> *What is removed drops horribly in a pail. . . .*

The extent of the influence of vernacular forces on the major writers of nineteenth-century America is only briefly suggested by the instances given here. Nothing has been said of the journalistic origins of the short story form which Hawthorne and Poe created; nor have we attempted to explore such obvious areas as the influence upon Whitman and Mark Twain of their years as newspaper editors. But enough has been said, perhaps, to indicate that a considerable part of the characteristically American quality in the work of our major writers stems from the influence of the vernacular tradition. Wherever we look in the writing of the nineteenth century we are likely to encounter one or more of the vernacular characteristics of utilitarian ethics, concern with the value of the individual, and the panoramic effort to comprehend a diversity of people and places in specific local and factual terms; and we are sure to find these characteristics developed in writing aimed at wide audiences—in personal narratives (from outright autobiographies like Franklin's to books like Melville's *Typee* and *Redburn* and Mark Twain's *Huckleberry Finn* and *Life on the Mississippi*), in books of information, in humorous writing, and in journalism.

Now let us see how some of these same vernacular qualities have manifested themselves in American painting, where the medium of expression is less subject to utilitarian demands than the written word.

7 Seeing Is Believing

After visiting the art gallery at the Philadelphia Centennial, William James wrote to his brother Henry to tell him how pleased he was with the high average of the American paintings. The great majority of them were landscapes, he noted, and in almost every case the animating spirit was "a perfectly sincere effort to reproduce a natural aspect" which in some special way had affected the painter's sensibility.

James's description of the animating spirit in these paintings is significant. It emphasizes the literalness in American paintings which almost all critics agreed was characteristic, whether or not they approved of it. William Dean Howells felt that the American paintings were "too often unstoried, like our scenery," and that their subjects "were seen, not deeply felt and thought." Similarly, the *Art Journal's* critic preferred the English landscape paintings to the American because so many of the best of ours appeared like pictures seen in the camera. (An odd converse to this statement appears in a comment by Hermann Wilhelm Vogel, one of the German judges, on the exhibit at Photographic Hall: the Americans, he noted, expect from the photographer "work which in Europe would belong to the artist.") As early as 1856 John Ruskin, complaining of the ugliness of some American paintings he had just seen, acidly noted that he could see "that they were *true* studies and that the ugliness of the country must be Unfathomable." The art critic James Jackson Jarves, too, objected to the literalness of our painters, and gave as an example Bierstadt's "Rocky Mountains," in which the realism was so factual "that the botanist and geologist can find work in his rocks and vegetation." And in 1879 S. G. W. Benjamin was complaining that the influence which had given birth to our landscape art had been prosaic, exacting, and uninspiring.

The "topographical and mechanical" notions of art to which Benjamin and the others objected, had—as a matter of fact—been come by honestly enough in the case of many of the painters. An extraordinary large percentage of American artists were originally apt in, or dependent upon, mechanical skill; Peale, Durand, Palmer, Chapman, and Kensett were all disciplined for pictorial work by workmanship in machinery, watchmaking, carving, or engraving. Several of our early sculptors, too, were mechanics by training. Joel Tanner Hart was a stonemason before he did his bust of Henry Clay (1847), based on exact measurements and a number of daguerreotype studies, and he later invented and patented a measuring machine to make his work more precise. Hiram Powers, late in his career, liked to reminisce in Florence about his early training in America as a mechanic simplifying and improving a machine for cutting clock wheels, and finishing brass plates for organ stops so smoothly and accurately that when one was laid on another and then raised, it would lift the other—as he proudly put it—"by mere cohesive attraction." So mechanically did Powers work in marble that he could sum up his philosophy of art by saying baldly that "He that can copy a potato precisely can copy a face precisely." The limitations of Powers' once-famous "Greek Slave" and other statues are evident enough to anyone who has seen them. But—like the familiar and universally popular "Rogers Groups" of the sixties[1]—they serve to illustrate the same sort of perfectly sincere effort to reproduce nature which James noted in American landscape painting.

In one of the most interesting studies of American painting Alan Burroughs makes it clear that a distinctively American—as distinguished from the parent English—ap-

[1] Typical examples were "The Returned Volunteer," "The Council of War," and "Weighing the Baby." John Rogers, their creator, had studied civil engineering, worked in a New Hampshire machine shop, and been boss of a railroad repair shop in the West.

proach to art had become apparent as early as 1750; and this distinction appeared not in the South but in New England, where the "best society" (that is, the patrons of art) was in close contact with the yeomanry. In painting, as in furniture design and architecture, there was a new emphasis on simplicity, reality, and serviceability. In the work of Copley, Smibert, and the other mid-eighteenth-century New England portrait painters, Burroughs writes, "what took the place of beauty and consciously artistic structure was simply good eyesight." And if one traces the course of American painting thereafter, it becomes clear that the only attitude which is traditional in American art is, as Burroughs concludes, "dependence on fact." There are, of course, different kinds of realism: realism of the eye, of the emotions, and of the mind; but there is only one fundamental attitude which permits any kind of realism, and that is respect for the thing seen, the feeling aroused, or the attendant thought.

This respect, this dependence upon fact, appears variously in the work of both the ablest and the least accomplished technicians. To analyze it carefully and fully would require more space than we have here at our disposal; but it will be familiar to anyone who has seen the work, for example, of William Sidney Mount, Winslow Homer, Thomas Eakins, or of the numerous so-called primitive painters.

American primitive paintings have been eagerly collected and frequently exhibited during the past few years, and more than a hundred of the best of them (from widely scattered private and public collections) have been reproduced by Jean Lipman in a handsome volume published by the Oxford University Press in 1942. Miss Lipman admires these paintings primarily because of what she calls their "purely aesthetic qualities of abstract design," which, she asserts, "entirely accounts for" the widespread contemporary interest in them. One may suppose, therefore, that she has selected for inclusion those pictures which best illustrate those qualities.

Yet anyone who examines the pictures soon discovers that there are two quite divergent types among them. On the one hand there are some which are indeed highly abstract and free from any apparent concern with visual reality, such as the formal little landscapes and still-life groups, frequently executed by means of stencils, or the conventionalized memorials like the one by Eunice Pinney (see Fig. 23), from Miss Lipman's own collection. These are in every sense abstract patterns of forms and colors. There is no optical reality about them.

On the other hand, a sizable majority of the paintings seem to represent a quite different attitude upon the part of the artist. In them one senses a diligent and often rather touching effort to make a literal and detailed record of the thing seen. Joseph H. Headley's oil on wood painting of Poestenkill (see Fig. 23) is obviously an attempt to record specific houses, barns, fences, roads, and landscape. Whatever deviations from actuality such a painting contains are imposed by the painter's lack of technical mastery. They are not the result of indifference to exact appearance, or of an instinctive preference for abstract design. If one of the barns in the painting is red, one feels sure that Headley did not paint it so because his sense of design required it but because that particular barn in Poestenkill in 1850 was red.

The point I am insisting on here is that in the two different types of primitives the absence of an accurate "representation of normal visible reality," which Miss Lipman and many other contemporary critics admire, results from two quite different causes. In pictures like Eunice Pinney's "Memorial" the painter had no intention of representing optical reality; she was out to create a lugubrious design, not a picture of a specific tomb. But in paintings like Headley's, actuality was the painter's primary concern—so much so that, within the limits of his craftsmanship, he often represented it even if he couldn't see it from where he stood, just because he *knew* it was there.

As one would expect, these two opposed attitudes are

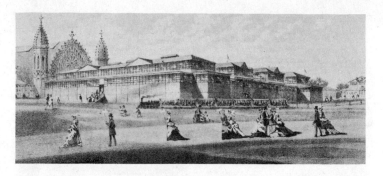

FIG. 19. THE POMOLOGICAL ANNEX AT THE CENTENNIAL. This picture, from Thompson Westcott's *Centennial Portfolio*, Philadelphia, 1876, is the only surviving record of the building. Of Agricultural Hall, in the background at the left, Westcott remarked that the exterior displayed "ornamentation sufficient to make the edifice attractive."

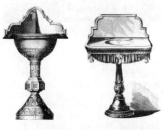

FIG. 20. DECORATIVE ART IN CAST IRON—CIRCA 1880. Iron washstands *(left, above)* and garden seat *(left, below)* by J. L. Mott Iron Works (from the *Illustrated Catalogue of the Plumbing and Sanitary Department of the J. L. Mott Iron Works*, New York, 1881; and Philip T. Sandhurst, *Industrial and Fine Arts*, Philadelphia, 1879).

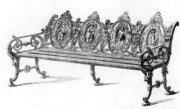

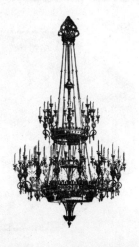

FIG. 21. INDUSTRIAL ART WORKMANSHIP—1876. Brass Chandelier by Mitchell, Vance and Co., New York (from *Masterpieces of the Centennial International Exhibition*, Philadelphia, 1876).

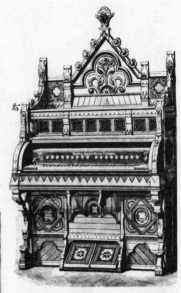

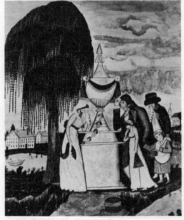

FIG. 23. TWO TYPES OF PRIMI-
TIVE PAINTING. (*Above*) *Memorial*,
a water color by Eunice Pinney,
done about 1815 (reproduced with
permission from the collection of
Jean and Howard Lipman); (*below*) *Poestenkill—Winter*, an oil-
on-wood painting by Joseph H.
Headley, done about 1850 (© Hal-
laday-Thomas Collection; reproduced with permission).

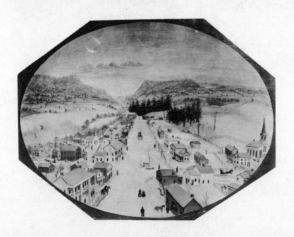

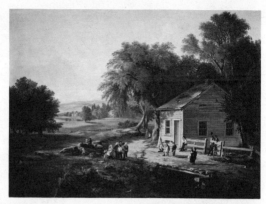

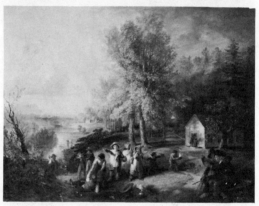

FIG. 24. THE VER-
NACULAR AND CUL-
TIVATED TRADITIONS
IN PAINTING. *(Above)*
The Old Schoolhouse
by James M. Hart,
1849 (reproduced
with permission from
the collection of Ira
W. Martin); *(below)*
Dismissal of School
on an October After-
noon, by Henry In-
man, 1845 (repro-
duced with permis-
sion of the Museum
of Fine Arts, Boston,
M. and M. Karolik
Collection).

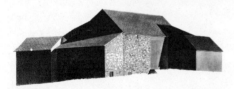

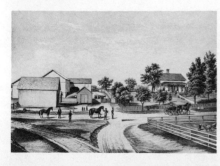

FIG. 25. THE PAINTER'S DIS-
COVERY OF VERNACULAR
FORMS. *(Above) Bucks County*
Barn—1923, water color with
pencil by Charles Sheeler (reproduced with permission from
the collection of Whitney Museum of American Art); *(be-*
low) Ohio Barns—1878, detail
of lithograph of *Residence and*
Stock Farm of J. F. Blair &
Son in Williams' *History of*
Ashtabula County, Ohio, Philadelphia, 1878.

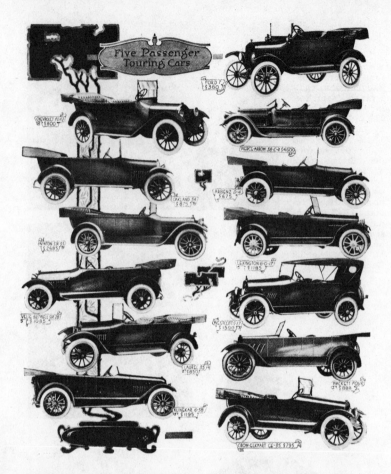

FIG. 26. AUTOMOBILE DESIGN—1916. A page of five-passenger touring cars from the "Before the Show" issue of the magazine *Motor World* (courtesy of the Chilton Company).

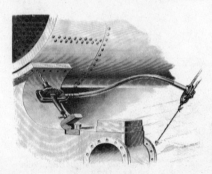

FIG. 27. FLEXIBLE POWER. The Stow flexible shaft (from *The Masterpieces of the Centennial*, Philadelphia, 1877).

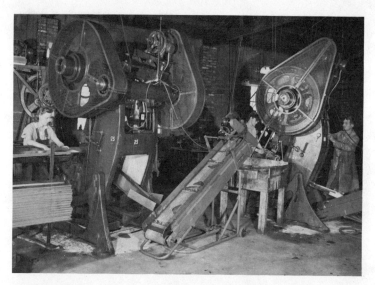

FIG. 28. FLEXIBLE FACTORY LAYOUT. Portable conveyor, electrically operated, receives stampings from chute of one punch press, carries them upward on cleated belt, and deposits them on tray by operator of next press, and so on through progressive operations (photograph of Press-Veyor installation at Dodge Tool and Manufactudring Company, courtesy of Rapids-Standard Co., Inc., Grand Rapids, Michigan).

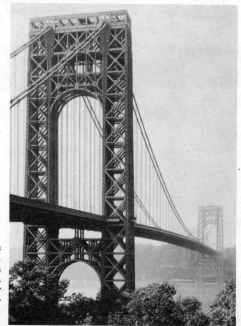

FIG. 29. ENGINEERING WITHOUT ARCHITECTURE. The George Washington Bridge over the Hudson River (photograph courtesy the Port of New York Authority).

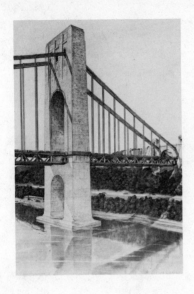
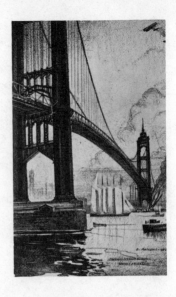

Fig. 30. Engineering and Architecture. *(Above left)* The George Washington Bridge towers as originally planned (Cass Gilbert's design, courtesy of the Port of New York Authority); *(above right)* Robinson and Steinman's Proposed Liberty Bridge over the Narrows, New York Harbor (from Steinman and Watson, *Bridges and Their Builders*, G. P. Putnam's Sons, New York, 1941, courtesy of David B. Steinman); *(below)* the Bronx-Whitestone Bridge; Aymar Embury, II, architect (courtesy of the Triborough Bridge and Tunnel Authority).

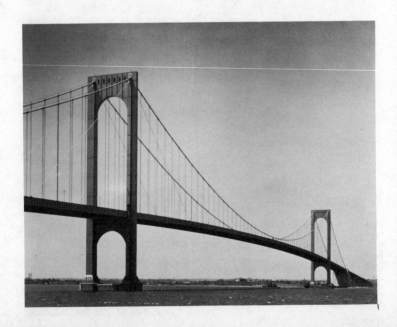

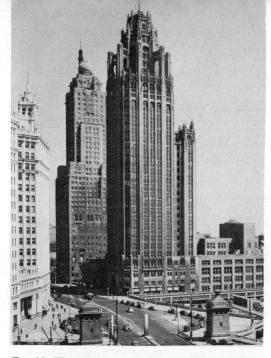

FIG. 31. "THIS BEAUTY STUFF IS ALL BUNK." *(Above)* The Chicago Tribune Tower, by Raymond Hood—1922 (photograph courtesy of the Chicago *Tribune);* *(below)* the McGraw-Hill Building, by Raymond Hood—1931 (photograph courtesy of McGraw-Hill Studio).

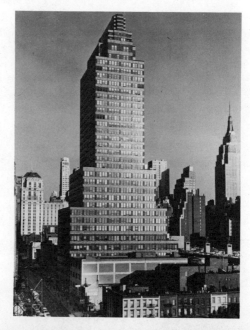

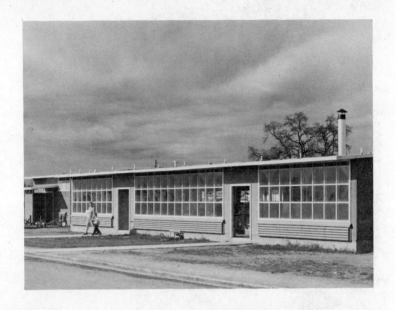

FIG. 32. THE TRIUMPH OF VERNACULAR FORM. *(Above)* Utilities Building, FSA Camp, Woodville, California (photograph courtesy of Library of Congress, Prints and Photographs Division); *(below)* Chrysler Tank Arsenal, designed by Albert Kahn (photograph by Hedrich-Blessing, courtesy of *Architectural Forum* and Hedrich-Blessing Studio).

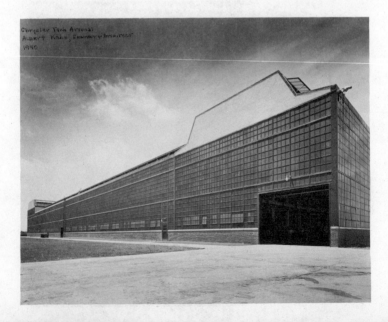

reflected in the kind of subject matter chosen. When the painter was concerned primarily with abstract design he drew his subjects from literature, or copied conventional designs in popular prints and pictures, or simply arranged stencils in agreeable patterns. But when the painter was concerned primarily with actuality, he turned for his subjects to real landscapes and to houses, ships, trains, and people that he knew.

In the former case composition is primarily the product of the artist's design sense, and the details are selected in terms of the design. In the latter, the composition exists almost independently of the artist; in a sense he merely selects or discovers it. One painter imposes a satisfying design upon pleasing conventionalized elements; the other imposes upon himself a satisfying relationship with an already existing design.

Those primitives in which fact is subordinate to design are always on the fringes of the cultivated tradition, and many of them are echoes if not mere unskilled imitations of professional work. The anonymous painting of "The Runaway Horse" (Plate 43 in Miss Lipman's volume) is an obvious echo of the academic English landscape school; Edward Hicks's notable "Penn's Treaty with the Indians" (Plate 69) is a memory image of Benjamin West's much-reproduced painting of the same scene; and the anonymous painting of "Cleveland's Public Square" (Plate 62) was certainly done by someone familiar with the expert aquatint engravings of the early nineteenth century. Amy, in Louisa May Alcott's *Little Women,* was in a sense the type of all the cultivated primitives. When she took up "poker-sketching," you may remember, "Raphael's face was found boldly executed on the under side of the moulding board, and Bacchus on the head of a beer barrel," and her later paintings were of swarthy boys and dark-eyed madonnas suggesting Murillo or "buxom ladies and dropsical infants" which were meant to look like Rubens. Even when she got the mania for "sketching from nature" she haunted river, field, and wood, "sighing for ruins to copy."

It seems clear, then, that there are two distinct categories of paintings which are generally lumped together as American primitives: unprofessional paintings reflecting the impact on the artist of some aspect of the cultivated tradition, and paintings which, seeking to reproduce optical reality, create a tone and feeling which relate directly to the thing seen.

These same qualities appear also in the work of our professional painters. Two pictures which provide a striking example of these divergent approaches were included in the loan exhibition, "Life in America," which was shown at the Metropolitan Museum of Art during the New York World's Fair in 1939, and are illustrated on facing pages of the catalogue of that exhibition. James M. Hart's "The Old Schoolhouse" and Henry Inman's "Dismissal of School on an October Afternoon" are similar in subject matter and were both painted in the 1840s. (See Fig. 24.) Both contain a schoolhouse among trees at the right of the scene, a group of children in the center foreground, and at the left a stream flowing into a distant landscape of hills and fields. In Inman's painting the whole effect is misty; the October atmosphere is an essential part of the artist's intention. The schoolhouse is partly obscured by trees; the children, though nearer to the artist than in Hart's painting, are less clearly observed and seem to be on loan from an inferior canvas by Sir Thomas Lawrence or George Romney; and the distant hills and fields are reminiscent of many of the romantic English landscapes of the period. Hart's schoolhouse, on the other hand, is sharply defined, revealing the warped and split clapboards and each shingle of the roof; the children look as country children may well have looked, not too tidy; and the landscape is familiar farmland.

Both Inman and Hart learned to paint in upstate New York, but Inman was taught by John Wesley Jarvis, the fashionable portrait painter, and became so successful that, under the patronage of wealthy admirers, he went to England in 1844 (the year before "Dismissal of School" was painted) and was warmly received by Mulready, Leslie, and other fashionable English artists. Hart, however, learned painting as a trade, both from his brother William, who was a carriage painter, and as an apprentice to a sign and banner painter. It was not until after "The Old Schoolhouse" was painted that he went to Düsseldorf for formal training.

No question of relative merit is involved in this discussion of these two canvases. The point is simply to demonstrate that the same diverse streams of art which we find in our architecture can be traced also in American painting. The fact happens to be that all during the nineteenth century and well into the twentieth art critics here and abroad have admired few of those painters, European or American, who have been dominated by a devotion to literal representation. Those who loved and understood the western European tradition of painting, and those who worked in it, were naturally drawn to Americans like Whistler and Mary Cassatt, whose work—done chiefly abroad—related directly to the development of that tradition. When Edgar P. Richardson made his scholarly study of *The Way of Western Art* (1939), he was concerned to "relate American art to the tradition to which it belongs." Inevitably, therefore, he omitted William Sidney Mount altogether, and gave only about a page each to Winslow Homer and Thomas Eakins.

Yet Homer and Eakins are towering figures in American painting, as Richardson would undoubtedly agree, and Mount's clear, explicit genre pictures and open-air landscapes are more and more coming to be recognized as an important link in a characteristic American tradition of precise representation. In 1846 Mount wrote in his journal: "There has been enough written on ideality and the grand style of Art, etc., to divert the artist from the true study of natural objects." But Mount was not to be diverted. Note after note in his journal records that his pictures were painted "out of doors," "on the spot," or "in the open air," and he designed an "artist's waggon," or portable studio with large glass windows, "to sketch and paint in during windy and rainy weather." It is this outdoor clarity which makes "Long Island Farmhouse" (Metropolitan) one of Mount's most effective paintings: an honest, literal record of plain structures in November sunlight.

Eakins saw his subjects with the eye of a trained scientist, rather than a mere observer, but his knowledge and understanding of them never led him to compromise with the absolute integrity of visual reality. As Lloyd Goodrich has said, he "worked from the core of reality out into art." Or, to say it another way, he knew—as Whitman knew—that "out from the well-tended concrete and physical—and in them and from them only—radiate the spiritual and heroic."

His interests were strongly scientific and mechanical. When, during his brief sojourn as an art student in Paris, he visited the International Exposition of 1867, it was the exhibits of locomotives and machinery which attracted him, rather than the art galleries. Throughout his life the most creative influence on his painting was the study of anatomy, in which he became almost a professional, contributing papers on his research to the published *Proceedings of the Academy of Natural Sciences of Philadelphia*. One of these papers, on "The Differential Action of Certain Muscles Passing More Than One Joint" (1894), clearly shows Eakins' mechanical-scientific bent. Having observed the muscles in a horse's leg when the beast was straining to start a horsecar, he noticed that they did not act as they would if they conformed to the description of them in standard works on muscular action. He therefore constructed "a model of the entire limb with flat pieces of half-inch pine board, catgut for tendons and ligaments, and rubber bands for muscles, all attached to their places and properly restrained." With this mechanism and with dissection on the leg of a dead horse, he demonstrated the true action of the muscles and showed how they must be considered not only in relation to the bones to which they are attached, "but with relation to the whole movement of the animal. . . . One is never sure," he concluded, "that he understands the least movement of an animal, unless he can connect it with the whole muscular system, making, in fact, a complete circuit of all the strains. . . . On the lines of the mighty and simple strains dominating the movement, and felt intuitively and studied out by him, the master artist groups, with full intention, his muscular forms. No detail contradicts. His men and animals live."

This interest in anatomical movement also led Eakins to carry out important experiments with photography. Muybridge's photographs of galloping horses, taken in California with a battery of twenty-four cameras, attracted a great deal of interest, and in 1884 (partly through Eakins' influence) he was invited to continue his experiments at the University of Pennsylvania. Eakins himself designed and helped to build a special camera which recorded successive phases of motion on a single film, thus approximating the effect of a series of movie stills.

Eakins' ideal of a painting was one in which "you can see what o'clock it is, afternoon or morning, if it's hot or cold, winter or summer, and what kind of people are there, and what they are doing, and why they are doing it." The great painter, he believed, learns what nature does with light, color, and form and appropriates these tools to his own use. They serve him, as he wrote to his father, as "a canoe of his own, smaller than Nature's, but big enough for every purpose," in which he can sail parallel to nature. But if the painter ever thinks he can "sail another fashion from Nature or make a better shaped boat, he'll capsize or stick in the mud." To many of Eakins' contemporaries, here and abroad, the study of light and atmosphere became an end in itself; but to him it was, like his knowledge of anatomy, merely an instrument. Speaking of the role of anatomical dissection in his teaching at the Pennsylvania Academy of Fine Arts he made it clear that for anatomy as such he cared nothing whatever. Dissection was hard and dirty work, of value to the artist simply because it increased his knowledge of how animals and human beings are put together and thus enabled him to "imitate" them. "Even to refine upon natural beauty—to idealize," he added, "one must understand what it is that he is idealizing; otherwise his idealization—I don't like the word, by the way—becomes distortion, and distortion is ugliness."

Eakins himself did not idealize; the unparalleled series of portraits he painted in the eighties and nineties are a record of his relentless understanding of human character and his objective respect for it. And "Max Schmitt in a Single Scull" (Metropolitan Museum of Art), with its precise representation of the light-modeled forms of the Girard Avenue Bridge in the background, and "The Agnew Clinic" (University of Pennsylvania), with the figure of Dr. Agnew standing out sharply against the background of student observers, are masterpieces of scientific realism in our nineteenth-century painting. Nor are they isolated phenomena, as they have sometimes been presumed to be. Something of the same point of view toward reality, with less depth of emotional understanding but none the less unmistakably, had appeared earlier in Audubon's paintings of animals and birds, and reappeared in isolated works of Eakins' own time, like Henry Alexander's "The Laboratory of Thomas Price" (Metropolitan Museum).

Related to Eakins' scientific realism was another pictorial approach which might be called reportorial or journalistic realism. The painter who best represented this approach was Winslow Homer, who found his way into painting through work as an illustrator-correspondent for *Ballou's Pictorial* and *Harper's Weekly* during the Civil War. It is in his early paintings, especially, that one senses the reporter's concern with visual accuracy. Precise and tight in brushwork, these pictures of rural schools, factories, and home scenes were less concerned with interpretation than were Eakins' paintings, but they searched out and recorded significant surfaces and forms with an integrity which not even Eakins could surpass. In "The

Morning Bell," for instance, there is something suggestive of Eakins in the way angular planes of light and shadow are employed to record the factory and the plank footbridge leading to it across the millpond. It is apparent that here, as in many of the unschooled primitive paintings of the same mid-century period, the arrangement of forms and colors was discovered and reported by the painter, rather than created by him. "When I have selected the thing carefully," Homer insisted, "I paint it exactly as it appears."

The tradition, if I may call it that, of respect for actuality can be traced in the work of many other painters than those mentioned here. It is clear that factualism has been a powerful force in the visual arts in this country, and that even when the influence of French painting asserted itself here at the turn of the century, men like Luks, Glackens, and Sloan (all of whom had, incidentally, been influenced by Eakins' teaching and all of whom also had been newspaper artists, trained in pictorial journalism) applied the techniques which they learned from abroad in reporting precisely and honestly what they saw about them.

Nor does the matter rest there. Horatio Greenough said a century ago that America had been born in the Age of Reason, and had been fed from the beginning with "the stout bread and meat of fact"; America was Europe's giant offspring, to be sure, but "every wry face the bantling ever made had been daguerreotyped." And this domination by fact is still effective. It appears most blatantly, perhaps, in the work of some of our popular illustrators like John Falter and Norman Rockwell. In describing his methods of painting Rockwell has said, in words reminiscent of those quoted from Winslow Homer, "It has never been natural for me to deviate from the facts of anything before me. . . . If a model has worn a red sweater, I have painted it red—I couldn't possibly have made it green. I have tried again and again to take such liberties, but with little success." And even an artist like George Grosz, who came here from Germany in 1932, found that his work became, as he described it, "more realistic." "I became easily influenced," he wrote ten years later, "by the great sense of fact in America."

But dependence on fact does not in itself make a tradition of art. At most it is only the traditional basis of an attitude toward painting, or sculpture, or architecture, or literature. Nor does "the American scene" or American subject matter provide the basis for an American tradition. Neither patriotic pictures like Leutze's "Washington Crossing the Delaware" nor the work of local-colorists like Grant Wood or Thomas Benton has sufficed.

The determinant in such a tradition in any art is, as Constance Rourke said of painting, not subject but form. It is by the use of form "that the individual artist makes his art distinctive. It is the consistent print of form in successive periods which gives a national tradition its character." Going one step beyond this, it is the consistent print of form which gives character to a civilization, and it is therefore to forms that we must look for the emergence of the vernacular tradition in our painting.

Seen from this perspective, it is no mere coincidence that good eyesight and respect for optical reality have been so large an element of American painting. Instinctively artists have known that they must discover forms which are significant to their contemporaries, and the search for such forms—indigenous to the new civilization—demanded respect for the thing seen and put a premium on good eyesight, on honest reporting, and on scientific analysis. America has, to be sure, produced important painters—and painters whose work was in other ways as distinctively American as Homer's or Eakins'—whose achievements depended not at all upon these qualities. But these have been isolated figures who, like Albert Pinkham Ryder, sought to express their own inner worlds of imagination rather than the concrete reality of the world about them.

Inevitably, perhaps, those Americans who achieved the

greatest technical mastery in painting were those like Whistler, Mary Cassatt, and La Farge who turned from the crude actualities of American life to the heritage of Europe and the Orient. And it was probably also inevitable that their work, divorced from dominant concerns of contemporary life and lacking the inner integrity of Ryder's dream canvases, should seem somehow thin and lacking in substance. On the other hand it was likewise inevitable that those who worked outside the older traditions would, like Mount, Homer, and Eakins, and even Ryder himself, have had to cope with technical limitations which sometimes encumber the structural interest of their work.

It is these limitations, one suspects, which in our own time lead a painter like Charles Sheeler to deny any stimulus from Homer or Eakins. Certainly the painters from whom Sheeler learned most have all been Europeans. But anyone who looks at his work will recognize that although the modes in which he paints have their chief source in France, in postimpressionism and cubism, the forms which give character to his work are the product of the vernacular tradition—the unself-conscious architecture of barns and factories, the unornamented furniture and buildings of the Shakers, the structure of ships and machines. His large drawing of "The Open Door" and the much earlier tempera painting of the "Bucks County Barn" (Fig. 25) are fine compositions, almost abstract in quality, not unrelated to the spatial and linear studies of the postimpressionists and cubists. But in a very real sense they have roots in the tradition of respect for actuality. They have something in common with even such utilitarian pictures as the lithographs which illustrated so many of the county histories published in the nineteenth century. Notice, for instance, in the detail from the anonymous 1878 lithograph of the "Residence and Stock Farm of J. F. Blair & Son" (Fig. 25) how the group of barns is rendered in terms of planes of light and shadow.

Many twentieth-century painters, in both Europe and America, have been primarily concerned with the prob-

lems of achieving formal strength. In Europe this interest
in the elements of structure in painting led chiefly to the
study of primitive art of all kinds—African sculpture, medieval stained glass, and prehistoric pictographs. In America it led chiefly to increased interest in vernacular forms,
particularly those of technology and industry. Even Lyonel
Feininger, who spent most of his creative life in Germany
before the war, as a member of the Bauhaus group, used
cubist line and plane to express that love of mechanical
and architectural form which he had developed as a young
man in New York. (See especially "Side Wheeler" in the
Detroit Institute of Arts, and "Old American Locomotive,"
both illustrated in the catalogue of the Museum of Modern Art's Feininger-Hartley exhibit in 1944.) It is not without significance that the good eyesight which goes into the
discovery of such forms was in Sheeler's case supplemented
by his meticulous and careful work as a photographer. Not
that he confuses the art of photography with the art of
painting; no one has more concretely defined the scope of
each. But his eye, like Eakins' before him, had been disciplined in part by the exactness of the camera lens. Whatever rank may be assigned to Sheeler's paintings, it seems
clear that in them, as effectively as in those of any of his
contemporaries, the cultivated and vernacular traditions
have merged into a distinctive creation.

8 The Artist's Dilemma

In the preceding chapters we have distinguished two differ-
ent traditions of art in nineteenth-century America, one
inherited from the older culture of Europe and the other
emerging in direct response to the actualities of a machine
civilization in a political democracy. We have observed
how these traditions interacted, each modifying the other,
and how a number of influences—geographical, political,
psychological, and social—have variously favored and resisted the development of each. And finally we have seen
that it was in the unself-conscious tradition of vernacular
expression that American people dealt most successfully
with the new and necessary facts of the emerging civilization.

Up to this point, then, we have been exploring a method
of approach to the problem of the arts in America. Now
let us see how that method might be applied to a consideration of the arts themselves. In what ways might it help
us to understand why our literature, for instance, has always seemed less American than our history? What light
can it shed on the resistances which the American environment offered to the creative imagination of the individual artist?

The arts are rooted in the civilization which produces
them, shaped in its image. Ranged behind the great masterpieces of the past—the temples of Greece, the paintings
of the Italian Renaissance, the plays of Shakespeare—
there had in each case been an immense and complete
reality of which they were the imaginative projection. For
a moment in the history of man's psychological adaptation
to his environment he had achieved an apparently stable
synthesis of his knowledge and belief, and the structure of
society itself—as embodied in its political, social, economic,

and religious institutions—seemed to reflect a coherent and enduring view of human destiny.

But in American civilization, as Emerson intuitively perceived and as Walt Whitman explicitly asserted, there was no such equilibrium between what men knew and what they believed, between fact and faith. As Whitman pointed out in *Democratic Vistas* (1871) our political institutions were based upon government of, by, and for those very people whom many of our social institutions encouraged us to distrust. The best-educated and most highly cultivated portion of the community looked upon the masses of people as a vulgar, untidy lump of humanity, with "gaunt and ill-bred" vices and virtues. At the same time our economic institutions and many of the social relationships of everyday life were being shaped by a technology and science which were at odds with the creeds and dogmas of our religious institutions and with the traditional amenities of cultivated society. The revolutionary impact of the•twin forces of democracy and science had only begun to be felt. The spirit of the new civilization, irresistibly reshaping the foundations of man's consciousness of himself and his world, still moved almost unnoticed beneath the surface of American life.

It was his awareness of this amorphous, self-contradictory quality in our civilization which brought Whitman to the recognition that there could be "no complete or epical presentation" of America until its distinctive spirit had permeated all aspects of its life. "How much is still to be disentangled, freed!" he said in *Democratic Vistas*. "How long it takes to make this American world see that it is, in itself, the final authority and reliance!"

We see the sons and daughters of the New World, ignorant of its genius, not yet inaugurating the native, the universal, and the near, still importing the distant, the partial, and the dead. We see London, Paris, Italy—not original, superb, as where they belong—but second-hand here, where they do not belong. We see the shreds of Hebrews, Romans, Greeks; but where, on her own soil, do we see, in any faithful, highest, proud expression, America herself? I sometimes question whether she has a corner in her own house.

In such a situation, he argued, America required "a new theory of literary composition for imaginative works." The poet must no longer be expected to round out and complete his vision in an artistic unity. The reader, not the poet, must himself or herself construct the finished poem —"the text furnishing the hints, the clue, the start or framework. Not the book needs so much to be the complete thing, but the reader of the book does." As he had said in the preface to the original edition of *Leaves of Grass* (1855), "the expression of the American poet is to be transcendant and new. It is to be indirect, and not direct or descriptive or epic. Let the age and wars of other nations be chanted, and their eras and characters be illustrated, and that finish the verse. Not so the great psalm of the republic. Here the theme is creative and has vista." So also, near the end of his life, he said: "I round and finish little, if anything, and could not, consistently with my scheme. . . . I seek less to state or display any theme or thought, and more to bring you, reader, into the atmosphere of the theme or thought—there to pursue your own flight."

In other words, Whitman saw that the function of the creative imagination in the new civilization differed essentially from that which was fulfilled in the older culture by artistic sensibility.

> . . . *each man and each woman of you I lead upon a knoll,*
> *My left hand hooking you around the waist,*
> *My right hand pointing to landscapes of continents and the public road.*

Not I, not any one else can travel that road for you,
You must travel it for yourself.
It is not far, it is within reach,
Perhaps you have been on it since you were born
and did not know.

It is not the artist who "rounds and finishes" that speaks in this passage from the "Song of Myself." It is rather the man who believed in the necessity of giving "positive place, identity" to his vision of America's destiny, revealing to each man the inner meaning and direction of an inchoate, revolutionary "future-founding" age.

To insist upon this aspect of Whitman's genius is not to deny that there are passages in his verse—and indeed whole poems—which rise into the concentrated intensity of lyric poetry. But there are many other passages—which an "artist" would have trimmed away, but which form an integral part of his design—where he is essentially the announcer with a megaphone on a cosmic sight-seeing bus, pointing out the landmarks to his fellow passengers as they roll along the open road. Few critics have been willing enough to take Whitman at his word when he asserted that no one can get at the real meaning of his *Leaves* "who insists upon viewing them as a literary performance, or attempt at such performance, or as aiming mainly toward art or aestheticism."

Probably no one who was driven solely, or even primarily, by the passion to integrate experience and give it order in artistic form could have flooded himself so completely, and even delightedly, as Whitman did "with the immediate age as with vast oceanic tides." Certainly there has been a marked tendency throughout our history for Americans with artistic talent to withdraw from direct contact with the everyday life about them. From Copley and Benjamin West to Whistler, Sargent, and Mary Cassatt it was almost habitual for American-born painters to become expatriates, and from the time of Greenough and Hiram Powers our sculptors have spent much of their creative lives abroad. In the field of literature, Henry James was the first eminent writer to become an actual expatriate, but many of his predecessors from Irving on down lived for considerable periods in England or on the Continent, and Lafcadio Hearn went to live in Japan. Even when our artists have not actually left the country, however, they have frequently sought some other means of isolating themselves from American society—whether in a lonely cabin at Walden Pond, like Thoreau, in an enclosed garden in Amherst, Massachusetts, like Emily Dickinson, or in a private solitude of vision like Albert Pinkham Ryder.

The work of any one of the writers or artists whom we have mentioned would provide us with ample material to illustrate the nature of the resistances which American civilization opposed to the artistic imagination. Yet we will do better, perhaps, to concentrate our attention here on someone who, for all that he was an essentially solitary and lonely genius, did not permit himself to become either a recluse or an expatriate.

Like most of his contemporaries, Nathaniel Hawthorne as a young man shared in the enthusiasm for creating a national literature, "hewing it, as it were, out of the unwrought granite of our intellectual quarries," discovering, if need be, new forms which would not be merely an "interminably repeated . . . reproduction of the images that were molded by our great fathers of song and fiction." As time passed, however, and as he concentrated more and more on the specific problems involved in shaping his own stories and novels, he made fewer and fewer overt references to the general problem of indigenous literary forms. Yet it would be a mistake to infer from this that he— or any other American artist—escaped the fundamental artistic problem involved in the conflict between the two traditions. Actually he ran head on into it. Over and over again in the prefaces to his books he reminded his readers of the difficulties involved in writing fiction about a land where actualities were "so terribly insisted upon" as they were—and needs must be—in America.

> In the old countries [he wrote in the preface to *The Blithedale Romance*], with which fiction has long been conversant, a certain conventional privilege seems to be awarded to the romancer; his work is not put exactly side by side with nature. . . . Among ourselves, on the contrary, there is as yet no such Faery Land, so like the real world that, in a suitable remoteness, one cannot well tell the difference, but with an atmosphere of strange enchantment, beheld through which the inhabitants have a propriety of their own. This atmosphere is what the American romancer needs.

It was in an effort to provide something of this atmosphere that Hawthorne always contrived settings for his novels which were somewhat removed from the everyday world about him—remote either in time or place from the main current of contemporary life. Even in *The House of the Seven Gables*, which—as Henry James observed—contained more of the "literal actuality" of American life than any of his other books, he deliberately intertwined the past and present through the agency of what he described as "a legend prolonging itself, from an epoch now gray in the distance, down into our own broad daylight, and bringing along with it some of its legendary mist"—a mist which would float almost imperceptibly about the characters and events of the novel to create the necessary atmosphere of strange enchantment.

Yet Hawthorne knew that his books were weakened by his inability to cope with the crude but vital elements of the emerging civilization. There was profound conviction behind his statement that, though he was unable to bring his creative imagination to bear on the world of commerce and trade in which for three years he played a part as surveyor of customs for the port of Salem, the fault was his own. "The page of life which was laid out before me," he wrote, "seemed dull and commonplace only because I had not fathomed its deeper import. A better book than I shall ever write was there. . . ."

One is struck by the fact that when he turned in his fiction to portraying the artist's role in American society he characteristically chose for his protagonists men who worked in art forms which were firmly rooted in the technological environment. Holgrave, for instance, in *The House of the Seven Gables,* was a daguerreotypist—a practitioner of the most "up-to-date" and scientific art; the hero of "Drowne's Wooden Image" was a carver of figureheads for ships; and in "The Artist of the Beautiful," Hawthorne's most elaborate allegory of the artist's role, Owen Warland was a young mechanical genius whose dream—and ultimate triumph—was "to spiritualize machinery, and to combine with the new species of life and motion thus produced a beauty that should attain to the ideal."

The sense of the past which permeates Hawthorne's novels and tales tends to obscure the relationships between his art and the main currents of life in his own time. Yet, if we follow the development in his fiction of the theme of conflict between past and present we will discover that it is closely related to his awareness of the artist's problem in the new civilization. In its barest form the theme was first stated in an idea for a story which he recorded in his notebook sometime during 1844. What he there proposed was "to represent the influence Dead Men have among living affairs." Dead men, he observed, by the terms of their wills control the disposition of wealth; the opinions of dead judges dominate the law courts. In short, "Dead Men's opinions in all things control the living truth; we believe in Dead Men's religion; we laugh at Dead Men's jokes; we cry at Dead Men's pathos; everywhere and in all matters, Dead Men tyrannize inexorably over us."

It was in *The House of the Seven Gables* (1851) that this theme found its most complete embodiment. The very language of the notebook entry appears there, considerably elaborated, in a speech which Hawthorne put into the mouth of Holgrave, the daguerreotypist, but which sums up the theme of the entire novel.

"Shall we never, never get rid of this Past?" cried he. . . . "It lies upon the Present like a giant's dead body! In fact, the case is just as if a young giant were compelled to waste all his strength in carrying about the corpse of the old giant, his grandfather. . . . Just think a moment, and it will startle you to see what slaves we are to bygone times,—to Death, if we give the matter the right word!"

Then follows an expanded version of the passage quoted above from the notebook, with this significant addition: "I ought to have said, too, that we live in dead men's houses; as, for instance, in this of the Seven Gables."

"But we shall live to see the day, I trust," went on the artist, "when no man shall build his house for posterity. . . . If each generation were allowed and expected to build its own houses, that single change . . . would imply almost every reform which society is now suffering for. . . . This old Pyncheon house . . . in my view, is expressive of that odious and abominable past, with all its bad influences, against which I have just been declaiming. I dwell in it for a while, that I may know the better how to hate it."

It is true that the idea as stated here is intended as an expression of Holgrave's character and is not presented as the author's own view. Indeed, speaking in his own person, Hawthorne in part disclaims it. Yet Holgrave, as we have seen, was one of the characters through whom Hawthorne projected his concept of the artist's role in America. Further, in a passage of the novel where Hawthorne comments in his own right on Holgrave's character, he explicitly states that "in his culture and want of culture . . . the artist might fitly enough stand forth as the representative of many compeers in his native land." And finally, the same ideas, in very nearly the same words, are expressed by another character in the novel who is also in some degree a projection of the author's own personality. For Clifford, the broken and defeated lover of the beautiful in whom Hawthorne represented many of those aspects of the artistic temperament which he recognized in himself, echoes Holgrave in his impassioned exclamation that the chief obstructions to human happiness are "these heaps of bricks and stones, consolidated with mortar, or hewn timber" which men build for themselves to die in and for their posterity to be miserable in.

Here, then, is the theme of conflict between past and present, fused in an architectural symbol which always had a peculiar fascination for Hawthorne. Long before he began to work on *The House of the Seven Gables* he had made something of a hobby of visiting old houses which had fallen into decay as the fortunes of the original owner declined. They seemed to him to suggest with special force the folly of attempting to establish hereditary patterns of family life amid the fluctuations of a democratic society. And when he first went abroad—two years after *The House of the Seven Gables* appeared—his impressions of England and Italy almost invariably crystallized around some architectural symbol of the older cultures.

Of course any American going abroad for the first time would inevitably receive his first and most overwhelming impressions of European culture from the buildings which embodied its aspirations and triumphs. Architecture, after all, is the most public and tangible expression of a civilization. As Catharine Maria Sedgwick had said, during her first visit to England in 1839, a miracle was wrought in the presence of a building like Winchester Cathedral, and the poems and paintings which had before seemed mere shadows—"a kind of magic mirrors, showing false images"— were suddenly revealed as divine forms "for the perpetual preservation of the beautiful creations of nature and art." But to Hawthorne the buildings of Europe had a special significance, deeply colored by the artistic problem with which he was so profoundly concerned.

His English and Italian notebooks are full of comments which embroider the theme he had explored in *The House of the Seven Gables*. Having observed in Coventry and other English towns that many buildings had "modern fronts" superimposed on Elizabethan frames and interiors, he remarked that they offered "a good emblem" of what England itself really was. Modern civilization, as he saw it there, was essentially only a modification of the old. The new elements in it were not only based and supported on the sturdy old things but were "often limited and impeded" by them. And yet, he concluded, "this antiquity is so massive that there seems to be no means of getting rid of it, without tearing the whole structure of society to pieces."

The great cathedrals and public buildings which still remained in their original glory filled him with the sense that "a flood of uncomprehended beauty" was pouring down on him. But he could not help feeling that the architecture of Westminster Hall, for instance, had more to do with the past than with the future. "Its beauty and magnificence," he noted, "are made out of ideas that are gone by." Still less was he impressed with Sir Charles Barry's adjacent attempt to resuscitate Gothic forms in the new Houses of Parliament. Granted that Barry had achieved magnificence, he said, he had nevertheless "contrived all his effects with malice aforethought," and thus missed the crowning glory "which God, out of his pure grace, mixes up with only the simple-hearted, best efforts of men."

From one point of view Hawthorne's comments on art are evidence of a philistinism which is only slightly less insensitive than that which still shocks the cultivated readers of Mark Twain's *A Tramp Abroad*. But the significant thing about them, in our present context, is that whenever he speculated about the arts of the Old World he tended to link them in his imagination with his own problems as an artist. On two separate occasions he went to see the Elgin marbles and the Assyrian and Egyptian stat-

uary at the British Museum. Both times his thought re-
curred to the theme of the domination of the past as
fused in the architectural symbol. "I wished," he wrote
after the first visit, "that the whole Past might be swept
away, and each generation compelled to bury and destroy
whatever it had produced. . . . When we quit a house,
we are expected to make it clean for the next occupant.
. . ." Seeing them again six months later he found himself wishing that the marbles and the frieze of the Parthe-
non itself "were all burnt into lime, and that the granite
Egyptian statues were hewn and squared into building
stones. . . . The present is burthened too much with the
past. We have not time, in our earthly existence, to appreciate what is warm with life, and immediately around
us."

If we bear in mind his sense that modern civilization
in England was overwhelmed by the past, there is a special
interest in his remarks about the iron and glass architecture of the famous Crystal Palace. His opinion of it differed on the several occasions that he saw it; at first it
seemed to him that no edifice built of glass could be anything but an overgrown conservatory, while two years later
he decided that it was "positively a very beautiful object."
But the thing that particularly impressed him was that this
earliest masterpiece of iron architecture was uncongenial
with the English character, "destitute of mass, weight, and
shadow, unsusceptible of ivy, lichens, or any mellowness
from age." One cannot miss the echo of that comment in
the preface to *The Marble Faun* where he gave his most
definite statement of the artists' problem in America. No
author, without a trial, he wrote, could conceive of the
difficulty of dealing with an environment which offered no
shadow or mystery. "Romance and poetry, ivy, lichens,
and wall-flowers, need ruin to make them grow."

In *The Marble Faun*, written in England after a two-
year visit to Italy, the theme of conflict between past and
present is transformed into somewhat different terms. As

it emerges there it is a study of conflict between European and American civilization as revealed in the fortunes of two young American artists who have gone to live in Rome. The theme as it develops in this instance is a subsidiary element of the novel, but the parallels it suggests are worth exploring. It was in Rome that Hawthorne himself had first come to the realization that "it needs the native air to give life a reality"—a truth, he recorded in his notebook, which he took home to himself regretfully, since he had little inclination to go back to the realities of his own. Hiram Powers and the other self-exiled American artists whom he had met there had seemed to him to be caught in the situation where they were always deferring the reality of life to a future moment, till by and by there would either be no future or they would go back to America and find that life had "shifted whatever of reality it had" to the country where they had lived as expatriates.

This realization permeates Hawthorne's handling of the theme of conflict in his novel. The theme as he develops it there is elaborated most explicitly in his portrayal of Hilda, the young New England painter who—like so many of her artistic countrymen—had gone to live in Italy in the belief that it was the only country where art could really flourish. Hilda is represented as passing through three distinct phases as an artist. Back in New England she had shown real talent and had done some very creditable work. Once arrived in Italy, however, she "seemed to have entirely lost the impulse of original design, which brought her thither."

No doubt [Hawthorne continued] the girl's early dreams had been of sending forms and hues of beauty into the visible world out of her own mind . . . through conceptions and by methods individual to herself. But more and more, as she grew familiar with the miracles of art that enrich so many galleries in Rome, Hilda had ceased to consider herself as an original artist. . . . It had probably happened in many other instances, as it did in Hilda's case, that she ceased to aim at original achievement in consequence of the very gifts which so exquisitely fitted her to profit by familiarity with the works of the mighty old masters.

That Hawthorne's own wife was a talented copyist of paintings may account for the elaborate justification which he subsequently offers for Hilda's abandoning her youthful ambitions. Granting all the noble and unselfish merits which he ascribes to her "for thus sacrificing herself to the devout recognition of the highest excellence" in the art of the past, there remains the inescapable fact that her youthful dreams were not unlike Hawthorne's own, and that he represents them as being drained from her by her subjection to the masterpieces of European culture. Nor is there any reason to suppose that Hawthorne was not fully aware of the implications of Hilda's change. For in the denouement of the novel Hilda arrives at a third stage in her development. Caught in a web of evil and wrongdoing which had not been of her own making, she grew "sadly critical" of many of the paintings she had formerly so much admired; she developed a new perceptive faculty which "penetrated the canvas like a steel probe, and found but a crust of paint over an emptiness." In the end she marries Kenyon, a young American sculptor to whom it had long seemed that in Italy, where generation after generation lived in the same house, "all the weary and dreary Past were piled upon the back of the Present," and when they decide to return to America, Hawthorne explains their decision in the very words he had used in his notebooks to describe the situation in which expatriates like Powers— and perhaps to some degree he also, now—found themselves.

When he returned to the United States in 1860 Hawthorne had already begun work on a novel which was to develop the international theme not as a minor element in the story but as its principal feature. The novel was never finished, but a number of unfinished versions of it remained in manuscript when he died in 1864, and some of these have since been published.

We cannot know what form Hawthorne might ultimately have given to his theme if failing health and the heartbreaking distractions of the Civil War had not prevented him from concentrating his full powers upon it, but we do know, from the number of attempts he made and the determination with which he persisted, that the theme was important to him. What he originally had in mind was to tell the story of a young American who has it in his power to join together the mysteriously broken thread of a tradition, part of which is known in England and part in the United States. In one version, for example, the hero was a descendant of a man who, wishing to disconnect himself from the past, emigrated from England to the new world and began life there under a new name. His descendant is fascinated by the strange legends woven around a small key which had been handed down from generation to generation in the American branch of the family. According to the legend, the key will open a cabinet containing a document that will clear up the mystery of his family's hereditary origin. The climax of the story is to be reached when, during a visit to England, he is led by a series of strange events to an old mansion which contains the very cabinet in which the secret is hidden.

The simple outline of the story had been suggested to Hawthorne by the number of Americans who had come to him while he was United States consul at Liverpool and asked him to help them establish their claims to some English estate. In his published account of his consular experiences he mentioned several instances of what he called "this diseased American appetite for English soil," and dwelt on them at some length because it seemed to him that they revealed a weakness which lay deep in the hearts of many of his countrymen. "The American," he observed, "is often conscious of the deep-rooted sympathies that belong more fitly to times gone by, and feels a blind, pathetic tendency to wander back again." But of all the "stray

Americans" whom he had encountered at the consulate, the one that interested him most was an old man whose story oddly paralleled that of Herman Melville's *Israel Potter*. For years the old fellow had been wandering around England trying to earn or beg enough money "to get home to Ninety-Second Street, Philadelphia."

> His manner and accent [Hawthorne remarked] did not quite convince me that he was an American, and I told him so; but he steadfastly affirmed,—"Sir, I was born and have lived in Ninety-Second Street, Philadelphia," and then went on to describe some public edifices, and other local objects with which he used to be familiar, adding, with a simplicity that touched me very closely, "Sir, I had rather be there than here!" . . . If, as I believe, the tale was fact, how very strange and sad was this old man's fate! Homeless on a foreign shore, looking always toward his country, . . . and at last dying and surrendering his clay to be a portion of the soil whence he could not escape in his lifetime.

Against the background of his experiences in the consulate and in Italy it was inevitable, then, that in planning his novel Hawthorne always conceived of the American's attempt to establish a firm link with the past as ending in some form of failure or disillusionment. He might find the cabinet which held the secret, but when he fitted his key to the lock he would discover something which he had better never have known. And curiously enough, the cabinet itself was fused in Hawthorne's imagination with the symbol which he so persistently associated with the domination of the past. For as he described it to himself it was one of those tall, stately, and elaborate pieces "that are rather articles of architecture" than of furniture—a miniature mansion "with pillars, an entrance, a lofty flight of steps, windows, and everything perfect."

But however the details of plot were to be worked out, it is clear that in the end the American would return to his own land. For the moral of the tale, as Hawthorne explicitly stated it at one stage of his experiment with the theme, was: "Let the past alone; do not seek to renew it; . . . and be assured that the right way can never be that which leads you back to the identical shapes that you long ago left behind you."

By thus isolating from its context in his work as a whole the single theme of the past's tyranny over the present we are able to throw into sharp focus the nature of Hawthorne's response to the civilization of his own time. It becomes clear that he fully sensed the necessity for new artistic forms suited to the unlineaged realities of a democratic and industrial social system. Yet every quality of his temperament which fitted him to be an artist in the traditional sense unfitted him to deal with the crude materials out of which the new forms could be created. The artistic sensibility and poetic insight which in *The Scarlet Letter* he could put to such effective use among the shadowy scenes of an imagined past were apparently useless in dealing with the glaring and turbulent realities of the present. Yet Hawthorne never lost his sense of the inherent value in the materials which proved so intractable to his genius. Late in his life he plied the young William Dean Howells with many questions about the West and said he would like to see some part of the country on which the "damned shadow" of Europe had not fallen. If his own experience finally convinced him that the arts as we had known them provided no tools powerful enough to shape the unwrought granite of American life, it never deluded him into thinking that the forms created by an older civilization could be imposed upon the actualities of the new one. "There is reason to suspect," he wrote in his last completed novel, "that a people are waning to decay and ruin the moment that their life becomes fascinating either in the poet's imagination or the painter's eye." There is a kind of magnificent courage in that observation. It is the statement of an artist who, like many others in his time, had gone down to defeat at the hands of immitigable facts, but who—unlike many of the others—had not turned and run.

The dilemma in which Hawthorne found himself was deeply colored by many factors peculiar to his own personality and to his own particular New England heritage. But the tension created by the conflict between inherited forms and present experience has been a dominant element, consciously or unconsciously, in the work of every creative artist who has attempted to deal with the American environment, whatever the artistic medium.

Thus we come face to face with the central fact in the development of the arts in America, whether we think in terms of the individual artist or of the people whose vision of life the artist finally expresses. For what men believed to be beautiful they knew—in their inmost hearts, at least —to be false. To paraphrase one of Hawthorne's most revealing remarks about old houses like the Pyncheon mansion, there was something so massive, stable, and almost irresistibly imposing in the forms which embodied the spirit of western European culture that their very existence seemed to give them a right to survive—at least, so excellent a counterfeit of right that few men had moral force enough to question it.

In Europe throughout the nineteenth century this right seemed to be substantiated by the fact that the foundations upon which the traditional forms had been erected had not been wholly wrecked by the upheaval of the Industrial Revolution. But in America the traditional forms stood on quicksand, no matter how earnestly the custodians of culture worked to put foundations under them, and something of the illusion of permanence departed from them. Furthermore it was in America, as we have seen, that the unembellished simplicity of vernacular forms, unself-consciously evolved by people who had no choice but to deal directly with the elements of the new environment, first emerged as a vivid challenge to creative artists. It was, of course, still possible for the minor poet, painter, or architect to create charming and delightful echoes of the past in conventional patterns. It is only when the creative imagination goes beyond talent and approaches genius that it becomes a moral force capable of rejecting all counterfeit majesty and confronting the naked majesty of the essential.

9 Space and Chance

When Hawthorne saw the great Gothic cathedrals of England in mid-century, he felt that they must be the most wonderful works that man had yet achieved. But there was something about those masterpieces of an earlier civilization which was alien to him, with which he could not feel at home. No matter how familiar he might become with their vast, intricate, yet harmonious shapes, he knew that he would never be able adequately to comprehend them, and would always be "remotely excluded from the interior mystery" of their beauty and grandeur.

A half century later one of the greatest American novelists found himself similarly excluded from the "mystery" of the great buildings which symbolized some of the strongest forces in contemporary American civilization—New York's skyscrapers. Henry James, revisiting America in 1904–06 after having lived abroad for more than twenty years, felt that the huge buildings—the most piercing notes, as he called them, in that "concert of the expensively provisional" which was the metropolis—left him staring at them "as at a world of immovably-closed doors." Behind those doors, to be sure, there was immense material for the artist, but he reluctantly concluded that it was beyond the reach of a writer who, like himself, had "so early and so fatally" withdrawn from contacts which might have initiated him into the life which the skyscrapers symbolized.

In these parallel reactions it is the shift of viewpoint which measures the change from the mid-nineteenth to the early twentieth century. It was common enough in Hawthorne's time for the American artist to be conscious that he was outside the European tradition and to try by whatever means he could devise to get inside. As for the vernacular tradition growing up around him, in so far as it had taken on any definite character, he either consciously rejected and resisted it, or simply took it for granted. Whatever influence it had upon his work was unconsciously assimilated. It would never have occurred to him to regret that he could not "get inside" such a formative tradition because it would not have occurred to him that it had anything whatever to do with art. By the time James revisited America in the early twentieth century, however, the vitality and energy of the vernacular had effectively displayed themselves in so many forms that the situation was almost exactly reversed. Artists like James, thoroughly immersed in the cultivated tradition, began to feel the need to make fruitful contact with the emerging tradition. But as James's career makes clear, the gap between the two was so wide that it could not easily be bridged.

Educated chiefly in Europe, lacking any close connection with the vital commercial, industrial, and technical elements of American life, James early discovered that the American scene was too restricted to supply materials for his art. As he wrote to Charles Eliot Norton in 1871, after returning to America from a year abroad, he concluded after looking about him that "the face of nature and civilization in this our country is to a certain point a very sufficient literary field. But it will yield its secrets only to a really *grasping* imagination." James *did* look about him, but as Hartley Grattan pointed out some years ago, in what is still one of the most perceptive studies of the novelist, he did not look in the places where we now know —and a few even then knew—that the secret and tremendous drives in American life were to be found. It was in the new factories, the new cities, the hustle and bustle of commerce and manufacturing and transportation that the American secret was hidden; business was a closed field for James, whose interest was in the leisure class—which in the America of the seventies was very small and almost exclusively feminine. In other words, by training and by taste he was concerned with the cultivated tradition. For

it was "matured and established" manners, customs, us-
ages, habits, and forms which, as he wrote to Howells,
were the very stuff upon which a novelist, in James's sense,
must work. It was inevitable that James, who of all American writers contributed most to the development of the
novel as a form of western European literature, taking rank
with George Sand, Balzac, Flaubert, and the other nineteenth-century masters, should have preferred "the denser,
richer, warmer European spectacle" to life in America. In
a famous passage from his critical study of Hawthorne
(1879) he enumerated the essential "items of high civilization" which were lacking in the United States:

> No sovereign, no court, no personal loyalty, no aristoc-
> racy, no church, no clergy, no army, no diplomatic
> service, no country gentlemen, no palaces, no castles, no
> manners, nor old country-houses, nor parsonages, nor
> thatched cottages, nor ivied ruins; no cathedrals, nor
> abbeys, nor little Norman churches; no great Universi-
> ties, nor public schools—no Oxford, nor Eton, nor Har-
> row; no literature, no novels, no museums, no pictures,
> no political society, no sporting class—no Epsom nor
> Ascot!

Not that he believed these things were necessarily the
proper subjects of fiction. As Grattan said, he simply found
that without these things present to him in the surrounding
air, his characters existed in a void. It was inevitable that
he chose England as his residence, and ultimately became
a British subject.

The recent revival of interest in James has done much
to combat the jingoistic prejudice which for a number of
years condemned him for "deserting" America and which
underrated his artistic achievements on the basis that they
were un-American. There was, to be sure, much in America
that he disliked, much which he could not understand,
and much of which he was afraid. Back in England, at
his home in Rye, after his last trip to the United States,

he remembered his homeland as giving "an immense impression of material and political power; but almost cruelly charmless, in effect, and calculated to make one crouch, ever afterwards, as cravenly as possible, at Lamb House, Rye." But James was too acute, and too brilliantly analytical, to confuse the issue as his detractors have done. What was taking place in America, as he observed, was "a perpetual repudiation of the past, so far as there had been a past to repudiate." But this repudiation—or as he elsewhere calls it, "the will to grow at no matter what or whose expense"—was not an exclusively American phenomenon. He had seen it, and hated it, on the other side of the world in a thousand places and forms; he was, indeed, aware that it was "the pipe to which humanity is actually dancing." In the United States, however, there was a difference; here, as he phrased it, it was a question of "scale and space and chance, margin and elbow-room." To some extent he meant this in the purely geographical sense. As he said in another connection, the nation seemed to him "too large for any human convenience," so large in fact that it could "scarce, in the scheme of Providence, have been meant to be dealt with" as he was trying to deal with it. But geography wasn't the whole of it. The bourgeois "will to grow" had more chance in America than in England, for instance, because here the influence of the aristocracy had been suppressed, and "a bourgeoisie without an aristocracy to worry it is of course a very different thing from a bourgeoisie struggling *in* that shade."

Actually, as we have repeatedly seen, and as James knew, Americans were by no means out from under the shadow of the cultivated tradition. Strether, the symbolic American of *The Ambassadors,* had fallen so deeply under the spell of Europe on his first visit that he had returned with the resolve to raise up "a temple of taste" by preserving, cherishing, and extending the germs of "the higher culture" he had seen abroad. And many of James's contemporaries had the same idea, as witness the founding of art schools and art museums and the wholesale acquisi-

tion of European *objets d'art* for American collections like
that of Mrs. Jack Gardner in Boston. It was the success
of these efforts, steadily increasing in audacity and ingenuity in the quarter century after the Centennial, which
was usually meant when people in the early 1900s referred admiringly to the increasing culture of America.

Curiously enough it was three of James's English contemporaries in literature who, on their visits to this country, were able to see beneath surfaces and discover, as he
had failed to do, the real sources of creative energy in
modern civilization. Oscar Wilde, who might be presumed
to have been even less well equipped than James to cope
with the vernacular environment, made some amazingly
acute observations in a lecture entitled "Impressions of
America" which he first delivered in September 1883,
shortly after returning to England.

There was little beauty to be found in American cities,
he said—nothing like "the lovely relics of a beautiful age"
which were to be found in Oxford, Cambridge, Salisbury,
or Winchester. And whatever beauty there was could be
found "only where the American has not attempted to
create it." Wherever the Americans had consciously sought
to produce beauty, he went on, they had signally failed.
Where they had succeeded—unconsciously—was in the
field of applied science:

> There is no country in the world [he told his British
> audiences] where machinery is so lovely as in America.
> I have always wished to believe that the line of strength
> and the line of beauty are one. That wish was realized
> when I contemplated American machinery. It was not
> until I had seen the waterworks at Chicago that I real-
> ized the wonders of machinery; the rise and fall of the
> steel rods, the symmetrical motion of great wheels is the
> most beautifully rhythmic thing I have ever seen.

But if cultivated Americans ever read what Wilde had
said about them, they apparently assumed that he was

merely being witty or paradoxical, for they continued to ignore the vernacular. Thirty years later the novelist Arnold Bennett reported that the most exacerbating experience that had befallen him during his visit to the United States had been to hear

> in discreetly lighted and luxurious drawing rooms, amid various mural proofs of trained taste, and usually from the lips of an elegantly Europeanized American woman with a sad, agreeable smile: "There is no art in the United States. . . . I feel like an exile." A number of these exiles, each believing himself or herself to be a solitary lamp in the awful darkness, are dotted up and down the great cities. . . . They associate art with Florentine frames, matinee hats, distant museums, and clever talk full of allusions to the dead.

It did not occur to them, he added (any more than it had to Henry James) to search for American art in the architecture of railroad stations or in the draftsmanship and sketch-writing of newspapers and magazines, because —as he scornfully put it—they had not the wit to learn that genuine art flourishes best in the atmosphere of genuine popular demand.

H. G. Wells, in a book about America published in the very year that Henry James left it for the last time, had been oppressed by the same sort of talk. At a meeting of a Boston book collectors' club which he attended it came to him with a horrible quality of conviction "that the mind of the world was dead, and that this was a distribution of the souvenirs"; and it seemed to him that all so-called American refinement, mysteriously enchanting and ineffectual as it was, was pervaded with "that Boston of the mind and heart" which, having eyes, did not see and, having powers, achieved nothing. It was an oppressive fact, but a fact none the less, that the full sensing of what was ripe and good in the past carried with it the quality of discriminating against the present and the future.

Outside of the realms dominated by this Boston of the mind and heart, however, there were signs which made Wells hopeful. There were the dynamos and turbines at the Niagara hydroelectric plant. Best of all there were men like Pierrepont Noyes, president of the Oneida Company —manufacturers of traps and plated silver. Noyes showed Wells around the factories; showed him the processes of manufacturing panther traps, bear traps, fox traps, and others; told him how the trap trade of all North America was in Oneida's hands, how they fought and won against British traps in South America and Burma. Time after time Wells tried to get Noyes going on politics. (His father, John Humphrey Noyes, the founder of the Oneida Community, had after all been a communist, even if a "non-political" one.) But the attempts came to nothing. As Wells described it, making a new world was to Noyes a mere rhetorical flourish about futile and troublesome activities, and politicians were merely a disreputable sort of parasite upon honorable people who made traps and chains and plated spoons. To see a man "so firmly gripped by the romantic constructive and adventurous element of business, so little concerned about personal riches or wealth," taught Wells something which he had never before understood about the American character—and which many people still do not comprehend. To such a man, Wells gathered, America was just "the impartial space, the large liberty," (space and chance, James had called it) in which Oneida grew. With America as a state or nation, in the European sense, such men had no concern. Yet back in 1906 Wells suspected—and he may still have been right—that it was with the services of such men that the World State, and peace, would one day be built.[1]

[1] Hugo Munsterberg, professor of psychology at Harvard, in a book about America published in Germany in 1904, commented in similar terms on the American attitude toward business. "The economic life means to the American a realizing of efforts which are in themselves precious. It is not the means to an end, but is its own end. . . . The merchant in Europe does not feel himself to be a free creator like the artist or scholar.

Underlying the devotion of men like Noyes to their manufacturing enterprises there was, of course, a whole-hearted acceptance of the industrial and technological environment which was instinctive with almost all Americans when they were not consciously struggling in the shadow of an imported (or transplanted) culture. As Joseph Wood Krutch once remarked, Europeans learned to use the machine as a middle-aged man learns to drive a car—dubiously and without ceasing to feel that it is alien to his nature; but Americans took to it with the enthusiasm of youth and manipulated its levers as if they were the muscles of their own bodies.

The American's affection for machinery has always been an outstanding characteristic. There is an amusing story, preserved by Julia Neal, of a Negro who received his freedom from the Shakers at South Union, Kentucky, in the early 1830s and went along with some of the Shaker merchants on a trip down the Mississippi to New Orleans. On the return trip he left his companions at Nashville and took a job on a river steamer at fifteen dollars per month. When the Shakers admonished him about leaving his religion he replied: "Talk to me about Eternal Life! Why Jesus Christ never saw a steamboat." Howard Paul, in some American sketches published in England in 1853, commented on the enthusiasm and devotion which the members of American fire companies lavished on their machines. The nearest thing to it in England, he said, was the devotion to favorite horses on Derby Day. The same sort of intense affection has been lavished on railroad locomotives, river steamers, automobiles, airplanes, and countless other machines and engines.

It is no accident that one of the most eloquent and moving elegies in American literature, Lee Strout White's

---

. . . The American merchant works for money in exactly the sense that a great painter works for money; the high price which is paid for his picture is a very welcome indication of the general appreciation of his art." *The Americans*, translated by Edwin B. Holt, New York, 1904, pp. 237–38.

"Farewell, My Lovely," is a lament for the passing of the Model-T Ford car. No other people in the world have adopted the automobile with such fervor as the Americans. In great part, of course, it was economic and geographic factors which accounted for the tremendous growth of the automobile industry here as compared with Europe.

To paraphrase the conclusions of David L. Cohn in his informal history of the automobile age, from 1900 to 1942 the industry produced 69,000,000 automobiles whose *wholesale* value was $44,000,000,000; to accommodate those cars we built hundreds of thousands of miles of road connecting 500,000 square miles of our national territory; fabulous industries were created or vastly expanded to serve the car, including petroleum, rubber, tourism, and installment finance; millions of people earned their living by making cars or servicing them and millions more used cars as an essential part of their daily lives. These are, as Mr. Cohn says, stupendous economic and social facts, "not comparable to anything else in our national life or in the experience of any other people." But, as Bergen Evans has argued with some plausibility, there is really no economic excuse for the amount of money and time which the average American citizen spends on and in his car. The whole business of car owning long ago exceeded the bounds of reason and took on the color and characteristics of something much closer to a love affair than a business proposition. And who counts the cost of a love affair?

Three reasons are commonly given for the American's passionate attachment to his car: that it serves him as a sort of mechanized magic carpet (in 1940, the American people drove their cars an estimated four hundred and ninety-eight *billion* passenger miles—an average of almost four thousand miles for every man, woman, and child in the country); that it vicariously gratifies his lust for power; and that it serves as a symbol of social prestige. All these are undoubtedly elements in the phenomenon, but there are at least two others which are even more important. For one thing, automobiles provide the majority of people with their most impressive firsthand experience of the machine civilization which shapes their lives. C. F. Hirschfeld estimated that in 1930 more than three quarters of the nation's prime-mover capacity (steam, hydroelectric, internal combustion, and all) was located under the hoods of pleasure cars! The defense plants, war machines, and airplanes built since then may well have reduced this percentage, but it is nevertheless true that an astounding proportion of the total mechanical power which our civilization has produced is owned and controlled by individual citizens.

The psychological results of this fact have never been adequately considered. Obviously the person who knows how to clean his own fuel-pump filter and to adjust his ignition timing will be hard to convince that "the machine" is his master. Merely understanding a few of your car's idiosyncrasies—the particular way to tease its worn-out windshield wiper into renewed activity, or the exact amount of pressure on the foot pedal which the brakes' adjustment requires—gives you a kind of secret intimacy with mechanical power which deprives it of the irrational terrors with which some people still like to scare themselves.

But in addition to providing a sense of familiarity with and personal control over "the machine," automobiles also happen to be among the most beautiful objects which modern civilization has produced, in spite of the chromium academicism of bulbous streamlining which the professional designers have imposed upon so many of them. Along with the skyscrapers, the grain elevators, the suspension bridges, and the huge transport planes, they are among the most aesthetically satisfying products of technology—and of all these objects they are the only ones which the average citizen can own.

In the early years, of course, the design of automobiles reflected the conflicting influences of the vernacular and cultivated traditions even more clearly than it now does.

Only reluctantly was the essentially technological character of the car acknowledged. Back in 1896, when cars
were still a rarity, Charles Duryea advertised his Duryea
Motor Carriage as "having a 'complete appearance'—not a
'carriage-without-a-horse look'—and yet not a machine in
appearance." But of course it *was* a machine, and no satisfactory solution of its design could disguise that fact.

When the history of automobile design is someday written, the Model-T Ford will surely turn out to have been
one of the most effective contributions to the evolution of
a distinctively automotive design. Here was a naked, un-
disguised machine for transportation, as free from extraneous ornament, as perfectly adapted to mass-production
techniques of manufacture as its modern successor in popular affection, the honest-to-God army jeep. If there ever
was an unabashed product of the vernacular tradition as
this book has defined it, the Model-T Ford was it.

Once established (in 1909), the design of the Model-T
was almost immutable, granted the business principle to
which Ford adhered for so many years. What he set out
to do was to manufacture a dependable, inexpensive, simple, and "completely utilitarian" car to meet the needs of
"the ninety-five percent" of the population who could not
afford fancy trimmings. Writing in 1923, he put it this
way:

It is considered good manufacturing practice, and not
bad ethics, occasionally to change designs so that old
models will become obsolete and new ones will have to
be bought. . . . Our principle of business is precisely
to the contrary. We cannot conceive how to serve the
customer unless we make for him something that, as far
as we can provide, will last forever. . . . We never
make an improvement that renders any previous model
obsolete. The parts of a specific model are not only interchangeable with all other cars of that model, but
they are interchangeable with similar parts on all cars
that we have turned out. You can take a car of ten

years ago, and buying today's parts, make it with very little expense into a car of today.

From the beginning, of course, some people were dissatisfied with the stripped utilitarianism of the Model-T's appearance. Industries grew up to supply the aesthetic deficiencies of the dowdy Ford, offering fancy radiator caps, wire wheels, special mudguards, and other ornamental gadgets. In 1916 a company in Detroit manufactured a complete transformation for Model-T. Heretofore, their advertisement said, "You have had to choose either Ford dependability and economy and put up with its appearance or pay a higher price for a better appearing car and stand its extravagant upkeep." Now, for $260, you could get a beautiful, luxuriously upholstered Beau Brummel Body to fit any Ford chassis. But of the millions of Model-T's sold, far and away the majority were appreciated for what they were, and were left in their natal, unornamented state.

For those who couldn't stomach the Ford's unashamedly vernacular design, there were a number of cars which carried on for several years the Duryea tradition of disguising or minimizing the mechanical nature of the automobile, at least in their advertising. There was the Apperson, with its "Old English Coach of 1820 lines," for instance, whose bright red with black trimmings was advertised as "an exact duplicate of color study as used in the latter days of George III before railroads had spanned countries." Yet by 1916 at the latest the basic "streamline" design of the modern car had been generally adopted. (See Fig. 26.) As the magazine *Motor World* summarized it in December 1916, "The year gone by has not been a remarkable one for engineering achievement. There has been no great change, no upheaval, in design or construction." What changes had been made were chiefly the addition of such "selling features" as dashboard clocks, Boyce Moto-Meters (on radiator caps to indicate water temperature), cigar lighters (not yet called cigarette lighters), and other items

designed to make the cars more "attractive and comfortable." Closed cars were rapidly increasing in popularity;
seventeen makes were regularly equipped with detachable
closed and open tops for summer and winter, and sedans
were being made in increasing numbers. But the important
fact was that, as any group of illustrations of 1916 models
will show, automobiles by then looked like automobiles
and nothing else.

The relative success of automobile design in thus early
rejecting the influence of the cultivated tradition can be
traced to a number of influences. For one thing, once the
"horseless carriage" idea was overcome it was recognized
that a car was an altogether new kind of vehicle, unde-
niably a machine, and as such it was enthusiastically
welcomed by all but a few of the conservatively wealthy.
(It was the big, expensive cars which held on longest to
the carriage and coach styles.) For another thing, the
mass-production techniques which Ford introduced into
the business tended, as they always do in the long run,
to simplify and standardize design.

Indeed it was chiefly the automobile industry as created
by Ford which, by the 1920s, seemed to many people to
symbolize America. The Frenchman, André Siegfried, for
instance, announced with "heart burnings and regrets" in
1927 that Americans were creating, on a vast scale, "an
entirely original social structure which bears only a superficial resemblance to the European"—and the basis of that
structure, as he saw it, was "Fordism." By Fordism, of
course, he meant industrial mass production, which, as he
rightly feared, meant doom for the kind of society to which
he, as a European, was accustomed.

For in Europe as well as in America the influence of
Fordism was strong. What appealed to American artists
and travelers abroad was, of course, "the Europe of
'dreaming spires,' divine Gothic, moss-grown castles, quaint
villages, special crafts, folk songs, gay peasant costumes,
and workingmen who love Wagner with their beer," but,
as Charles Beard wrote in 1929, only a blind man could

contend that that was any longer the creative and dynamic Europe. The truth was, as he pointed out, that Europe was at war with herself, and that the American invasion —spearheaded during the twenties by tourists, expatriates, and commercial and financial expansionists—was merely adding weight to the winning side.

Actually, Europe had been at war with herself in this sense ever since the Industrial Revolution got under way in England toward the end of the eighteenth century. That America had by the late 1920s become synonymous with modern civilization, while Europe was still regarded (and on the whole regarded herself) as the custodian of the older culture, was—as James had observed—merely the result of the fact that here the new forces had found more space and chance. But the inevitable result was that when Europeans became aware of the new civilization's growing domination in their own countries they tended to identify it with American influence.

To some extent, of course, it *was* American influence. Industrial mass production, though it was the logical and inevitable outgrowth of forces which had their origins in eighteenth-century Europe, evolved so much more rapidly in the United States that its techniques were largely of American origin by the time Europe began to adopt it on a large scale.

The first great American influence on European industry was not "Fordism" however, but "Taylorism," and it is revealing to look briefly at what that influence involved. It began in 1903, when the Philadelphia engineer and inventor Frederick Winslow Taylor published an article called "Shop Management" in the *Transactions of the American Society of Mechanical Engineers*. The article was translated and published in almost every European country, as was the book *The Principles of Scientific Management* (1911) in which Taylor subsequently expanded his ideas.

If Taylor is remembered now, it is usually only as the man who introduced time and motion studies into factory

management, but his contribution was a much more significant one than that. What it involved was a recognition
that the worker was an integral part of the industrial process—that increased productivity involved not only the improvement of machines and of factory layout but also the
increased efficiency of the men and women who tended
them. Essentially, as Taylor said in his testimony before
a special congressional investigating committee in 1912,
scientific management was not a mere bunch of efficiency
devices. It was, rather, an attitude toward production
which involved a complete mental revolution on the part
of both workers and management. Both must take their
eyes off the division of the surplus resulting from their
joint labors and concentrate instead on increasing the surplus. Both must substitute "exact scientific investigation
and knowledge" for individual judgments or opinions,
either of the workman or boss, in all matters relating to
production.

In other words, Taylor was working toward a unifying
conception of the total industrial process, based on scientific rather than empirical knowledge. By many of his contemporaries, however, his system was accepted as simply
a new kind of wage system or a collection of "efficiency
devices" in the crude sense, and Taylor himself was partly
to blame for the misunderstanding. To get his system
adopted, he had to sell the idea to management and he
therefore tended to emphasize the ways in which it would
increase management's immediate profits. Labor, consequently, got the notion that the system exploited the workers, and labor leaders viciously attacked the man who
proposed it. Labor's attacks in turn led Taylor, who was
hotheaded and frequently tactless, to say and do things
which confirmed the impression that he was anti-labor.

Taylor never formally stated his basic philosophy, but
there are enough scattered clues to indicate the democratic bases of his thought. In his book, for instance, he
thus summarized the characteristics of the kind of indus-

trial system he advocated as distinguished from current practice:

Science, not rule of thumb.
Harmony, not discord.
Cooperation, not individualism.
Maximum output, in place of restricted output.
The development of each man to his greatest efficiency
and prosperity.

These are social objectives, far removed from the "public be damned" attitude of the finance-capitalists who, at that time, were largely in control of American industry. But Taylor made his outlook even clearer in a letter written in the same year that his book was published. In it he pointed out that workmen and employers are only two of the parties in the industrial process; that it is the whole people who eventually pay both wages and profits; and that "the rights of the people are therefore greater than those of either employer or employee." The aim of scientific management was, therefore, the broadly social one of maximum production in the interests of the whole people. That maximum was to be achieved by over-all planning in terms of exact knowledge of all production factors—including the workers.

What Taylor's work amounted to was the systematic formalization of industrial procedures which up to that time had evolved in hit-or-miss fashion out of the everyday experience of many scattered shops and factories. That it failed to achieve the harmony and co-operation which he aimed at was perhaps inevitable in a time when the entire industrial and economic system was thought of as something distinct from the rest of human life, having nothing to do with the values expressed in political and social institutions, to say nothing of the arts. Full recognition of the interrelationships between the industrial system and the rest of society had to await the now famous experiments undertaken in the late twenties by F. J. Roeth-

lisberger of Harvard and W. J. Dickson of the Western
Electric Company at Western Electric's Hawthorne plant
in Chicago. Those experiments, together with the subsequent studies directed by Elton Mayo, make it clear that
Taylor's emphasis on techniques to promote human efficiency must give way to an emphasis on techniques of
human co-operation.

But in his own time it was, as we have said, Taylor's
efficiency techniques which were seized upon by industry,
and it was these which were borrowed most eagerly in
Europe. The pressures toward increased industrial efficiency growing out of the First World War created widespread interest in American methods of production, and
as Taylor's biographer, F. B. Copley, has shown, Taylorism became the focal point of that interest. In France the
Michelin Foundation sought to promote Taylorism by
courses given in the advanced technical colleges and by
public lectures, and in a circular dated February 26, 1918,
signed by Clemenceau, the French Ministry of War declared "an imperative necessity" that all heads of military
establishments should study Taylorism, and ordered that
in every plant there should be created a planning department whose directors should consult Taylor's books. In
Vienna there appeared a periodical called *Taylor-Zeit-
schrift*. In Russia *Pravda* for April 28, 1918, carried a long
article by Lenin on "The Urgent Problems of Soviet Rule"
in which he declared that the new Russia "should try out
every scientific and progressive suggestion of the Taylor
system."

The spread of Taylorism and later of Fordism to Europe
and the rest of the world has, of course, been more often
lamented than welcomed by those who cherish the values
inherent in the older cultures. To many it has seemed, as
it did to André Siegfried, that mankind was giving up a
system in which the individual was considered as an independent ego, and substituting for it one which sacrificed
the individual to material conquests. Certainly there is little enough in the history of the rise of Fascism in Italy

and Germany, or of Soviet Communism in Russia, to contradict this gloomy view. It is no wonder, after the horrors of the last fifteen years (1933–48), that the "Americanization" of Europe or Asia is regarded with dread—if to Americanize means merely to adopt or imitate our technology rather than to adopt those attitudes and motives which made that technology possible.

That it has meant this, in many instances, is one of the greatest tragedies of our time, a tragedy which results from a fundamental misconception of the American experience. For underlying that experience and running through every phase of our history, as we have seen in our tracing of the vernacular tradition, the technological influences have been inextricably interwoven with those of democracy. It was our democratic political and social institutions that gave our industrial system its special characteristics, while at the same time it was our technological achievements that strengthened and extended our political and social democracy. Neither could have existed without the other in anything like its present form.

It would be pointless to defend such an assertion as anything more than a useful generalization. The present writer has no interest in trying to foster the notion that American industrialists have been uniformly democratic and humane. It is absurd, however, to assume as many people do that industrial technology is everywhere the same in its character and influence. Anyone who reads the British government's postwar surveys of the need for increased productivity in British industry, or who studies the so-called Monet plan for industrial modernization in France, will find ample evidence of the astonishing divergences between British and French technology and that of the United States. Only in the most superficial sense is it true that an automobile plant or electric motor factory is the same sort of thing in Britain or France as in America. Even the most cursory reading of prewar and postwar technical and industrial publications will confirm the impression that both in its administrative aspects and in its

technology American industry has been shaped by vernacular influences to a much greater degree than that of
Europe.

It will be apparent, for instance, that the differences
between European and American technical practice grow
out of the differing social contexts in which industry has
developed there and here. Consider in this connection the
conclusions of Wallace Clark, consulting management engineer, after three and a half years of experience in France,
Germany, England, Poland, and several other countries
during the boom years of 1927–30. He was impressed by
the fact that European industrialists had long persisted in
the belief "that the purchase of the most efficient machinery and equipment" was all that was required to bring
them American prosperity, and were only beginning to
learn that the attitudes and methods of American management were "quite as important as machines and processes."
Throughout Europe he found that there was a barrier
between the administrator and the practical mechanic
which was almost never crossed. Plant executives, from
the superintendent up, invariably had engineering degrees
which represented good theoretical training, but they had
seldom had any actual shop experience. Workers, on the
other hand, had so little reason to expect promotion to
positions of responsibility that they did nothing to fit themselves for it. There were, of course, variations in this pattern from place to place, but as Mr. Clark piles up illustrations of his point in plant after plant and country
after country it becomes apparent that the degree to which
the gap between management and worker is unbridgeable
in any nation reflects the relative rigidity of class lines in
other social spheres. Not, as he said, that executives in
European industry actively opposed promotions from the
ranks when he suggested them. It was simply that under
normal circumstances such things were very rare. To put
it in Mr. Clark's own words, "it does not occur to anyone
that they can be done."

What this means is that in countries where distinctions

between social classes were established by long tradition before modern industrialism was introduced, the technology of production tends to be administered by an elite which deliberately cuts itself off from practical experience. In America, on the other hand, despite the increasing concentration of economic power which industrial development has produced in this as in other countries, control of production is still largely in the hands of men who have had actual shop experience.

Similarly, vernacular influences have molded the technology of American industry, with the result that the organization of production still retains its characteristic flexibility and adaptability. In an earlier chapter we noted how belts and pulleys were early substituted for toothed gears and shafts in transmitting power in American factories, thus permitting greater flexibility in layout. At the Centennial Exhibition in 1876 one of the most striking inventions exhibited was the Stow flexible shaft (Fig. 27) —ancestor of the cordlike shaft on a modern dentist's drill— which, with its various attachments, enabled power to be transmitted readily to all positions and applied in any desired direction. Two years later, at the Paris exhibition, the London *Times* correspondent singled it out as the very type of Yankee contrivances. Watching its operator holding what seemed at first sight to be a small garden hose with an auger at its end, with which he could bore in every direction, the *Times* writer declared that it "upsets all one's ideas of rigidity."

With the coming of the electric motor, flexibility of factory layout was further increased. When each machine and power tool had its own direct source of power, and it was no longer necessary to arrange them in relation to fixed lines of shafting, the old standard factory aisles could be broken up and the machines could be grouped in functional units.

The degree to which this flexibility has been carried in recent years can be illustrated by the setup in a plant like that of the Spicer Manufacturing Company of Toledo,

Ohio, makers of truck and bus parts, which was described by Mike Kallaher in the June 1943 issue of *Factory*. The nature of the company's business required major changes in its production lines every four or five months, and lesser changes—involving on the average twenty machines—every week. The plant was housed in a one-story building with monitor roof so constructed as to provide adequate natural light in all parts of the interior, thus imposing no limitations on the location of machines because of light requirements. The factory floor was made of asphalt-impregnated wood blocks over which heavy machines could be slid without injury to them or to the floor. Suspended from the roof at regular intervals were electric power ducts, which could be plugged into at any point. The machines themselves, each driven by an individual motor, got their electric current from the overhead ducts through lead-in wires carried in flexible cable rather than in rigid pipe, as in other plants. This system did not make for tidiness of appearance, but it saved a lot of pipe-fitting time when changes in layout were made. As a result of these various features it was possible for a tractor and its operator and one millwright to haul and shove a machine from one location to another in a very brief time, the electrician merely pulling the plug out of one junction box on the overhead ducts and plugging it into another. A department of fifty machines, many of them heavy gear cutters, was thus moved in a single day by two tractors plus their operators, two millwrights, and two electricians.[2]

This factory was, of course, a somewhat special case. Many plants do not require such frequent changes of layout. But throughout American industry one can find evidence of essentially the same sort of adaptability. The magazine which contained the description of the Spicer

[2] For an earlier example of the same sort of flexible layout, with belt-driven machines, see "Migration of Presses into Grouped Production Units," *The Iron Age*, November 13, 1930, which describes practices at the Acklin Stamping Company of Toledo, Ohio.

plant carried in the same issue an article on the decentralization of the maintenance department at a Douglas Aircraft Company plant, an outgrowth of the need for more flexible operations; and an entire section of the magazine was devoted to a review of portable factory equipment which had been introduced during the preceding year. Another technical magazine, *Mill and Factory*, brought out a special 684-page issue in May 1947, in which were presented thousands of recently introduced devices and techniques, many of which—like portable conveyor systems, shop trucks and tractors, and free-moving cranes—greatly increase the flexibility of plant layout. (See Fig. 28.)

A notable development in this area was the new theory of machine design proposed by two young Canadian physicists, Eric W. Leaver and John J. Brown, both of whom worked for a number of years in the United States. Their experience in Canada's wartime radar program stimulated their interest in the application of electronics to industrial processes. In the past, they argued in an article in *Fortune* (November 1946), machines were designed to turn out a certain *product* rather than to perform a certain function, and this point of view resulted in increasingly uneconomic specialization. As an example of this they mention a machine made during the war to mass-produce aircraft cylinder heads.

It was ninety feet long, a marvel of precision and ingenuity, and cost in the neighborhood of $100,000. Rough castings went in one end, and finished cylinder heads dropped out the other at the rate of one a minute. The machine is now just scrap metal; that type of cylinder head is no longer made.

What Leaver and Brown proposed was a theory of design which concentrated on basic operations rather than on products. Briefly summarized, their idea was that machines should be made up of groups of small units plugged together, each unit designed to perform one function. Various combinations of these basic units would comprise machines to make the various parts of a given product. A number of such machines, electronically controlled and linked by conveyors, would produce and assemble a complete product.

In discussing the significance of their proposal, they and the editors of *Fortune* placed the chief emphasis on the automatism which would be achieved in a factory that used such machines—the H. G. Wellsian concept of a factory whose production floor, "as clean, spacious, and continuously operating as a hydroelectric plant," is barren of men, the only human presences being a few engineers and technicians who walk about on a balcony before a great wall of master control panels. But automatic production is by no means new. In the processing of raw materials it was achieved more than a century and a half ago, as we know from the accounts of Oliver Evans' flour mill (quoted in Chapter 2), and it has been common practice in bulk manufacturing—of bread, gasoline, and many other products—for a number of years. Even in large-scale assembly operations it is well beyond the experimental stage.

Almost thirty years ago the A. O. Smith Corporation of Milwaukee, Wisconsin, completed an automatic factory for manufacturing automobile frames, and by 1930 the company's assistant works manager, A. W. Redlin, was able to report to the members of the American Society of Mechanical Engineers that every operation from raw steel stock to the assembled and painted frame, including nearly all handling, was done with automatic machinery. The scope of the engineering imagination involved in designing such a factory is suggested by the fact that each frame was composed of more than a hundred parts, and that fabricating and assembling those parts required more than five hundred separate operations, all of which had to be perfectly synchronized. The raw materials had to be automatically tested by special machines and then distributed mechanically to more than a hundred different places in the plant, where as many different machines fabricated the various parts. These parts in turn had to be conveyed mechanically to meet on precise schedule at one place where other machines automatically assembled them at the rate of a completed frame every eight seconds. In a twenty-four-hour day the plant could turn out ten thousand frames, the machines performing approximately four million synchronized, automatic operations.

Yet for all the engineering genius displayed in the A. O. Smith factory, its automatism may well prove to have been a dead-end solution to an essentially anachronistic problem. Nothing, surely, could be more inflexible, more mechanically rigid, than a factory so arranged. Nowhere in modern industry has mechanical specialization been carried so far.

From our point of view, therefore, it is not the automatic feature of the Leaver and Brown proposal that is significant, but their idea that machines should be "highly adaptable, with easily detachable components designed to be shuffled and rearranged at any time to build an entirely different product." This interchangeability of basic units would permit a factory to accommodate itself to changes in the market with an ease unknown in contemporary production, and would remove one of the most binding restrictions on the introduction of new products. The great problem with mass production has always been that the cost of the plant can be justified only by large demand. But for a new product the demand is rarely great. Leaver and Brown take as an instance the dilemma of the manufacturers of helicopters. The demand for these aircraft would undoubtedly increase if the price could be cut to that of an automobile. But the only way to get the price down is to mass-produce, and that would involve an investment of millions of dollars in specialized machines. If such an investment were made now, when helicopter design is changing rapidly, the whole factory might be obsolete before a single helicopter was sold. Under a system of flexible machine units, however, changes in design could easily be made.

Putting the Leaver and Brown proposal into practice would create some painful social and economic consequences, including technological unemployment and the scrapping of costly current equipment—consequences which cannot be lightly dismissed. But the suggestion commands our attention here because it so dramatically extends the traditional adaptability and flexibility of American industry.

Signs of the same sort of adaptability have appeared also in recent developments in the administrative and financial branches of industry. One of the most interesting experiments along this line got its start in 1940 when a young physicist named Richard S. Morse set out to organize a company which would depend for its economic success on turning out one new process or product after another. At first glance there may not appear to be anything very revolutionary about that. Introducing new products and processes has long been a source of profit to manufacturers and businessmen, and has kept our economic system supple and expanding. But if the history of American business demonstrates anything, it demonstrates that once a company turns out an idea which is a financial success it tends to lose interest in other ideas and concentrate on exploiting the successful one already launched. As Mr. Kettering of the General Motors research laboratories once put it, "the human family in industry is always looking for a park bench along the road of progress where it can sit down and rest."

Despite the loud wailing of some of our crusading liberals, there is no unholy conspiracy of corporate evil involved in the reluctance of an established producer to introduce a new process or product. He faces the prospect of putting out of business some of his equipment, of having to spend money to train men in new processes, of having to shut down his plant, of incurring expenses for new machinery, and hence of losing money. Even with an automatic factory like that proposed by Leaver and Brown, change would involve the risk of some losses, and in present practice the losses are often great. Obviously these are disquieting prospects, and it is not surprising that few businessmen feel they can afford to act in terms of the perfectly obvious but remote fact that such losses would be temporary, and that in the long run an improved product or process would be more profitable than the old one.

As long as business remained in the hands of a great many relatively small companies, many of which went bankrupt or simply went out of business every generation and were replaced by new enterprises, the economic system as a whole did not suffer much from the natural tendency of established business to shy away from new talent and new techniques. In a highly competitive field there was nearly always someone who would take a chance on the long-run profits, someone who would be able to take Mr. Kettering's advice that the surest way to sell a new device to one company is to sell it first to a competitor.

But what if there is no competitor? The history of American business has been the story of a larger and larger proportion of our economic activity coming under the control of fewer and fewer large corporations. This long-term trend was markedly accelerated by the war, and the restrictive pressures—the clogs on progress—inevitably have become greater and greater. On all sides we see symptoms of hardening of the economic arteries, from devices aimed at getting around the anti-trust laws to an increasing reliance on salesmanship.

Everyone agrees, of course, that we must continue to have a healthy and expanding economy, with the rising standard of living it implies. But only constant, progressive change in the techniques of manufacture and distribution can keep the economic system healthy. And that is why it is worth looking at a company which, like Morse's National Research Corporation, attempts to find an organizational basis which will make change profitable.

Basically, Morse's company was designed as a producing unit built around scientific and technical research. The core of the company was to be ideas rather than products. His intention was that production should stimulate research rather than that research should merely assist production. If things went according to plan the company would set up subsidiary companies to manufacture the products or to exploit the processes which the research outfit develops. (Only one such subsidiary had been set up when this chapter was written, but others were in the offing.) Obviously, if the subsidiaries were very successful there would be a tendency for the tail to wag the dog unless the parent company automatically divested itself of its interests in the subsidiary after a fixed interval, and some such arrangement would be inevitable if the parent company was to be put in a position where continued profits require the constant development of new methods and new products.

Since creative scientific research is "a young man's game," as Vannevar Bush has said, a company sparked by research must remain in the control of young men. Morse decided that high salaries and early retirement for research men were essential to the future of his company, and it was intended that the older members of the original outfit should move over into administrative positions in the subsidiaries as those were set up, thus making room for younger research men to replace them.

Whatever the outcome of this particular experiment in enterprise, it called attention to the continuing need for fresh solutions to the conflict between the profit-making necessities of established units in our business system and the experimentation and innovation which renews the system's lifeblood. Whether or not this particular solution works, interest in the problem is widespread. Edwin H. Land of the Polaroid Corporation took this sort of organizational scheme as the subject of his talk at the Standard Oil Development Company's 1944 forum on the "Future of Industrial Research." More recently, in 1946, a group of businessmen and scientists, originally led by Ralph E. Flanders—machine-tool manufacturer, former president of the Federal Reserve Bank of Boston, and senator from Vermont—formed the American Research and Development Corporation to provide financial support and research facilities for small companies trying to introduce "new ideas and developments which give promise of expanded production and employment, and an increased standard of living for the American people." These and other financial and organizational experiments, coupled with technological proposals like those of Mr. Leaver and Mr. Brown, suggest that the adaptability and flexibility of American industry are by no means played out, and that the one-time bugaboo of a "mature economy" was more a depression-born slogan than an industrial reality. As long as our civilization rests upon an industrial system which remains quick on its feet and readily adaptable there will be space and chance for those who are "firmly gripped by the romantic constructive and adventurous element of business." The danger comes, as the so-called Americanization of Europe and a number of grim episodes in our own history have demonstrated, when the instruments of technological civilization come under the control of those who use them to perpetuate the forms and values of a moribund social structure.

10 *Stone, Steel, and Jazz*

A civilization shaped by technical and industrial forces like those we have considered in the last chapter, working in collaboration with social and political institutions which —in spite of two world wars and a cataclysmic depression —have retained a degree of democratic equality and personal liberty unparalleled elsewhere, implies cultural values and artistic forms which are not only different from those appropriate to the agricultural and handicraft-commercial civilizations of the past, but have also originated in an altogether different way. For the process by which technological civilization has taken form has reversed that which operated in earlier cultures.

Hitherto, as Santayana pointed out in *Reason in Society* (1905), civilization has consisted in the diffusion and dilution of habits arising in privileged centers: "It has not sprung from the people; it has arisen in their midst by a variation from them, and it has afterward imposed itself on them from above." But civilization in America, in so far as it can be identified with the vernacular influences this book has sought to define, *has* sprung from the people. What was "imposed on them from above" was the transplanted tradition of an older culture.

From the point of view of those who have been trained in the cultivated tradition, the emergence of a civilization from popular roots has been a phenomenon of dubious merit. The fear of what is often called "popular culture," in all its manifestations, is a notable feature of much historical and critical writing. To Santayana himself it seemed certain that "a state composed exclusively of such workers and peasants as make up the bulk of modern nations would be an utterly barbarous state." Indeed, those who think of culture as "the diffusion of habits arising in

privileged centers" are led almost unavoidably to the conclusion reached by an anonymous writer in *Harper's* in
1928, that the future of culture in America is "clearly
quite hopeless" because there is no church or aristocracy
or other authority to modify or restrain what is assumed
to be the human race's "natural taste for bathos."

Back in the 1880s this attitude was already firmly established. Cultivated people everywhere tended to agree
with writers like Sir Edmund Gosse that it was from America that the real threat to established values came.

> Up to the present time, in all parts of the world [Sir
> Edmund wrote in 1889], the masses of uneducated or
> semi-educated persons . . . though they cannot and do
> not appreciate the classics of their race, have been con-
> tent to acknowledge their traditional supremacy. Of
> late there have been certain signs, especially in America,
> of a revolt of the mob against our literary masters. . . .
> The revolution against taste, once begun, will land us
> in irreparable chaos.

Here was one aspect of that "perpetual repudiation of the
past" that Henry James had observed. But what Gosse did
not see, and could not have accounted for if he had seen,
was that this revolt was by no means confined to the mob.
Eight years before Gosse wrote, the conservative and staid
North American Review had published Walt Whitman's
famous essay on "The Poetry of the Future" in which he
argued that until America produced its own great poetry
the "feudalistic, anti-republican poetry" of Shakespeare
and the other great writers of the past "will have to be
accepted, such as they are, and thankful they are no
worse." Even the decorous William Dean Howells was
publicly asserting a few years later that at least three
fifths of the literature called classic, in all languages, was
as dead as the people who wrote it and was preserved
only by "a superstitious piety." What was happening, of
course, was much more than a mere revolution *against*

taste. It was a revolution *in* taste—and it had its roots in the changing bases of civilization itself.

The man who, perhaps more clearly than anyone else in his time, understood what was going on was the engineer, George S. Morison, designer of the first of the great bridges across the Mississippi at Memphis and of many other bridges throughout the country. A powerful man, physically and intellectually, Morison had early abandoned what promised to be a successful career in law to go into engineering. He went to work under Octave Chanute, chief engineer of the Kansas City bridge, in 1867, and by the time the bridge was completed in June 1869, Morison had risen to be associate engineer. By 1875 he was internationally famous as the man who—eighty-six days after fire destroyed the great wooden trestle which carried the Erie Railroad across the Genesee River at Portage—had designed and constructed the steel bridge which replaced it, and at the time of his death in 1903 he was widely recognized as one of the world's great engineers.

Oddly enough, however, few people remember Morison's book, *The New Epoch as Developed by the Manufacture of Power,* published just after he died but completed—and the preface dated—in Chicago in 1898. It is a strange, forcefully clear book, and an important one, though no historian of our civilization, so far as the present writer has discovered, has taken any note of it. Briefly, it argued that with the discovery of ways to manufacture power mankind entered a new ethnical epoch which would transform civilization. What ultimate form the new epoch would take he did not specify, but he saw clearly that the new mechanical and technical era would in the long run bring about fundamental changes in men's relationship with one another and with their environment. In many ways, he realized, the new epoch would inevitably open as an era of destruction. By its very nature it would destroy "many of the conditions which give most interest to the history of the past, and many of the traditions which people hold most dear." There would be destruction in both the physical and intellectual world—of customs and ideas, systems of thought, and methods of education as well as of old buildings, old boundaries, and old monuments. How this destruction would occur, and how much time it would take, he did not care to guess. The important thing, he argued, was that it would come—"not because the things which are destroyed are themselves bad, but because however good and useful they may have been in the past, they are not adaptable to fulfill the requirements of the new epoch."

Meanwhile there was danger. Some time might elapse after the old had been destroyed before the new was established in its place, and the trouble would lie in the gap between the two. "The next two or three centuries," he warned, "may have periods of war, insurrection, and other trials, which it would be well if the world could avoid." One of the greatest dangers, in this connection, would be the fact that the new epoch would destroy ignorance, spreading education not only to all classes in civilized countries but to savage and barbarous races as well. The most terrible period of all would be that time "when the number of half-educated people is greatest, when the world is full of people who do not know enough to recognize their limitations, but know too much to follow loyally the direction of better qualified leaders."

Whatever the limitations of Morison's 134-page historical essay, it nevertheless succeeded as few if any of its more ponderous successors have done in diagnosing the causes of unrest and chaos in our time. If we bear his thesis in mind we will no longer have any difficulty in understanding the link between Gosse and other cultivated writers of the genteel tradition in the eighties and nineties and their vigorous critics in the 1920s. On the surface, of course, men like J. E. Spingarn, H. L. Mencken, and Ludwig Lewisohn were in open rebellion against almost everything that the exponents of the genteel tradition had stood for. But essentially the writers of the twenties were, in Lewisohn's phrase, trying as their predecessors had done to awaken Americans to "the peril of cutting ourselves off from the historic culture of mankind." Even Irving Babbitt and the new humanists were doing their best to reinforce traditional standards which would correct that "unrestraint and violation of the law of measure" which was at the root of our cultural deficiency. The finest literary talent of a generation was dedicated to the task of setting up some authority which would restrain what inevitably seemed, to anyone who cherished the values inherent in European culture, to be the American's "natural taste for bathos."

Almost nobody among our writers seemed to realize, as Morison did, that destruction of those values was inevitable, however regrettable it might be, and that the great job to be done was to help discover and establish those new values, based upon the actualities of political democracy and industrial technology, which must one day—after who knows what misery and devastation—take their place. Those who sensed that this was so were left to struggle with the problem alone, till many were overcome by the fear of futility. There is no more pitiful record of this fearful loneliness than Sherwood Anderson's *Perhaps Women* (1931). Listen to the note of desperation in these words, for instance:

. . . when mechanical invention ·followed mechanical invention . . . I at least had not tried to get out of it all by fleeing to Europe.

I had at least not gone to Paris, to sit eternally in cafes, talking of art.

I had stuck and yet . . . all my efforts had been efforts to escape.

Time and again I had told the story of the American man crushed and puzzled by the age of the machine. I had told the story until I was tired of telling it. I had retreated from the city to the town, from the town to the farm.

Watching an intricate machine at work, Anderson thought that the men who designed and built it might "some day be known to be as important in the life swing of mankind as the man who built the Cathedral of Chartres." And yet, he asked, can man, being man, actually stand, naked in his inefficiency before the efficient machine? And his answer was no, it cannot be done—not yet in any event. "They are too complex and beautiful for me. My manhood cannot stand up against them yet."

In his loneliness Anderson questioned whether men any longer had the power to make new values to replace those which the machine was destroying, and the point of his book was the despairing hope that perhaps women could do it for them. But he at least faced up to the challenge, which one woman had thrown at him, to "go and look" at the factories and machines which were shaping the new age, and to "stay looking."

Those who might have been expected to help in the exploration of new values too often spent their time ridiculing or denouncing or lamenting what they called America's bourgeois taste. People like James Truslow Adams, whose study of the downfall of the Puritan theocracy in colonial New England should have taught him better, wrote articles urging "the upper class" to refine and elevate the middle class and not be swamped by its "obscurantist prejudices, its narrow and ignoble prepossessions, its dogmatism, self-righteousness, self-sufficiency." In an article published in a popular monthly in 1932—after Radio City and the George Washington Bridge had both been built—one of the future editors of the *Reader's Digest* declared that anyone who looked at American architecture and manners could see that for a decade or more we had been in the throes of an "uprising of serfs." The middle class, he announced, had delusions of upper-class grandeur to which it was giving expression in structures like the Automat restaurant up near the Bronx with its huge cathedral window and elaborate vestibule, in huge, "insincerely magnificent" movie palaces such as New York's Roxy and Paramount, and in overelaborate business offices designed to cater to what he contemptuously called "the demand for the dignity of industrial pursuits."

That demand was real enough, and the amount of money spent in an effort to satisfy it is a measure of its intensity. It is certainly true that there were plenty of inappropriate guesses as to how that dignity should be expressed. But the failure to find appropriate expressions, in architecture and elsewhere, should not have been taken as evidence that the demand itself was contemptible. The onus for buildings like the Roxy, the Gothic Automat, and the ornate business offices belonged not to those who demanded beautiful surroundings for recreation and work without knowing how to achieve them, but to those who could not, or would not, share Louis Sullivan's faith that it was the architect's job to affirm that which the people really wish to affirm—namely, the best that is in them. For as Sullivan knew, "the people want true buildings, but do not know how to get them so long as architects betray them with architectural phrases."

As one looks back at the twenties and thirties in the light of the argument which this book has developed, there is something rather touching about the desperate efforts Americans made to put utilitarian architecture behind them and to build beautiful things. We had been effectively taught, by those who we readily agreed were our betters in aesthetic matters, that what was useful was not beautiful. The architecture of the Chicago school—the highest manifestation of the vernacular tradition yet achieved—was discussed by Thomas E. Tallmadge in a chapter of his 1927 history of American architecture entitled "Louis Sullivan and the Lost Cause." Such architecture was doomed, he said, because of its demand for originality and for freedom from traditional styles. "What is the culture and genius of America?" he asked; and promptly answered, "It is European."[1]

[1] Nine years later, in a revised edition of his book, Mr. Tallmadge changed the title of his chapter on Sullivan to "Louis

It was no wonder, then, that the ordinary citizen who wanted beauty in his dwelling frequently turned, not to the vernacular for inspiration, but to the cultivated tradition, convinced that to be beautiful a design must be both European and useless. It was in this mood that Americans built during the twenties those genial horrors that Charles Merz described in *The Great American Bandwagon:* the Italian wells that pumped no water, the Spanish balconies for houses with no rooms upstairs, and all the rest of the amiable but pointless lies of the Coral Gables era.

There were, of course, fine things being done all through this period. We were still building grain elevators and industrial plants which, as the German architect Walter Gropius had written in the *Jahrbuch des Deutschen Werkbundes* in 1913, had a natural integrity deriving from their designers' independent and clear vision of these grand, impressive forms, and which were "not obscured by sentimental reverence for tradition nor by other intellectual scruples which prostrate our contemporary European design." But in the twenties this mechanical architecture, as Lewis Mumford pointed out at the time, had a vocabulary without a literature. When it stepped beyond the elements of its grammar—that is, when it moved from pure engineering construction into the field of architecture proper, it usually could only "translate badly into its own tongue the noble poems and epics which the Romans and Greeks and medieval builders left behind them."

A dispassionate study of the relationships between engineering and architecture in the twentieth century would be of great value to an understanding of our civilization. What apparently happened was that the engineers, feeling the need for something more than the purely utilitarian satisfactions which their designs provided, turned to the architects for help, while at the same time the architects, sensing the vitality of engineering construction in contrast

---

Sullivan, Parent and Prophet"—a change which concisely expresses the shift in "official" attitudes toward the vernacular from the twenties to the thirties.

with the sterility of traditional architecture, turned increasingly to the problems of giving architectonic expression to the forms evolved by the engineers.

Any study of these interrelationships would, to be sure, have to reckon with certain questions which are posed by such a structure as the George Washington suspension bridge across the Hudson at New York. As it stands, the bridge is concededly one of the most beautiful structures in America. Other great suspension bridges, like the Golden Gate Bridge, have more spectacular settings; but there is something about the George Washington's lofty yet sturdy towers, curving cables, and slender floor[2] which, as the eminent bridge designer David B. Steinman said, has made this bridge, to the younger generation of Americans, a symbol of our civilization. (See Fig. 29.) Yet, as it stands, it is unfinished; the original design worked out by the engineers and the consulting architect has never been completed.

The bridge as originally designed was the work of O. H. Amman, chief engineer; Allston Dana, engineer of design; and Cass Gilbert, architect. According to the *First Progress Report* on the bridge, issued by the Port of New York Authority January 1, 1928, the guiding motives of the design, from the engineering point of view, were "purity of type, simplicity of structural arrangement, and ease and expediency of construction"—motives which, as we have frequently observed, are characteristic of the vernacular tradition. But, the *Report* continues, in designing this bridge "it was realized that more than the usual attention must be paid to the aesthetic side," because of its monumental size and conspicuous location and because the bridge "should be handed down to posterity as a truly monumental structure, which will cast credit upon the aesthetic sense of the present generation." Here were the reverence for tradition and the intellectual scruples which Gropius had lamented in European design, and which ap-

[2] The second level of this bridge was not added until 1961.

peared in America wherever the cultivated tradition retained influence. The general outlines and proportions were purely vernacular in origin, dictated, as the *Report* said, "by engineering requirements." But the towers, anchorages, and approaches "called for careful architectural treatment and dignified appearance." It was here, especially in the towers, that the cultivated tradition would be called upon to create the beauty which it was assumed the vernacular alone could not achieve. The steel skeletons of the towers, designed to carry the entire dead and live load of the completed structure, were nevertheless to be imbedded in a concrete casing faced with granite, in the design of which the architect had decorated the main arch with imposts, springers, and voussoirs and had provided other ornamental details which had no reference to the structural forces at work. (See Fig. 30.)

However, as the 635-foot steel skeletons of the towers rose from the shores of the river, something unprecedented happened. The "unexpected" functional beauty of the naked steelwork fascinated people, and there was a widespread popular protest against applying the masonry covering which, according to the original plan, was to be the chief element in the aesthetic appeal of the bridge.[3] So far as the present writer knows, the Port of New York Authority has never taken formal action to abandon the

---

[3] After this chapter was written the author came upon a discussion of this incident in Le Corbusier's book, *When the Cathedrals Were White* (1947). M. Le Corbusier agrees that the George Washington is "the most beautiful bridge in the world," and that it would have been utterly spoiled if the towers had been faced with stone "molded and sculptured in 'Beaux Arts' style" as the architect had planned. But he seems to have picked up an impression that it was the farseeing wisdom of a single "sensitive" individual which caused the original design to be abandoned. Further, he fails to consider the implications of the fact that the bridge as it stands is a *pure* engineering achievement in the sense that the designer had no aesthetic intentions, but was merely solving functional problems and providing a structure upon which the aesthetic "treatment" could be hung.

original design, and it is still theoretically possible that the towers will be cased in concrete and stone.[4] The protest which prevented the "aesthetic" treatment of the towers was, after all, almost entirely a popular one, and the time may come when our betters in these matters will decide to go ahead with the design which they believed would best cast credit on our generation's taste. For to many people, apparently, it still seems difficult to believe that pure mathematics and engineering expediency can by themselves produce something beautiful. Even Chief Engineer Amman himself, in his final report on the bridge in 1933, still insisted that the appearance of the towers would be "materially enhanced by an encasement with an architectural treatment" like Cass Gilbert's, though he admitted that the steel towers as they stand lent the structure "a much more satisfactory appearance" than he or anyone else connected with the project had anticipated.

Nor is Mr. Amman the only civil engineer who is unable to accept the statement made fifty years ago by George S. Morison, past president of their society, that "architecture, which as a fine art would consign itself to the museum, . . . will find its highest development in correct construction." For even in suspension bridges designed since the George Washington, the engineers have usually felt the need of some sort of architectural treatment for the towers, such as the step-back of Joseph Strauss's Golden Gate Bridge or the steel cupola and spire indicated in Robinson's and Steinman's studies for the proposed Liberty Bridge over the Narrows of New York Harbor. (See Fig. 30.) On the other hand, when architects have had a large part in bridge design they have shown increased confidence in the aesthetic force of unadorned engineering

[4] The fact that Cass Gilbert's designs for the anchorages and approaches of the bridge were ultimately discarded in favor of much simpler designs by Aymar Embury II suggests, however, that Gilbert's designs for the towers may also have been permanently shelved. The Port Authority will not, however, make public any information on this point.

forms, as witness the design by Aymar Embury II of the sheet-steel towers of the Bronx-Whitestone Bridge. (See Fig. 30.) Mr. Embury, it is perhaps worth noting, was trained as an engineer before he began his work as an architect.

One of the most illuminating architectural careers of this period was that of Raymond M. Hood, who died in 1934. The buildings Hood designed from 1914 to the time of his death offer a startling record of the change from architecture conceived in terms of the cultivated tradition to architecture as the exaltation of vernacular forms.

Born in Pawtucket, Rhode Island, educated at Brown University and the Massachusetts Institute of Technology, Hood worked for a year as a draftsman in the office of Cram, Goodhue and Ferguson, then went to the Beaux-Arts in Paris. After his return to this country in 1911, he worked for a while in an architect's office in Pittsburgh, then in 1914 set up as an architect on his own in New York. For years he found little work to do, managing to keep himself going only with sustaining jobs like designing radiator covers. In 1922, however, he suddenly leapt into fame as the co-author of the prize-winning design in the Chicago *Tribune's* $50,000 competition. (See Fig. 31.) The contrast between Hood's and Howell's tower, with its drapery of Gothic flying buttresses, and the design submitted in the same competition by the Finnish architect Eliel Saarinen, has often been pointed out. Saarinen's design—"a soaring pile of receding pyramidal masses"—made no compromise with the essential nature of a skyscraper; Hood's tried its best to hide the fact that it was made of concrete and steel and glass.

How much Hood's later work was influenced by the bold design which was defeated by his own in the *Tribune* competition it is impossible now to say. His next big skyscraper was the black and gold American Radiator Tower in New York (1924), which was simpler than the Tribune Tower but essentially in the same vein. Even as late as 1929, in the Scranton Masonic Temple, he was still echo-

ing the Gothic which he had learned in the office of Cram,
Goodhue and Ferguson. Then suddenly in 1930 he produced the Daily News Building, with its red stripes ac-
centuating the vertical quality of its step-backed mass, and
a year later the McGraw-Hill Building (his favorite) in
which the wide strips of windows are separated by horizontal bands of green-blue. (See Fig. 31.) Those two great
buildings were the last, except for his share of the Rockefeller Center project, before he died.

What happened to Hood between the Tribune Tower
and the McGraw-Hill Building would make a profoundly
interesting study. No doubt it was in part the influence of
his friend Joseph Urban which encouraged him to use
color as an integral part of design. It is probable too that
his partnership with the engineer André Fouilhoux taught
him a great deal about steel, concrete, and glass construction. But such influences do not by any means answer the
questions which his astonishing career raises. What we
need to know, and someday may know when Hood's life
is properly written, is what he meant when he said, late
in life, to Kenneth Murchison, "This beauty stuff is all
bunk." On the evidence of his two greatest buildings it
seems safe to assume that he meant something very like
what the Shaker elder, Frederick Evans, had meant back
in the 1870s when he told Charles Nordhoff that Shaker
buildings ignored "architectural effect and beauty of design" because what people called "beautiful" was "absurd
and abnormal." Like the Shakers, the designer of the
McGraw-Hill Building had an eye to "more light, a more
equal distribution of heat, and a more general care for
protection and comfort. . . . But no beauty"—if beauty
was something apart from such things as these.

In all branches of architecture the influence of the vernacular has been increasingly effective during the past
twenty years. First the depression and then the war created pressures which tended to overcome the retarding
influence of the cultivated tradition and to encourage a
bold acceptance of vernacular forms and techniques. There

is increasing awareness that the best work in American architecture grows directly out of the democratic and technological necessities which force us to think in terms of economy, simplification, and fitness for human purposes.

Writing in 1941, Talbot Hamlin listed some of the architectural high spots of the preceding five years: the Farm Security Administration's camps for migratory workers; the Hunter College building; Rockefeller Center; the Bronx-Whitestone Bridge; the new buildings of the Massachusetts General Hospital; the Kaufman house—Falling Water; the planned community of Greenbelt, Maryland; the Norris Dam and its powerhouse; the high school at Idaho Springs, Colorado; the Santa Rita housing project at Austin, Texas; and Frank Lloyd Wright's buildings for the Taliesin Fellowship. Of all these structures, as Mr. Hamlin observed, only Wright's Kaufman house was a private dwelling; all the rest were designed for some socially constructive purpose.

In a technical discussion of the FSA camps in a professional architectural journal Mr. Hamlin observed that the details of actual construction of these buildings were of extraordinary interest "because they show how the need for economy, creatively conceived, can itself become a means to new and beautiful architectural forms," as, for example, in the use of ventilating louvers as an important element of design in the Utilities Building at the Woodville, California, camp. (See Fig. 32.)

Apparently [he continued] the San Francisco architectural office of the FSA approached every problem of architectural design, in big as in little ways, with complete freshness and innocence of mind. It had no fixed ideas as to windows or doors or interiors or exteriors. Nothing seems to have inhibited its logical approach to each problem; no foreordained picture of what had been done or what was usual held it back.

Very much the same sort of freedom characterizes the best of our industrial plants, especially those built during the war, and here too it is economy which provided the impetus to imaginative construction. The late Albert Kahn, engineer and architect of such magnificent structures as the Chrysler Tank Arsenal in Detroit (see Fig. 32), the Olds Foundry at Lansing, Michigan, and many others, stated the matter very clearly in an article written for the *Atlantic Monthly* in 1942. Strict economy must, by the nature of the case, prevail in designing factories, especially those which were then called "defense projects." All non-essentials, everything which is not "purely utilitarian," must be eliminated.

The very observance of this requirement, however, often makes for successful design [Mr. Kahn continued]. As a rule, the most direct and straightforward solution produces the best-looking structure. . . . Just as the mere clothing of the skeleton of a modern airplane by designers with an eye for line and a sense of fitness produces an object of beauty, so the frank expression of the functional, the structural, element of the industrial building makes for success.[5]

The triumph during the second quarter of this century of vernacular forms which emerged from a hundred years of firsthand experiments in patterning the elements of a new environment could be traced in many fields besides construction. In writing, for example, it would be easy to show how the tradition of reportorial journalism which first attained literary quality more than a hundred years ago in Dana's *Two Years Before the Mast* had become, since Mark Twain's time, one of the principal shaping forces in our literature and could be traced as clearly in John Dos Passos' *U.S.A.* trilogy as in John Gunther's *Inside U.S.A.* Indeed, journalism in this sense has become a distinctively American phenomenon. As Georges Bataille

[5] It is interesting to observe how the structural forms of Kahn's steel and glass factories were prefigured seventy years earlier in the temporary wood and glass exhibition building shown in Fig. 19.

said in the critical journal which he publishes in France, writing like John Hersey's account of the atom bomb's aftermath in Hiroshima illustrates a characteristic American effort "to give reportage a foundation of rigorously factual detail" which is almost unknown elsewhere.

In the movies, again, one could observe the origin and development of an almost purely vernacular art form, the direct product of technology and the commercial organization of popular culture. Those who were sensitive to the changing character of our civilization had anticipated something like the movies long before the technical means had been discovered. As early as 1888 David Goodman Croly, newspaper editor and sociologist, wrote a curious book called *Glimpses of the Future* in which—fifty years before publication of *Finnegan's Wake*—he prophesied the disintegration of the novel as an art form and suggested the use of colored pictures (in his day, chromolithographs of course) to take the place of descriptions of people and places, and of phonographs to reproduce the conversations between characters. That was as near as he could come, at that stage of technical development, to foreseeing the Technicolor talking picture. But the point worth noting is that long before movie cameras or color film had been invented those who were aware of the vital forces in the new civilization recognized that the traditional art forms would be superseded by forms appropriate to a technological environment.

A study of the development of the movies, furthermore, would provide a striking example of the interaction between the cultivated and vernacular traditions. Earlier in this book that interaction was discussed in terms of architecture, and we saw how the forms which had been inherited from an older civilization were modified by such vernacular influences as balloon-frame construction. In the case of the movies, however, the process was reversed, and a vernacular form was modified by cultivated influences. In the early stages movies were produced without any conscious aesthetic aim; the men and women who

made them were in the business of providing mass enter-
tainment in a medium which had been created by machines and science. Then, sometime in the twenties, cultivated critics began discussing the films of D. W. Griffith
and Charlie Chaplin as artistic achievements of the first
rank. The movie makers themselves began to wonder if
they weren't artists and shouldn't behave as such, and
artists who had been trained in the techniques of older
art forms like the theater began to move over into movie
making. With the coming of the talking picture in the late
twenties the movies became more and more like photo-
graphed plays, and the confusion between what can properly be called cinema values and those of the theater still
marks much of Hollywood's output in spite of the success
of such movies as *The Informer* and a few of the great
documentary films like Pare Lorentz' *The River*.

The role of the vernacular in creating new art forms
and altering the basis of old ones could be traced, too, in
other fields: in modern dance, in the evolution of the ani-
mated cartoon, of the comic strip, and of the radio serial,
and in the effect of photographic techniques and movie
scenarios upon fiction and poetry. But it is in music, especially in the music loosely known as jazz, that we can
most clearly perceive both the extent to which vernacular
forms and techniques have succeeded in modifying older
traditions and the degree to which the newer forms and
techniques are still limited.

Jazz is a subject about which many people have very
intemperate opinions, and it will be well, for the purposes
of this present discussion, if we can avoid the heated con-
troversies which constantly rage not only between those
who dislike it and those who like it, but even between the
various cults of its admirers. We may as well avoid, in
so far as possible, such bitterly disputed points as the precise relationship between jazz and the music of primitive
African tribes and the extent to which jazz has been improved or degraded by its divergence from the instrumen-

tal music produced by colored bands in New Orleans sporting houses fifty years ago.

To begin with, then, let us agree that by jazz we mean American popular dance music, exclusive of waltzes, *as it has been performed* for the past quarter century or so. By this definition we mean to include not only the spontaneous instrumental or vocal improvising called hot jazz, epitomized by such a performer as Louis Armstrong, but also the carefully rehearsed performances, featuring improvised solos and "breaks," which professional dance bands like Benny Goodman's or Tommy Dorsey's give to everything they play—whether it be Tin Pan Alley tunes composed in the old operetta or ballad traditions, or melodies lifted from western European concert music, or pieces composed by Tin Pan Alley in imitation of hot-jazz improvisations. In this broad sense jazz is a product of the interaction of the vernacular and cultivated traditions, but its distinctive characteristics as a form of musical expression are purely vernacular.

Jazz is fundamentally a performer's art, and in this it marks itself off decisively from the music of the western European tradition. The composer, who is the dominant figure in Western concert music, is of almost no importance to jazz, for in jazz—in its most distinctive form—invention and performance occur simultaneously as the players have their way with the melodic or rhythmic pattern. It is true, of course, that musical improvisation has flourished in other cultures, and that even Western music of the cultivated tradition had its roots in improvisatory processes. But never before have conditions favored the universal availability of a performer art. The emergence of jazz as what might be called the folk music of the American people is inextricably bound up with such technological advances as phonographic recording and radio broadcasting.

Nor is it only in making jazz available that these technological devices have been important. In the early development of jazz, for example, the player piano not only contributed to the dissemination of ragtime (a rhythmic type which popularized many of the elements of jazz) but also imposed certain characteristics of rhythmic precision and even of tonal quality which became distinctive elements of its techniques. Anyone familiar with the playing of accomplished jazz pianists knows how they can use "pianola" style, though usually only for humorous effect in these latter, more sophisticated days. Similarly, the microphone of the recording and broadcasting studios has had its effect upon the instrumental and vocal performance of jazz. The vocal techniques of singers as diverse as Louis Armstrong and Bing Crosby, Bessie Smith and Dinah Shore, have been devised—often with remarkable inventiveness and sensitivity—to exploit the full range of possibilities in the microphone, and it is largely to the microphone's limitations and possibilities that the typical jazz band owes both its characteristic make-up and its distinctive instrumental techniques. Indeed, these techniques have become such an integral part of jazz that it is seldom performed without the use of a microphone even in small quarters like night clubs and even when the band is not on the air.

It was precisely with the beginning of recorded jazz, in 1918 and the years immediately following, that the instrumentation of jazz bands began to undergo the changes which in the early twenties produced the orchestral combination that is still standard. As long as jazz remained a localized phenomenon in the Storyville district of New Orleans, it retained the instrumentation which had first crystallized with Buddy Bolden's band in the 1890s: a combination of trumpet, valve trombone, clarinet, string bass, drums, and banjo. But as it spread to other parts of the country, and as recordings became increasingly popular after the phenomenal success which Victor made with its records by the Original Dixieland Band in 1918, new instruments were added (notably the piano and saxophone) and the balance of instruments within the ensemble underwent important changes. From about 1921 on the standard jazz orchestra has consisted of three units: the brass (trumpets and trombones), the reeds (saxophones and a clarinet), and the rhythm section (piano, guitar or banjo, string bass or tuba, and drums). All kinds of variants have been tried on this basic arrangement; big "symphonic" bands have been organized, and there have been recurrent experiments with various "small band" combinations built around a piano, and even some highly successful trios, quartets, sextets, and so on. But the three-unit instrumentation remains the standard for both hot and sweet (or commercial) bands.

One of the most interesting aspects of jazz instrumentation is that the rhythm section tends to remain intact, whatever variations may be made in the other units. A fifteen-piece band has four men in the rhythm section, and so has an eight-piece band. What this amounts to, of course, is a recognition of the fundamentally rhythmic nature of jazz. For it is its rhythmic structure that distinguishes it from other types of music.

It is precisely this distinctive rhythmic structure which makes jazz such an extraordinarily effective musical form in our civilization, and we will be better able to understand its significance if we acquaint ourselves with the two rhythmic characteristics which give it its special quality.[6] These characteristics are syncopation and polyrhythm.

Syncopation, in the simplest terms, is the upsetting of rhythmic expectation by accenting a normally unstressed beat and depriving a normally stressed beat of its emphasis. As such it is a device which is fairly common in western European music, and consequently people who do not understand jazz frequently assume that jazz performance has merely borrowed a stock effect from traditional music and done it to death. But in a Brahms quartet, for example, syncopation is a special effect, consciously used for its striking qualities, whereas in jazz it is—as Winthrop

[6] Far and away the most useful analysis of jazz as a musical form is that by Winthrop Sargeant in the revised and enlarged edition of his book, *Jazz: Hot and Hybrid*, published in 1946. I draw heavily on Mr. Sargeant's work in this chapter.

Sargeant says—"a basic structural ingredient which permeates the entire musical idiom."

Even so, syncopation by no means accounts for the special nature of jazz. If it did, musicians trained exclusively in the cultivated tradition would produce jazz merely by continuously employing a device with which they are already familiar—whereas all they would actually produce would be *corn*. For in addition to syncopation jazz is characterized by superimposing of conflicting rhythms which creates a peculiar form of polyrhythm. This polyrhythm, as Don Knowlton was apparently the first to recognize, consists of imposing a *one*—two—three rhythmical element upon the fundamental one—two—three—four rhythm which underlies all jazz.

This formula of three-over-four, with its interplay of two different rhythms, seldom is baldly stated in jazz melody, but it almost invariably affects jazz phraseology and gives it its unique stamp. Here, as in the case of syncopation, we are using a term which is familiar in the cultivated tradition of Western music; but, as with syncopation, the term has a distinctive meaning in relation to jazz. As Sargeant points out, the commonest form of polyrhythm in European concert music—two-over-three—*never* appears in jazz, and the almost universal three-over-four of jazz is very rare indeed in Western music. Furthermore, in European polyrhythm there is no upset of normal rhythmic expectation; strong beats remain stressed and no accent is placed upon unstressed beats. But jazz polyrhythm has the effect of displacing accents in somewhat the same way that syncopation does so.

The domination of jazz by these two characteristics means, as Sargeant makes clear, that the relation between jazz rhythms and those of music composed in the western European tradition is "so slight as to be negligible." In other respects, of course, jazz has been strongly influenced by the cultivated tradition. Both its scalar and harmonic structure are largely borrowed or adapted from western

European sources, though even in these aspects jazz has developed certain peculiarities—notably the "barbershop" or "close" harmony which it shares with other types of American music including that of the cowboys and the hillbillies.[7] But rhythmically jazz is a distinctive phenomenon.

The source of jazz polyrhythm is almost certainly to be found in the Afro-American folk music of the Southern Negroes. But from the point of view of our discussion, the important fact is that almost all American popular music, the commercial "sweet" as well as the hot variety, has wholeheartedly adopted both polyrhythm and syncopation, *and that both of these are devices for upsetting expected patterns.* In other words this music which originated in America and spread from there to the rest of the world depends for its distinctive quality upon two rhythmic devices which contribute to a single effect: the interruption of an established pattern of alternation between stressed and unstressed beats.

This interruption of rhythmic regularity in jazz is perhaps most clearly exemplified by the so-called "break" or "hot lick"—the improvised solo bridge passage of two or four measures which frequently fills the interval between two melodic phrases. During the break the fundamental four-four beat is silenced and the solo goes off on its independent rhythmic and melodic tangents, until suddenly the band picks up the basic four-four beat again right where it would have been if it had never been interrupted. The effect is brilliantly described in the following paragraph from Winthrop Sargeant's book:

[7] Sargeant makes a convincing case for the idea that this barbershop harmony is not an echo of the post-Wagnerian chromatic effects of European music, but was developed from the structural characteristics of accompanying instruments like the guitar and banjo. It merely uses the chords you get by sliding the hand up and down the neck of the instrument while holding the fingers in the same relative position. Cf. *Jazz: Hot and Hybrid,* pp. 198–200.

In this process the fundamental rhythm is not really destroyed. The perceptive listener holds in his mind a continuation of its regular pulse even though the orchestra has stopped marking it. . . . The situation during the silent pulses is one that challenges the listener to hold his bearings. . . . If he does not feel the challenge, or is perfectly content to lose himself, then he is one of those who will never understand the appeal of jazz. The challenge is backed up by the chaotic behavior of the solo instrument playing the break. It does everything possible to throw the listener off his guard. It syncopates; it accents everything *but* the normal pulse of the fundamental rhythm. . . . The listener feels all the exhilaration of a battle.

It is essentially this same sort of battle between unexpected, challenging melodic rhythms and the regularity of the fundamental beat which characterizes all jazz. In hot jazz, when almost all the players are improvising all the time and nobody really knows what anybody is going to do next, the exhilaration is more intense than in rehearsed performances spiced with improvised solos and breaks. But the difference is one of degree, not of kind.

Now a musical form which exploits and encourages this kind of free-for-all might logically be expected to be chaotic and disorderly in the extreme. As Louis Armstrong once wrote, you would think "that if every man in a big sixteen-piece band had his own way and could play as he wanted, all you would get would be a lot of jumbled up, crazy noise." And with ordinary performers that is exactly what you would get—which is why most orchestras play from scores in which, with varying degrees of success, an arranger has incorporated hot phrasing. But, as Armstrong concludes, when you have "a real bunch of swing players" they can pick up and follow one another's improvisations "all by ear and sheer musical instinct." It is the essence of good jazz performance to be able to cut loose from the score, and to know—or feel—"just when to leave it and when to get back on it."

Benny Goodman, explaining the basis of organization for the famous band he got together in 1934, put the matter thus: what he wanted was, first of all, "a good rhythm section that would kick out, or jump, or rock or swing," and secondly, musical arrangements that would be adequate vehicles for such a rhythmic section and at the same time would "give the men a chance to play solos and express the music in their own individual way." In other words, Goodman intuitively recognized that it is the rhythmic structure of jazz which reconciles the demands of group performance (the arrangement) and individual expression (the solos).

What we have here, then, is an art form which within its own well-recognized limits comes closer than any other we have devised to reconciling the conflict which Emerson long ago recognized as the fundamental problem in modern civilization—the conflict between the claims of the individual and of the group. Everybody in a first-class jazz band seems to be—and has all the satisfaction of feeling that he is—going his own way, uninhibited by a prescribed musical pattern, and at the same time all are performing in a dazzlingly precise creative unison. The thing that holds them together is the very thing they are all so busy flouting: the fundamental four-four beat. In this one artistic form, if nowhere else, Americans have found a way to give expression to the Emersonian ideal of a union which is perfect only "when all the uniters are isolated."

By its resolution of this basic conflict jazz relates itself intimately with the industrial society out of which it evolved. The problems with which Armstrong and Goodman are concerned have much less to do with the problems of the artist, in the traditional sense, than with those of industrial organization. It is not in traditional art criticism that we will find comparable values expressed, but in passages like this from Frederick Winslow Taylor's *Principles of Scientific Management,* published just seven years before the first jazz recordings were issued:

> The time is fast going by for the great personal or individual achievement of any one man standing alone and without the help of those around him. And the time is coming when all great things will be done by that type of cooperation in which each man performs the function for which he is best suited, each man preserves his own individuality and is supreme in his particular function, and each man at the same time loses none of his originality and proper personal initiative, and yet is controlled by and must work harmoniously with many other men.

In other ways, also, jazz relates itself to the vernacular tradition out of which it came. Like all the patterns which that tradition has created, it is basically a very simple form. Harmonically it is little more than the repetition of four or five extremely simple and rather monotonous chord sequences. Melodically, it consists of the repetition of extremely simple tunes which, however lovely or amusing they may often be, are not subject to elaborate development, as are the themes of western European music. They may be worried and fooled with in hot solos till they are practically dismantled, but they are not thematically developed. Finally, even in its rhythm, where jazz displays so much ingenuity, it is restricted to four-four or two-four time.

As a musical form, then, jazz is so simple as scarcely to be a form at all. The "piece" being played always has, of course, at least an elementary formal pattern—a beginning, middle, and end; but the jazz performance as such usually does not. It merely starts and then—after an interval which has probably been determined more by the duration of phonograph records than anything else—it stops. But this structural simplicity accords with the other vernacular characteristics that jazz displays. The polyrhythmic and syncopated flights of hot solos and breaks, with their abrupt, impulsive adjustments to ever-changing rhythmic situations, give jazz an extraordinary flexibility; but they could exist only in a simple, firmly established musical framework. Similarly, it is the structural simplicity of jazz which makes it, like other vernacular forms and patterns, so suitable for mass participation and enjoyment and so universally available.

In these terms one can understand Le Corbusier's brilliantly perceptive observation that the skyscrapers of Manhattan are "hot jazz in stone and steel." Jazz and the skyscrapers! It is these two, and jazz in a "more advanced" form than the other, which to one of the world's greatest living architects and city planners "represent the forces of today." And both, as we have seen, are climactic achievements of the vernacular tradition in America. Neither implies anything resembling the cultivated tradition's negation of or contempt for the actualities of a civilization founded upon technology and shaped by democratic political and social institutions. (It is no mere coincidence that in Nazi Germany and Communist Russia, and wherever authoritarian regimes have existed, the men in power have attempted to discourage if they have not forbidden the performance of jazz.)

Let it be clear that in making these points we are not implying the aesthetic superiority of jazz over western European music or of Rockefeller Center and the McGraw-Hill Building over the cathedrals of Chartres and Salisbury. Such comparative valuations have no place in the context of this book, whether or not they have validity elsewhere. Judged strictly in its own terms, jazz is admittedly limited in its emotional range. Like other vernacular forms, notably journalism and radio serials, it is pretty much restricted to moods of humor, sentimental sadness, and sexual excitement; it is difficult to conceive of a jazz performance which would evoke the moods of tragedy, of awe, or of spiritual exaltation which are found in the masterpieces of western European music. Furthermore, there is some question whether jazz is capable of evolutionary development. To many critics it seems that jazz today is in all essential respects precisely what it was at the moment when it emerged from the New Orleans sporting houses to sweep the country. Others might agree with the present writer that works like George Gershwin's *An American in Paris* and parts of his score for *Porgy and Bess,* and more recent works like Robert McBride's *Quintet for Oboe and Strings,* give evidence of an evolutionary process whereby the vernacular jazz tradition interacts creatively with the cultivated tradition, losing none of the former's vitality and immediate relevance but greatly augmenting its expressive range.

Certainly skyscraper architecture at its best owes more than a little of its success to cultivated influences which have modified its vernacular qualities. But the essential fact is that both of these forms fully acknowledge their vernacular roots. Both are forms of artistic expression which have evolved out of patterns originally devised by people without conscious aesthetic purpose or cultivated preconceptions, in direct, empirical response to the conditions of their everyday environment.

It is clear that these vernacular forms and the others we have touched upon in this essay do not—by themselves— yet offer a medium of artistic expression adequate to all our needs. Forms inherited from an older tradition still must play an important role if we are not to be aesthetically starved, or at least undernourished. Opera and poetic drama, for example, may be as moribund as their most candid critics assert, but there will inevitably be periodic attempts to rejuvenate them. And such attempts will be made not only because of the cultural (and social) prestige which attaches to these and many other heirlooms of the cultivated tradition but also because we cannot yet afford to let them die.

Meanwhile the techniques and forms of the vernacular are rapidly attaining widespread influence and prestige, and their popularity throughout the world serves to remind us once again that it is not their specifically American quality, in any nationalistic sense, which gives them their fateful significance. The products of the vernacular in America do, of course, bear the stamp of the national character, just as the artistic achievements of other peoples display certain national characteristics. But these are superficial features. The important thing about the vernacular is that it possesses inherent qualities of vitality and adaptability, of organic as opposed to static form, of energy rather than repose, that are particularly appropriate to the civilization which, during the brief life span of the United States, has transformed the world. By an accident of historical development it was in America that this tradition had the greatest freedom to develop its distinctive characteristics. It should, however, temper any undue nationalistic pride which that fact might induce in us, to remind ourselves that people in other lands have sometimes been more ready than we to appreciate the human and aesthetic values of vernacular modes of expression. Foreign movies have, after all, frequently surpassed ours in creative realization of the cinema's potentialities, and European and South American architects sometimes seem to be more alive than our own to the expressive possibilities of vernacular construction.

As a nation we have often been hesitant and apologetic about whatever has been made in America in the vernacular tradition. Perhaps the time has come when more of us are ready to accept the challenge offered to the creative imagination by the techniques and forms which first arose among our own people in our own land.

List of Sources and References

The following chapter-by-chapter list includes A: *books* and articles quoted or mentioned in the text, arranged alphabetically by author, if the author's name appears in the text, or otherwise by subject; *and* B: a selection of books and articles which, though not specifically quoted or referred to, were directly useful to the writer and which may be of interest to the reader. [A few titles have been added, covering the revisions in the paperback edition; but no attempt has been made to bring the bibliography up to date.]

1. ART IN AMERICA

A. SOURCES QUOTED OR MENTIONED

Beard, Charles, "Is Western Civilization in Peril?" *Harper's Magazine*, August 1928.

Burke, Kenneth, *Counter-Statement*, New York, 1931.

Fiske, John, *The Beginning of New England*, Boston, 1889.

Hall, James: see John T. Flanagan, *James Hall*, Minneapolis [1941].

Hubbell, Jay B., "The Frontier," *The Reinterpretation of American Literature*, edited by Norman Foerster, New York [1928].

James, Henry, *The American Scene*, New York, 1907.

Longfellow, Henry Wadsworth, *Kavanagh: A Tale*, Boston, 1849.

Lowell, James Russell, *The Bigelow Papers*, 2d Series, Boston, 1867.

——, *A Fable for Critics*, Boston, 1848.

——, "Leaves from My Journal in Italy," *Graham's Magazine*, April, May, and June 1854.

Mackay, Alexander, *The Western World,* 2 vols., Philadelphia, 1849.

Marryat, Captain Frederick, *Diary in America,* 3 vols., London, 1839.

Martineau, Harriet, *Retrospect of Western Travel,* 2 vols., New York, 1838.

——, *Society in America,* 3 vols., London, 1837.

Richards, I. A., *Science and Poetry,* New York, 1926.

Sherman, Stuart P., *The Genius of America,* New York, 1923.

Trollope, Frances, *Domestic Manners of the Americans,* 2 vols., London, 1832.

B. ADDITIONAL REFERENCES

Brooks, J. G., *As Others See Us,* New York, 1908.

Burlingame, Roger, *The March of the Iron Men,* New York, 1938.

Kouwenhoven, John A., "Arts in America," *Atlantic Monthly,* August 1941 (the first statement of the general theory which this book explores).

Mumford, Lewis, *The Culture of Cities,* New York, 1938.

——, *The Golden Day: A Study in American Experience and Culture,* New York, 1926.

Nevins, Allan, *American Social History as Recorded by British Travellers,* New York, 1923.

Polanyi, Karl, *The Great Transformation,* New York, 1944.

Rourke, Constance, *The Roots of American Culture and Other Essays,* edited by Van Wyck Brooks, New York [1942].

2 . WHAT IS VERNACULAR?

A . SOURCES QUOTED OR MENTIONED

American watches—comparative tests: Edward Knight, "Clocks and Watches," *Reports of the United States*

Commissioners to the Paris Universal Exposition, *1878*, Washington, 1880, Vol. IV.

Anderson, William, "Railway Apparatus," *Reports of the United States Commissioners to the Paris Universal Exposition, 1878*, Washington, 1880, Vol. IV.

Arnold, H. L., and Faurote, F. L., *Ford Methods and Ford Shops*, New York, 1915.

Atlantic Monthly, September 1876.

Barnard, Charles, "English and American Locomotives," *Harper's Monthly Magazine*, March 1879.

Bartholdi, Frédéric Auguste: see Robert Stowe Holding, *George H. Corliss of Rhode Island*, The Newcommen Society of England, American Branch, New York, 1945.

Burlingame, Roger, *The March of the Iron Men*, New York, 1938.

Centennial, member of German delegation to: see Siegfried Giedion, "American Development in Design," *New Directions 1939*.

Centennial, typical account: *Souvenir of the Centennial Exhibition*, Hartford, 1877.

Collins plow: see Horace Greeley and Others, *The Great Industries of the United States*, Hartford, 1873, p. 139.

Colt, Samuel: Charles T. Haven and Frank A. Belden, *The History of the Colt Revolver*, New York, 1940; Bernard De Voto, *The Year of Decision*, Boston, 1943, pp. 215–16; and Jack Rohan, *Yankee Arms Maker*, New York [1948].

Cooper, James Fenimore, *Notions of the Americans: Picked up by a Travelling Bachelor* (first published 1828), New York, 1850.

Crystal Palace: see *Great Exhibition, 1851. Official Descriptive and Illustrated Catalogue*, 3 vols., London, 1851.

Durfee, W. F., report on Pratt and Whitney machines in *United States Centennial Commission, Reports and Awards, Group XXI*, Philadelphia, 1877.

Evans, Oliver, *The Young Mill-Wright and Miller's Guide*, 5th ed., Philadelphia, 1826, pp. 201–10, 275–77. See also: Greville and Dorothy Bathe, *Oliver Evans*, Philadelphia, 1935.

Flint, Charles L., "Agriculture in the United States," *Eighty Years Progress of the United States*, New York and Chicago [1861].

Ford, Henry (in collaboration with Samuel Crowther), *My Life and Work*, New York, 1923.

Fritz, John: see F. B. Copley, *Frederick W. Taylor, Father of Scientific Management*, 2 vols., New York, 1923, Vol. 1, p. 110.

Giedion, Siegfried, *Mechanization Takes Command*, New York, 1948.

Hall, James: see John T. Flanagan, *James Hall*, Minneapolis [1941].

Josiah Allen's Wife as a P.A. and P.I.: Samantha at the Centennial [by Marietta Holley], Hartford, 1877.

Lewis, H. L. B.: advertisement reproduced in Edward Hungerford, *From Covered Wagon to Streamliner*, New York [1941].

London *Times*, August 22, 1878.

Mackinnon, Captain, "English and American Ocean Steamers," *Harper's Monthly Magazine*, July 1853.

Manufacturer and Builder, Vol. VIII, No. 6, June 1876.

Martineau, Harriet, *Retrospect of Western Travel*, 2 vols., New York, 1838. (Vol. 2, p. 45.)

Mauritius *Commercial Gazeteer*: see Carl C. Cutler, *Greyhounds of the Sea*, New York [1930].

McHardy, David: *United States Centennial Commission, Reports and Awards, Group XV*, Philadelphia, 1877.

McKay, Donald: see Carl C. Cutler, *Greyhounds of the Sea*, New York [1930].

Monroe, Harriet, *A Poet's Life; Seventy Years in a Changing World*, New York, 1938.

Pendred, Vaughan, *The Railway Locomotive*, New York, 1908.

Porter, William T., "Machines and Machine Tools," *Reports of the United States Commissioners to the Paris Universal Exposition, 1878*, Washington, 1880, Vol. IV.

Randall, G. P.: advertisement in *Vermont Watchman and State Journal*, Montpelier, January 15, 1846.

Richards, John, *Treatise on the Construction and Operation of Woodworking Machinery*, London, 1872.

Roe, Joseph W., "Early American Mechanics—Philadelphia," *American Machinist*, December 17, 1914.

Royal Small Arms factory at Enfield: see Hubbard (below under B).

Scientific American Supplement, No. 19, May 6, 1876.

Sellers, William: see F. B. Copley, *Frederick W. Taylor, Father of Scientific Management*, 2 vols., New York, 1923, Vol. 1, p. 110.

"Shreve, Henry Miller," *Democratic Review*, Vol. XXII, No. CXVI, February 1848. For a recent scholarly evaluation of Shreve's work, see Louis C. Hunter, *Steamboats on the Western Rivers*, Cambridge, 1949, pp. 15–17, 75–76, and 127.

Steel spade used by member of the American Institute: see *Transactions of the American Institute of the City of New York for the Year 1854*, Albany, 1855, pp. 231–32.

Steers, George: see Carl C. Cutler, *Greyhounds of the Sea*, New York [1930].

Stevenson, David, *Sketch of the Civil Engineering of North America*, London, 1838.

True Guide: *The British Mechanic's and Labourer's Handbook, and True Guide to the United States*, London, 1840.

Whitney, Eli: see Jeanette Mirsky and Allan Nevins, *The World of Eli Whitney*, New York, 1952; and also Robert S. Woodbury, "The Legend of Eli Whitney and Interchangeable Parts," *Technology and Culture*, Summer, 1960.

Willis, Robert, *The Principles of Mechanism*, London, 1841.

Wilson, Joseph M., "The Mechanics and Science of the Centennial Exhibition," *The Masterpieces of the Centennial Exhibition*, 3 vols., Philadelphia [1877].

B.   ADDITIONAL REFERENCES

Alexander, E. P., *Iron Horses. American Locomotives 1829–1900*, New York [1941].

Art and Industry as Represented in the Exhibition at the Crystal Palace, New York—1853–54, revised and edited by Horace Greeley, New York, 1853.

Bishop, J. L., *A History of American Manufactures from 1608 to 1860*, 3 vols., Philadelphia, 1866.

Burlingame, Roger, *Machines That Built America*, New York [1953].

Butterworth, Benjamin, *The Growth of Industrial Art*, Washington, 1892.

Clark, Arthur H., *The Clipper Ship Era*, New York, 1910.

Clark, Victor S., *History of Manufactures in the United States*, 3 vols., New York, 1929 (especially Vol. 1, Chapters XVI and XIX).

Dorsey, Edward B., *English and American Railroads Compared*, New York, 1887.

Eighty Years Progress of the United States (by various authors), New York and Chicago, 1861.

Galton, Douglas, report to British commission on American railroads, *United States Centennial Commission, Reports and Awards, Group XVIII*, Philadelphia, 1877.

Howe, Henry, *Memoirs of the Most Eminent American Mechanics*, New York, 1844.

Hubbard, Guy, "Development of Machine Tools in New England," *American Machinist*, August 30, 1923, and January 24, 1924.

Hubbel, William Wheeler, "First Eight-Wheel Locomotive," appendix to Charles B. Stuart, *Lives and Works of Civil and Military Engineers of America*, New York, 1871.

Knight, Edward H., *Knight's American Mechanical Dictionary*, New York, 1875.

———, *Knight's New Mechanical Dictionary*, Boston, 1884.

———, "Mechanical Progress," *The First Century of the Republic*, New York, 1876.

Mumford, Lewis, *Technics and Civilization*, New York, 1934.

Riddle, Edward, "Report on the World's Exposition," *Report of the Commissioner of Patents for the Year 1851. Part I. Arts and Manufactures*, Washington, 1852, pp. 347–485.

Roe, Joseph W., *English and American Tool Builders*, New York, 1926.

White, George S., *Memoir of Samuel Slater*, Philadelphia, 1836.

8. TWO TRADITIONS IN CONFLICT

A. SOURCES QUOTED OR MENTIONED

Allen, Lewis F., *Rural Architecture. Being a Complete Description of Farm Houses, Cottages, and Out Buildings, etc.*, New York, 1852.

Appleton's Journal, April 10, 1869 (on iron architecture, p. 58).

Balloon frame denounced: S. B. Reed, *House-Plans for Everybody*, New York, 1879, pp. 73–74.

Bancroft, Hubert H., *The Book of the Fair*, 2 vols., Chicago, 1893.

Beecher, Catherine E., and Stowe, Harriet Beecher, *The American Woman's Home*, New York, 1869.

Bode, Wilhelm: see Siegfried Giedion, *Space, Time and Architecture*, Cambridge, Mass., 1941, pp. 285–90.

Bogardus, James: see Carl Condit, *American Building Art*, New York, 1960, pp. 33–38. See also J. A. Kouwenhoven, *The Columbia Historical Portrait of New York*, 1953, pp. 244 and 493.

Bridges, Lyman: see James H. Bowen, "Report upon Buildings, Building Materials, and Methods of Building," *Reports of the United States Commissioners to the Paris Universal Exposition, 1867*, Washington, 1869.

Browne, D. J., "Construction of Farm Cottages," *Sixth Annual Report of the American Institute*, Albany, 1848.

Clarke, Thomas C., "American Iron Bridges," *Scientific American Supplement, No. 32*, August 5, 1876.

Ducker Portable House Co., *Illustrated Catalogue. Ducker Portable Houses*, New York [1888].

Dwyer, C. P., *The Immigrant Builder; or, Practical Hints to Handy-men*, Philadelphia, 1872.

Eads bridge: see Steinman and Watson, *Bridges and Their Builders*, New York [1941].

Emerson's farmer-neighbor on wooden houses: see R. W. Emerson, "Agriculture in Massachusetts," in *Natural History of Intellect and Other Papers*, Boston, 1893, pp. 221–22.

Etzler, John Adolphus, *The Paradise Within the Reach of All Men, Without Labor, by Powers of Nature and Machinery*, Pittsburgh, 1833, pp. 65–67.

Etzler (of England): T. De Witt Talmage, *The Abominations of Modern Society*, New York, 1872.

Ferguson, James, quoted in *Scientific American Supplement, No. 11*, March 11, 1876.

Field, Walker, "A Re-examination into the Invention of the Balloon Frame," *Journal of the American Society of Architectural Historians*, Vol. 2, No. 4, October 1942.

Fowler, Orson S., *A Home for All, or, The Gravel Wall and Octagon Mode of Building* (original ed. 1849), New York, 1854.

Gems of the Centennial Exhibition, New York, 1877.

Giedion, Siegfried, *Space, Time and Architecture*, Cambridge, Mass., 1941.

Great Industries of the United States, The (by Horace Greeley and Others), Hartford, 1873.

Hamlin, Talbot, *Architecture Through the Ages*, New York [1940].

Hunt, Richard Morris, "Architecture," *United States Centennial Commission, Reports and Awards, Group XXVI*, Philadelphia, 1877.

Industrial Chicago, 6 vols., Chicago, 1891–96, Vols. 1 and 2.

Iron fronts: see George W. Howard, *The Monumental City, its past history and present resources*, Baltimore, 1873; *Fifth Annual Review of the Commerce, Manufactures, and the Public and Private Improvements of Chicago, for the Year 1856*, Chicago, The Democratic Press, 1857, pp. 7–8; and *The St. Louis Riverfront. An Exhibition of Architectural Studies*, St. Louis Public Library, 1938.

Kettell, Thomas P., "Buildings and Building Material," *Eighty Years Progress of the United States*, New York and Chicago, 1861.

Klondike. The Chicago Record's Book for Gold Seekers, Boston, 1897.

Lafever, Minard, *The Architectural Instructor*, New York, 1856.

New and Complete American Encyclopaedia; or, Universal Dictionary of Arts and Seiences, The, New York, 1805–11, Vol. 1, p. 504.

Parton, James, *Triumphs of Enterprise, Ingenuity, and Public Spirit*, New York, 1872, p. 55.

Pope, Thomas: see David B. Steinman and Sara Ruth Watson, *Bridges and Their Builders*, New York [1941], pp. 116–17.

Putnam's Magazine, March 1854 ("New York Daguerreotyped").

Reed, S. B., *House-Plans for Everybody*, New York, 1879.

Robinson, Solon, "How to Build a Balloon House," *Transactions of the American Institute of the City of New York for the Year 1854*, Albany, 1855.

Roebling, John A.: quoted in Steinman and Watson, *Bridges and Their Builders*, New York [1941]. See also Hamilton Schuyler, *The Roeblings: A Century of Engineers, Bridge-Builders and Industrialists*, Princeton, 1931.

Ruskin, John, *The Seven Lamps of Architecture* (originally published 1849), New York, 1871.

Skillings, D. N., and Flint, D. B., *Illustrated Catalogue of Portable Sectional Buildings*, Boston and New York [1862].

Stevenson, David, *Sketch of the Civil Engineering of North America*, London, 1838, pp. 192–95.

Sullivan, Louis, *Kindergarten Chats and Other Writings*, New York, 1947.

Sullivan, Louis, to Claude Bragdon: see Claude Bragdon, *More Lives than One*, New York, 1938.

[Thoreau, Henry], "A Mechanical Utopia," *Democratic Review*, November 1843.

Vaux, Calvert, *Villas and Cottages*, New York, 1857.

Wahl, William H., *Building and Engineering* [no place, no date], Arts and Sciences Publishing Co. (Internal evidence indicates a date circa 1889.)

Washington, George, *The Writings of George Washington*, edited by Jared Sparks, Boston, 1838, Vol. IX, p. 115.

Woodward, G. E. and F. W., *Woodward's Country Homes*, New York, 1866.

Woollett, William M., *Old Homes Made New*, New York, 1878.

Wright's Suntop Homes: Henry-Russell Hitchcock, *In the Nature of Materials. The Buildings of Frank Lloyd Wright*, New York, 1942.

B. ADDITIONAL REFERENCES

Coolidge, John, *Mill and Mansion, A Study of Architecture and Society in Lowell, Massachusetts, 1820–1865*, New York, 1942.

Hamlin, Talbot, *Greek Revival Architecture in America*,

New York, 1944 (especially Appendix A, "The
American Development of Greek-Inspired Forms,"
pp. 339–55).

Jarves, James Jackson, *The Art Idea: Sculpture, Painting,
and Architecture in America*, New York, 1864.

Mumford, Lewis, *The Brown Decades*, New York [1931].

Schuyler, Montgomery, *American Architecture*, New York,
1892.

——, "Glimpses of Western Architecture," *Harper's
Monthly Magazine*, August 1891.

Tallmadge, Thomas E., *The Story of Architecture in
America*, rev. ed., New York [1936].

4.   THE PRACTICAL AND THE AESTHETIC

A.   SOURCES QUOTED OR MENTIONED

Abbey, E. A.: see E. V. Lucas, *Edwin Austin Abbey*, New
York, 1921.

Benjamin, S. G. W., "Fifty Years of American Art,"
Harper's Monthly Magazine, October 1879.

——, "Present Tendencies of American Art," *Harper's
Monthly Magazine*, March 1879.

Benson, Eugene, "Museums of Art as a Means of Instruction," *Appleton's Journal*, January 15, 1870.

Blake, J. L., *The Family Encyclopedia*, New York, 1834
(article on "Taste").

[Curtis, George W.], "The Editor's Easy Chair," *Harper's
Monthly Magazine*, April 1876.

Ellsworth, William H., *A Golden Age of Authors*, Boston, 1919.

Greenough, Horatio, "American Architecture," *Democratic
Review*, August 1843 (not identical with chapter
on same subject in *The Travels, Observations, etc.*,
see below).

——, and Emerson: see *The Letters of Ralph Waldo*

Emerson, ed. by Ralph L. Rusk, New York, 1939, Vol. IV, p. 312.

——, *Letters of Horatio Greenough to His Brother Henry Greenough*, edited by Frances B. Greenough, Boston, 1887.

——, "Remarks on American Art," *Democratic Review*, July 1843 (not identical with the material included in *The Travels, Observations, etc.*, see below).

——, *The Travels, Observations, and Experience of a Yankee Stonecutter*, by Horace Bender, New York, 1852.

Harper's Bazaar, July 1, 1876.

Hone, Philip, *The Diary of Philip Hone*, edited by Allan Nevins, New York, 1936.

Howells, William Dean, *Criticism and Fiction*, New York, 1891.

Jarves, James Jackson, *The Art Idea: Sculpture, Painting, and Architecture in America*, New York, 1864.

Jig saw: see "Fret-Sawing and Woodcarving," *Harper's Monthly Magazine*, March 1878.

Johnson, Robert Underwood, *Remembered Yesterdays*, Boston, 1923.

Lathrop, George Parsons, "The Study of Art in Boston," *Harper's Monthly Magazine*, May 1879.

Lourdelet, M., "Industries and Commercial Machinery of the United States," translated from the French and printed in the report of U. S. Consul Frank H. Mason, Marseilles, May 10, 1884, *Reports from the Consuls of the United States*, No. 42, June 1884, Washington, D.C.

Pomological Annex at Centennial: see Thompson Wescott, *Centennial Portfolio*, Philadelphia, 1876, p. 12.

Simonin, L., *A French View of the Grand International Exposition of 1876*, translated from the *Revue des Deux Mondes* by Samuel H. Needles, Philadelphia, 1877.

Smith, Walter, "Industrial Art," *The Masterpieces of the Centennial Exhibition*, Philadelphia [1877], Vol. II.

Tryon, Dwight W.: see Henry C. White, *The Life and Art of Dwight William Tryon*, New York, 1930.

Tuckerman, Henry T., *American Artist Life*, New York, 1870.

B. ADDITIONAL REFERENCES

Benjamin, S. G. W., "American Art Since the Centennial," *New Princeton Review*, Vol. IV, 1887.

Clarke, I. E., "Art and Industrial Education," *Education in the United States*, edited by Nicholas Murray Butler, Albany, 1900, Vol. II.

Jarves, James Jackson, *Art Hints*, New York, 1869.

LaFollette, Suzanne, *Art in America*, New York, 1929.

Oppé, A. P., "Art," *Early Victorian England, 1830–1865*, edited by G. M. Young, 2 vols., London, 1934.

5. THE FIGURE IN THE CARPET

A. SOURCES QUOTED OR MENTIONED

Downing, Alexander J., *The Architecture of Country Houses . . . with Remarks on Interiors, Furniture, etc.*, New York, 1850.

"Editor's Table," *Harper's Monthly Magazine*, August 1859.

Emerson, Ralph Waldo, "Art," *Essays, First Series*, Boston, 1841.

———, *The Conduct of Life*, Boston, 1860.

Great Industries of the United States, The (by Horace Greeley and Others), Hartford, 1873.

[Holley, Marietta], *Josiah Allen's Wife as a P.A. and P.I.: Samantha at the Centennial*, Hartford, 1877.

Humphreys, Mary Gay, "The Progress of American Decorative Art" (from the London *Art Journal*), *Household Art*, edited by Candace Wheeler, New York, 1893.

Illustrated London News, June 17, 1876.

Nordhoff, Charles, *The Communistic Societies of the United States*, New York, 1875.

Poe, Edgar Allan, "The Philosophy of Furniture," *Burton's Gentleman's Magazine*, May 1840.

Shaker laundry at Canterbury: see J. W. Meader, *The Merrimack River: Its Sources and Tributaries*, Boston, 1869.

[Stephens, Ann S.], *High Life in New York*, Philadelphia, 1854.

Twain, Mark, *Life on the Mississippi*, New York, 1883.

Whitman, Walt, *The Uncollected Poetry and Prose of Walt Whitman*, edited by Emory Holloway, Garden City, 1921, Vol. II, pp. 311–12.

Wyatt, Sir Matthew Digby, *Industrial Arts of the Nineteenth Century*, London, 1853.

B. ADDITIONAL REFERENCES

Gilman, Roger, "The Romantic Interior," *Romanticism in America*, edited by George Boas, Baltimore, 1940.

Morse, Florence, "About Furnishings," *Household Art*, edited by Candace Wheeler, New York, 1893.

Robsjohn-Gibbings, T. H., *Good-bye, Mr. Chippendale*, New York, 1944.

Wharton, Edith, and Codman, Ogden, *The Decoration of Houses*, New York, 1897.

6. TO MAKE ALL THINGS NEW

A. SOURCES QUOTED OR MENTIONED

Appleton's Journal ("Table Talk"), April 3, 1869.
——, ("Table Talk"), July 10, 1869.
Barnum, P. T., *Struggles and Triumphs*, Buffalo, 1872.
Brown, Herbert Ross, *The Sentimental Novel in America, 1789–1860*, Durham, N.C., 1940.
Brownson, Orestes, "Origin and Ground of Government," *Democratic Review*, August 1843.

Burlesque writer: see Walter Blair, "Burlesques in Nineteenth-Century American Humor," *American Literature*, November 1930.

Byles, Mather, "Bombastic and Grubstreet Style," *American Magazine and Historical Chronicle*, January 1745.

Carlyle, Thomas: see *The Correspondence of Thomas Carlyle and Ralph Waldo Emerson*, 2 vols., Boston, 1888.

Channing, William Ellery, "Honor Due to All Men," *The Works of William E. Channing*, new and complete ed., Boston, 1875.

——, "The Present Age" (1841), Ibid.

——, "Remarks on National Literature," Ibid.

Chase, Dr. A. W., *Dr. Chase's Recipes; or, Information for Everybody* ("Seventy-third edition"), Ann Arbor, Mich., 1876.

Crockett, Davy: see Constance Rourke, *Davy Crockett*, New York, 1934.

Crowe, Pat, *Pat Crowe. His Story, Confession and Reformation*, New York, G. W. Dillingham Co. [1906].

Drake, Daniel, *A Systematic treatise, historical, etiological, and practical, on the principal diseases of the interior valley of North America, etc.*, 2 vols., Cincinnati, 1850.

Drake, Daniel: see Charles D. Drake's introduction to Daniel Drake, *Pioneer Life in Kentucky*, Cincinnati, 1870; Ralph L. Rusk, *The Literature of the Middle Western Frontier*, New York, 1926, Vol. I, pp. 206–07; and Geddes Smith, *Plague on Us*, New York, The Commonwealth Fund, 1943.

Eggleston, Edward, *The Circuit Rider*, New York, 1874.

Emerson, Ralph Waldo, "Art," *Essays*, Boston, 1841.

——, *The Journals*, edited by Edward Waldo Emerson and Waldo Emerson Forbes, 12 vols., Boston, 1909–12.

——, *Representative Men*, Boston, 1850.

Fuller, Margaret: see Ossoli, below.

Garland, Hamlin, *A Son of the Middle Border*, New York, 1917.

Goodrich, S. G., "The Peddler. A Chapter from an Unpublished Romance," *Cyclopaedia of Wit and Humor*, edited by W. E. Burton, 2 vols., New York, 1857.

Great Industries of the United States, The (by Horace Greeley and Others), Hartford, 1873.

Hill, Thomas E., *Hill's Manual of Social and Business Forms* (Thirty-ninth edition), Chicago, 1883.

Howells, William Dean, *Criticism and Fiction*, New York, 1891.

Jemison, Mary: James E. Seaver, *A Narrative of the Life of Mrs. Mary Jemison*, 1824 (and many subsequent editions; see *The Colophon*, Part Seven, 1931).

Kerr, Orpheus C.: see Rourke, Constance, *American Humor*, below.

Lippard, George, *New York: Its Upper Ten and Lower Million*, Cincinnati, 1854.

Longfellow, Henry Wadsworth: see Lawrance Thompson, *Young Longfellow*, New York, 1938.

Lowell, James Russell, "Emerson the Lecturer," *The Complete Writings of James Russell Lowell*, 16 vols., Boston, 1904.

Lutes, Della T., "We Had a Book," *Saturday Review of Literature*, November 27, 1937.

[J. Milton Mackie], "Forty Days in a Western Hotel," *Putnam's Magazine*, December, 1854. This was later revised and included in his book *From Cape Cod to Dixie and the Tropics*, New York, 1864.

Melville, Herman, "Hawthorne and His Mosses," *Literary World*, August 17, August 24, 1850.

——, *Israel Potter*, New York, 1855.

——, letter to Abraham Lansing, January 2, 1877, in *Family Correspondence of Herman Melville*, edited by V. H. Paltsits, New York Public Library, 1929.

Mencken, H. L., *The American Language*, 4th ed., New York, 1945; and *The American Language. Supplement I*, New York, 1945.

Olson, Charles, *Call Me Ishmael*, New York [1947].

Ossoli, Margaret Fuller, *Woman in the Nineteenth Century and Kindred Papers*, Boston, 1855 (review of *Ellen: or, Forgive and Forget*, pp. 269–75).

Poe, Edgar Allan, letter to Charles Anthon: see Arthur Hobson Quinn, *Edgar Allan Poe*, New York, 1941.

——, review of Hawthorne's *Twice-Told Tales* and *Mosses from an Old Manse*, in *Godey's Lady's Book*, November 1847.

Rourke, Constance, *American Humor*, New York, 1931.

——, "The Shakers," *The Roots of American Culture and Other Essays*, edited by Van Wyck Brooks, New York [1942].

Rusk, Ralph L., *The Literature of the Middle Western Frontier*, 2 vols., New York, 1926.

Schlesinger, Arthur M., Jr., *The Age of Jackson*, Boston, 1945.

Scott, Walter, *The Messiahship, or Great Demonstration, Written for the Union of Christians, etc.*, Cincinnati, 1860.

Scott, Walter: see A. S. Hayden, *Early History of the Disciples in the Western Reserve*, Cincinnati, 1876.

Sedgwick, Catharine Maria, "Our Village Post Office," *The Token*, Boston, 1838.

——, *The Poor Rich Man and the Rich Poor Man*, New York, 1836.

Simms, William Gilmore, "Dedication" (dated September 1856) of *The Wigwam and the Cabin*, 1857.

Sinclair, Upton, "Letters to Editor," *Atlantic Monthly*, October 1946, p. 29.

Turner, Frederick Jackson, *The Frontier in American History*, New York, 1920.

Twain, Mark, *Mark Twain's Letters*, edited by Albert Bigelow Paine, 2 vols., New York, 1917.

Whitman, Walt, "Democratic Vistas," *Complete Prose Works*, Philadelphia, 1892.

———, "Elias Hicks," Ibid.

———, "Specimen Days," Ibid.

Winslow, Ola Elizabeth, "Books for the Lady Reader," *Romanticism in America*, edited by George Boas, Baltimore, 1940.

Yankee Smith's American Broad Grins, No. I, London, R. MacDonald [no date].

B. ADDITIONAL REFERENCES

Blair, Walter, *Native American Humor*, New York [1937].

Blegen, Theodore E., *Grass Roots History*, Minneapolis [1947].

Case, Victoria and Robert Ormond, *We Called It Culture. The Story of Chautauqua*, New York, 1948.

De Voto, Bernard, *Mark Twain's America*, Boston, 1932.

Holbrook, Stewart, *Lost Men of American History*, New York, 1946.

Horner, Charles F., *The Life of James Redpath and the Development of the Modern Lyceum*, New York, 1926.

Kittredge, George L., *The Old Farmer and His Almanack*, Boston, 1904.

Matthiessen, F. O., *American Renaissance*, New York [1941].

McLean, J. P., *A Bibliography of Shaker Literature*, Columbus, O., 1905.

Pond, F. E., *Life and Adventures of "Ned Buntline,"* 1919.

7. SEEING IS BELIEVING

A. SOURCES QUOTED OR MENTIONED

Alcott, Louisa M., *Little Women*, Boston, 1868.

Art Journal, 1876 ("Paintings at the Centennial Exhibition," pp. 283–85, signed by "S.N.C.").

Benjamin, S. G. W., "Fifty Years of American Art," *Harper's Monthly Magazine*, October 1879.

Burroughs, Alan, *Limners and Likenesses*, New York, 1936.

Eakins, Thomas, "The Differential Action of Certain Muscles Passing More than One Joint," *Proceedings of the Academy of Natural Sciences of Philadelphia*, 1894.

Feininger, Lyonel: see *Lyonel Feininger . . . Marsden Hartley*, Museum of Modern Art [1944].

Goodrich, Lloyd, *Thomas Eakins, His Life and Work*, New York, 1933.

Greenough, Horatio, "American Architecture," *Democratic Review*, August 1843.

Grosz, George: see George Heard Hamilton, "A European Artist's Reaction to the American Scene," New York *Times Book Review*, April 29, 1945.

Hart, Joel Tanner: see *Dictionary of American Biography*.

Homer, Winslow: see William H. Downes, *The Life and Works of Winslow Homer*, Boston, 1911.

Howells, William Dean, "A Sennight at the Centennial," *Atlantic Monthly*, July 1876.

James, William: see Ralph Barton Perry, *The Thought and Character of William James*, Boston, 1935, Vol. I.

Jarves, James Jackson, *The Art Idea*, New York, 1864.

Lipman, Jean, *American Primitive Painting*, New York, 1942.

Mount, William S.: see B. Cowdrey and H. W. Williams, Jr., *William Sidney Mount*, New York, 1944.

Powers, Hiram: see Henry W. Bellows, "Seven Sittings with Powers, the Sculptor," *Appleton's Journal*, June 12, June 19, June 26, July 10, August 7, August 28, and September 11, 1869.

Richardson, Edgar P., *The Way of Western Art, 1776–1914*, Cambridge, Mass., 1939.

Rockwell, Norman: see Arthur L. Guptill, *Norman Rockwell, Illustrator*, New York, 1946.

Rourke, Constance, *Charles Sheeler, Artist in the American Tradition*, New York [1938].

Sheeler, Charles: see Rourke, Constance, above.

Vogel, Hermann Wilhelm, "Photographs at the Centennial Exhibition," *Scientific American Supplement, No. 40*, September 30, 1876.

Whitman, Walt, "Good-bye, My Fancy," *Complete Prose Works*, Philadelphia, 1892.

B. ADDITIONAL REFERENCES

History of Ashtabula County, Ohio, Philadelphia, 1878.

Isham, Samuel, *The History of American Painting*, new ed., New York, 1927.

LaFollette, Suzanne, *Art in America*, New York, 1929.

Saint-Gaudens, Homer, *The American Artist and His Times*, New York, 1941.

Taft, Lorado, *The History of American Sculpture*, New York, 1903.

Tuckerman, Henry T., *American Artist Life*, New York, 1870.

8. THE ARTIST'S DILEMMA

A. SOURCES QUOTED OR MENTIONED

Hawthorne, Nathaniel, *The American Notebooks*, edited by Randall Stewart, New Haven, 1932.

——, "The Ancestral Footstep," *The Dolliver Romance, Fanshawe, and Septimius Felton*, Boston, 1883.

——, "The Artist of the Beautiful," *Democratic Review*, June 1844 (included in *Mosses from an Old Manse*, 1846).

——, *The Blithedale Romance*, Boston, 1852.

——, *Dr. Grimshawe's Secret*, Boston, 1883.

——, *The English Notebooks*, edited by Randall Stewart, New York, 1941.

——, *The House of the Seven Gables*, Boston, 1851.

——, *The Marble Faun*, Boston, 1860.

——, *Passages from the French and Italian Notebooks*, London, 1871.

——, *The Scarlet Letter*, Boston, 1850.

——, "A Select Party," *Democratic Review*, July 1844 (included in *Mosses from an Old Manse*).

James, Henry, *Hawthorne*, Boston, 1879.

Sedgwick, Catharine Maria, *Letters from Abroad*, 2 vols., New York, 1841.

Whitman, Walt, "A Backward Glance O'er Travel'd Roads," *Leaves of Grass*, Philadelphia, 1891–92.

——, "Democratic Vistas," *Complete Prose Works*, Philadelphia, 1892.

——, "Preface, 1855," Ibid.

——, "Preface, 1876," Ibid.

B. ADDITIONAL REFERENCES

Kouwenhoven, John A., "Hawthorne's Notebooks and *Dr. Grimshawe's Secret*," *American Literature*, January 1934.

9. SPACE AND CHANCE

A. SOURCES QUOTED OR MENTIONED

American Research and Development Corporation (a brochure), Boston, January 1, 1947.

Beard, Charles A., "The American Invasion of Europe," *Harper's Magazine*, March 1929.

Bennett, Arnold, *Your United States*, New York, 1913.

Clark, Wallace, "European Manufacturing Plants Slowly Emulating American Methods," *Iron Age*, December 18, 1930.

Cohn, David L., *Combustion on Wheels*, Boston, 1944.

Copley, F. B., *Frederick W. Taylor, Father of Scientific Management*, 2 vols., New York, 1923.

Evans, Bergen, "Auto-intoxication," *Harper's Magazine*, May 1947.

Ford, Henry, *My Life and Work*, New York, 1923.

Grattan, C. Hartley, *The Three Jameses, A Family of Minds*, New York, 1932.

Hawthorne, Nathaniel, *The English Notebooks*, edited by Randall Stewart, New York, 1941.

——, *Our Old Home*, Boston, 1863.

Hirschfeld, C. F.: see *Toward Civilization: A Symposium*, edited by Charles Beard, New York, 1930.

James, Henry, *The American Scene*, New York, 1907.

——, *Hawthorne*, Boston, 1879.

——, *The Letters of Henry James*, edited by Percy Lubbock, 2 vols., New York, 1920.

Kallaher, Mike, "How to Change Layouts Often," *Factory*, March 1943.

Krutch, Joseph Wood, "Still Innocent and Still Abroad," *Harper's Magazine*, April 1931.

Land, Edwin H., "Research by the Business Itself," *The Future of Industrial Research*, Standard Oil Development Co., 1945.

Leaver, Eric W., and Brown, John J., "Machines Without Men," *Fortune*, November 1946.

Mayo, Elton, *The Social Problems of an Industrial Civilization*, Boston, 1945.

Mill and Factory, May 1947 (special issue).

Morse, Richard S.: see National Research Corporation.

Motor World ("Before New York Show Issue"), December 27, 1916.

National Research Corporation: see John A. Kouwenhoven, "An Experiment in Enterprise," *Harper's Magazine*, October 1944.

Neal, Julia, *By Their Fruits. The Story of Shakerism in South Union, Kentucky*, Chapel Hill, N.C., 1947.

Paul, Howard, *Dashes of American Humor*, New York, 1853.

Redlin, A. W., "Handling Materials in an Automatic Frame Plant," *Transactions of the American Society of Mechanical Engineers*, New York, 1930, Vol. 52, Part II.

Roethlisberger, F. J., and Dickson, W. J., *Management and the Worker*, Cambridge, Mass., 1934.

Siegfried, André, *America Comes of Age*, New York, 1927.

Stow flexible shaft: see Charles E. Emery, "Motors, Hydraulic and Pneumatic Apparatus, etc.," *Reports and Awards, Group XX*, United States Centennial Commission, Philadelphia, 1878. For London *Times* comment see: *Reports of the United States Commissioners to the Paris Universal Exposition, 1878*, Washington, 1880, Vol. I, p. 449.

Taylor, Frederick Winslow, *The Principles of Scientific Management*, New York [1911].

Wells, H. G., *The Future in America*, New York, 1906.

White, Lee Strout (pen name of E. B. White and Richard Lee Strout), "Farewell, My Lovely," *New Yorker*, May 16, 1936.

Wilde, Oscar, *Impressions of America*, edited by Stuart Mason, Sunderland, 1906.

B. ADDITIONAL REFERENCES

Bourdet, Claude, "The Battle for Post-war France," *Harper's Magazine*, April 1948.

Bush, Vannevar, *Endless Horizons*, Washington, D.C. [1946].

Economic Development in Selected Countries. Plans, Programmes and Agencies, United Nations, Department of Economic Affairs, Lake Success, October 1947.

Hayes, Samuel P., Jr., "France," *Towards World Prosperity*, edited by Mordecai Ezekiel, New York [1947].

Lloyd, E. M. H., "Modernization of Industry in Britain," *Towards World Prosperity*, edited by Mordecai Ezekiel, New York [1947].

Product Engineering (special issue on "Designs for Material Conservation"), April 1942.

Recent Social Trends in the United States. Report of the

President's Research Committee on Social Trends, 2 vols., New York, 1933.

Science and Life in the World (The George Westinghouse Centennial Forum), 3 vols., New York [1946].

Wartime Technological Developments. A Study Made for the Subcommittee on War Mobilization of the Committee on Military Affairs, 79th Congress, 1st Session, Senate Subcommittee Monograph No. 2, May 1945.

10. STONE, STEEL, AND JAZZ

A. SOURCES QUOTED OR MENTIONED

Adams, James Truslow, "Our American Upper Class," *Harper's Magazine*, January 1932.

Amman, H. O.: see American Society of Civil Engineers, *George Washington Bridge Across the Hudson River at New York*, Port of New York Authority, 1933, p. 51.

Anderson, Sherwood, *Perhaps Women*, New York, 1931.

[Anonymous], "The Future of America," *Harper's Magazine*, June 1928.

Armstrong, Louis, *Swing That Music*, New York, 1936.

Babbitt, Irving, "The Critic and American Life," *Literary Opinion in America*, edited by Morton Dauwen Zabel, New York, 1937.

Bataille, Georges, "On Hiroshima" (translated by R. Raziel from an article in *Critique*), *politics*, July–August 1947.

Croly, David Goodman, *Glimpses of the Future*, New York, 1888.

Future editor of *Reader's Digest:* Ferguson, Charles W., "High Class," *Harper's Magazine*, March 1932.

Goodman, Benny (and Irving Kolodin), *The Kingdom of Swing*, New York, 1939.

Gropius, Walter: see Siegfried Giedion, *Space, Time and Architecture*, pp. 265–66.

Hamlin, Talbot, "Architecture in America Today," *New Republic*, August 4, 1941.

——, "Farm Security Architecture," *Pencil Points*, November 1941.

Hood, Raymond M.: see "Raymond M. Hood," *Architectural Forum*, February 1935.

Howells, William Dean, *Criticism and Fiction*, New York, 1891.

Kahn, Albert, "Architects of Defense," *Atlantic Monthly*, March 1942.

Knowlton, Don, "The Anatomy of Jazz," *Harper's Magazine*, April 1926.

Le Corbusier, *When the Cathedrals Were White*, translated by F. E. Hyslop, Jr., New York, 1947.

Lewisohn, Ludwig, "Literature and Life," *A Modern Book of Criticism*, edited by Ludwig Lewisohn, Modern Library, New York [n.d.].

Merz, Charles, *The Great American Bandwagon*, New York, 1928.

Morison, George S., *The New Epoch as Developed by the Manufacture of Power*, Boston, 1903. See also: George Abbot Morison, *George Shattuck Morison, 1842–1903, A Memoir*, Peterborough [N.H.] Historical Society, 1940.

Mumford, Lewis, *Sticks and Stones*, New York, 1924.

Port of New York Authority, *First Progress Report on Hudson River Bridge at New York*, January 1, 1928.

Santayana, George, *Reason in Society*, New York, 1905.

Sargeant, Winthrop, *Jazz: Hot and Hybrid*, new and revised edition, New York, 1946.

Steinman, David B., and Watson, Sara Ruth, *Bridges and Their Builders*, New York [1941].

Sullivan, Louis, "What Is Architecture?" *Kindergarten Chats and Other Writings*, New York, 1947.

Tallmadge, Thomas E., *The Story of American Architecture*, New York, 1927.

Taylor, Frederick Winslow, *The Principles of Scientific Management*, New York, 1911.

Whitman, Walt, "Poetry Today in America—Shakespeare —The Future" (1881), *Complete Prose Works*, Philadelphia, 1892.

B. ADDITIONAL REFERENCES

Architectural Forum (special issue, "Design Decade"), October 1940.

Borneman, Ernest, "The Jazz Cult" (Parts I and II), *Harper's Magazine*, February and March 1947.

Gaines, M. C., "Narrative Illustration, The Story of the Comics," *Print, A Quarterly Journal of the Graphic Arts*, Vol. III, No. 2, Summer, 1942.

Harap, Louis, "The Case for Hot Jazz," *Musical Quarterly*, January 1941.

Hobson, Wilder, *American Jazz Music*, New York, 1939.

Jacobs, Lewis, *The Rise of the American Film*, New York [1939], Chapters III and IV.

Johnson, Philip, *Machine Art*, Museum of Modern Art, New York, 1934.

MacDonald, Dwight, "A Theory of Popular Culture," *politics*, February 1944.

Seldes, Gilbert, *The Seven Lively Arts*, New York, 1924.

Smith, Charles Edward, and Others, *The Jazz Record Book*, New York, 1942, pp. 1–125.

Waugh, Colton, *The Comics*, New York, 1947.

Index